HISTORY OF THE INTERNATIONAL UNION OF PSYCHOLOGICAL SCIENCE (IUPsyS)

History of the International Union of Psychological Science (IUPsyS)

Mark R. Rosenzweig
University of California at Berkeley, USA

Wayne H. Holtzman
University of Texas, Austin, USA

Michel Sabourin
Université de Montréal, Canada

David Bélanger
Université de Montréal, Canada

Psychology Press
Taylor & Francis Group

LONDON AND NEW YORK

First published 2000 by Psychology Press Ltd
27 Church Road, Hove, East Sussex, BN3 2FA

Simultaneously published in the USA and Canada
by Taylor & Francis Inc
2 Park Square, Milton Park, Abingdon, Oxfordshire OX14 4RN

First issued in paperback 2015

Psychology Press is an imprint of the Taylor and Francis Group,
an informa business

British Library Cataloguing in Publication Data
A catalogue record for this book is available from the British Library

ISBN 13: 978-1-138-87739-9 (pbk)
ISBN 13: 978-1-84169-197-8 (hbk)

Cover design by Leigh Hurlock
Typeset in Palatino and Korinna by Facing Pages, Southwick, West Sussex

Contents

Illustration credits

Page 17. Julian Ochorowicz.
Photograph reproduced with the permission of Archiwum Ilustracji Wydawnictwa Naukowego PWN S.A., Warsaw.
Page 25. Christine Ladd-Franklin.
Photograph taken from The Scientific Monthly. (1930, p. 30). Washington, DC: American Association for the Advancement of Science.
Page 26. Jozefa Joteyko.
Photograph reproduced with the permission of Archiwum Ilustracji Wydawnictwa Naukowego PWN S.A., Warsaw.
Page 33. Carl Stumpf.
Photograph taken from C. Murchison (1930). *A history of psychology in autobiography,* vol. 1. Worcester, MA: Clark University Press.
Page 45. Charles S. Myers.
Photograph taken from C. Murchison (1936). *A history of psychology in autobiography*, vol. 3. Worcester, MA: Clark University Press.
Page 47. Gerardus Heymans.
Photograph taken from C. Murchison (1932). *A history of psychology in autobiography*, vol. 2. Worcester, MA: Clark University Press.
Page 48. James McKeen Cattell.
Archives of the History of American Psychology, Photograph File—The University of Akron. Reproduced with permission.
Page 63. James Drever Snr.
Photograph taken from C. Murchison (1932). *A history of psychology in autobiography, vol. 2.* Worcester, MA: Clark University Press.
Page 65. David Katz.
Photograph taken from Langfeld, H.S., Boring, E.G., Werner, H., & Yerkes, R.M. (1952). *A history of psychology in autobiography*, vol. 4. Worcester, MA: Clark University Press.
Page 86. Congress participants, Brussels.
Photograph taken from the Proceedings of the 15th International Congress of Psychology, Brussels, Belgium, 28 July–3 August, 1957. Amsterdam: North-Holland Publishing Company, 1959.
Page 102. Congress participants, Washington.
Photograph taken from the Proceedings of the 17th International Congress of Psychology, Washington, DC, USA, August 20–26, 1963. Amsterdam: North-Holland Publishing Company, 1964.
Page 126. Eugene Jacobson.
Photograph reproduced with the permission of Michigan State University, USA.
Page 135. George Drew.
Photograph reproduced with the permission of the British Psychological Society (BPS).

Foreword

This book aims to trace the development of the International Union of Psychological Science (IUPsyS), not only since its founding at the 14th International Congress of Psychology at Stockholm, 1951, but going back to 1881 when a young Polish psychologist first proposed the ideas of an international congress and of an international association of psychological societies. These ideas soon bore fruit in the 1st International Congress of Psychology in 1889 and the formation of the International Congress Committee. These, in turn, led to the long series of international congresses which continue today and, eventually, to formation of the Union.

To trace this history, we have consulted the published proceedings of every International Congress of Psychology to date, and also the extensive archives of minutes of the Assemblies and meetings of the Executive Committees of the IUPsyS. Reports of some of these meetings have been published by the Secretaries-General of the IUPsyS, but the majority are available only in the archives, so this book reveals much information that has previously been unavailable to the public.

We regret that this historical project started only in 1998 when it was no longer possible to obtain first-hand accounts from the first generation of officers and members of the Executive Committee of the IUPsyS. We hope that current and future officers and members of the Executive Committee will contribute pertinent accounts and correspondence to the archives, and that officers of national psychological organizations will also preserve records of future historical value.

As a first step of organizing this history, David Bélanger, Wayne H. Holtzman, and Mark R. Rosenzweig met together at Berkeley in August 1998 and also in San Francisco with members of the Executive Committee. Later David Bélanger had to reduce the time he had hoped to devote to the project, and Michel Sabourin joined the authors. First drafts of Chapters 1–6 were prepared by Rosenzweig, Chapters 7–9 by Sabourin, Chapters 10–14 by Holtzman, and Chapter 15 by Pierre Ritchie, Secretary-General of the IUPsyS. All chapters were reviewed by all authors and by officers of the IUPsyS. We are indebted especially to Géry d'Ydewalle, President of the IUPsyS, and to Pierre Ritchie, for help at many points during preparation of the manuscript. We also thank some members of the Executive Committee—Bruce Overmier, Cigdem Kagitcibasi, and John Adair—for contributing draft paragraphs on topics of their expertise. We would also like to thank Luis Montoro González (1982) and Maria José González Solaz (1998) for providing us with copies of their informative unpublished doctoral theses from the University of Valencia on the International Congresses of Psychology (1889–1960 and 1963–1984, respectively). Thanks are due to all those who provided photographs of psychologists and participants at the international congresses. Finally, we thank colleagues at Psychology Press for their help and cooperation in the rapid and expert preparation of the book in time for the Stockholm Congress.

We would enjoy hearing from those who may have additional records or information about the history of the IUPsyS and the international congresses of psychology, both to supplement our own knowledge and so that the archives of the IUPsyS may be as complete as possible.

Mark R. Rosenzweig
Wayne H. Holtzman
Michel Sabourin
David Bélanger

Preface

At the annual meeting of the Executive Committee of the International Union of Psychological Science (IUPsyS) in Stockholm in 1997, we considered various ways to commemorate the 50th anniversary of IUPsyS, which is to be celebrated at the occasion of the 27th International Congress of Psychology in Stockholm in July 2000. At that time, the archives of IUPsyS were being transferred from Leuven (Belgium) to Montréal (Canada); while packing, we realized how rich the history of IUPsyS is. Admittedly, going through the minutes of the Executive Committee and Assembly meetings over the almost 50 years of its existence is a rather boring exercise; still, they do contain immensely valuable information from the past and important lessons to be drawn for future activities of IUPsyS. The critical problem was to find colleagues willing to process the available information and to transform it into a text which could be both read enjoyably as the history of IUPsyS and also contain sufficient detail for archival purposes. The idea emerged to invite a few Honorary Life Members of the IUPsyS Executive Committee as authors. It was a nice way to get them involved once again in the activities of IUPsyS; also, we could profit from their extended past experience with the Union. We contacted Mark R. Rosenzweig and Wayne Holtzman (both Past-Presidents), and David Bélanger (past Treasurer); they all immediately accepted the invitation. Michel Sabourin (current Treasurer) joined the authors. We do realize how much time and work were involved in order to get the book ready for the Stockholm congress. On behalf of the whole IUPsyS Executive Committee, I wholeheartedly thank them. I also wish to convey our thanks to Psychology Press, who were willing to publish a book appealing mainly to readers interested in international psychology and in the history of psychology.

Leuven, February 29, 2000
Géry van Outryve d'Ydewalle
IUPsyS President

The International Union of Psychological Science today

1.

The International Union of Psychological Science (IUPsyS) is the main international body of psychology. As indicated in Figure 1.1, it groups together organizations that represent psychology in 66 countries (as of early 2000), and the memberships in these national organizations total more than 500,000 psychologists. The IUPsyS represents psychology in such organizations as the International Social Science Council (ISSC) and the International Council for Science (ICSU); it also has consultative relations with the Economic and Social Council and the Department of Public Information of the United Nations and with the World Health Organization

FIGURE 1.1

Relations of the International Union of Psychological Science (IUPsyS) with other organizations

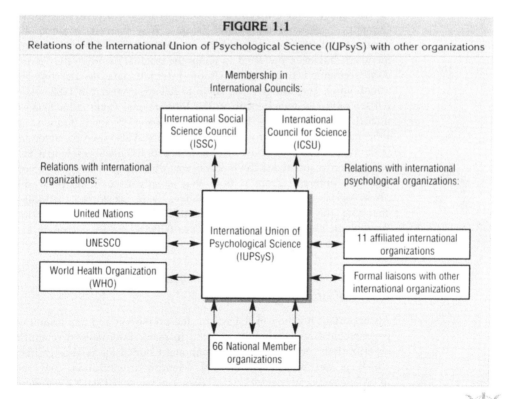

(WHO). The IUPsyS aims to represent psychology in all the countries in which it is developed and to foster the development of psychology as a science and a profession around the world.

The Assembly of IUPsyS is its legislative body and final authority. The Assembly consists of the members of the Executive Committee and one or two delegates per national member. It meets every 2 years, at the site of an international congress of the IUPsyS or at the site of an international congress of the International Association for Applied Psychology (IAAP). As is the rule for most international scientific unions, the IUPsyS is composed of national member organizations, not more than one national member per country. Since 1951, IUPsyS has grown steadily to a membership of 66 national members (as of May 2000). A detailed history of the IUPsyS and of the international congresses of psychology is given in later chapters of this book.

Changes in name and acronym of the IUPsyS

Over its history, the Union has changed its name and its acronym. The original name, from 1951 to 1965, was the International Union of Scientific Psychology (IUSP). The name was changed to the International Union of Psychological Science (IUPS) in 1965. Most members of the Executive Committee preferred the change because they wanted to avoid the implication that some psychology is not scientific. French-speaking members, however, preferred to retain the original name, so the French name remained unchanged (Union Internationale de Psychologie Scientifique). The change of acronym to IUPsyS occurred in 1982, when IUPsyS assumed membership in the International Council for Science (ICSU). The International Union of Physiological Sciences, founded in 1952, had been a member of ICSU since 1955 and also used the acronym IUPS. When psychology posed its candidacy for full membership in ICSU, a condition required for the election was that the psychological union choose a different acronym from that already used in ICSU by the physiological union. Various alternatives were considered, including changing the name back to the International Union of Scientific Psychology. Finally it was agreed to use IUPsyS, and that acronym has now become familiar.

Participation of the IUPsyS in major international organizations

An important function of IUPsyS for the promotion and application of psychological science is participation in major international scientific organizations, especially the International Council for Science (ICSU), which is the major international scientific organization, and the International Social Science Council (ISSC), of which IUPsyS is a founding member. As a member of ICSU, IUPsyS receives grants for some research projects, and it collaborates with the ICSU Committee on Data for Science and Technology (CODATA). IUPsyS is also developing cooperative relations with other scientific unions in ICSU, such as the International Brain Research Organization (IBRO) and the International Geographical Union (IGU). IUPsyS and IBRO recently received a major grant from ICSU to organize a Brain Imaging Workshop in conjunction with the International Congress of Psychology in 2000 in Stockholm, and it will hold a joint symposium with IGU at the Stockholm Congress.

IUPsyS cooperates with ISSC and its member organizations in several research programs and International Issue Groups, in the program on Human Dimensions of Global Environmental Change, in Working Groups, and in a number of UNESCO-sponsored projects, particularly those involving developing countries. ISSC provides IUPsyS grants for certain projects. IUPsyS has also cooperated with UNESCO on several projects of mutual interest.

Organizations affiliated with the IUPsyS

The IUPsyS maintains relations with several other international or regional psychological organizations. Its affiliates include the following organizations: the International Association of Applied Psychology (IAAP), the Interamerican Society of Psychology/Sociedad Interamericana de Psicologia (SIP), Association de Psychologie Scientifique de Langue Française (APSLF), International Council of Psychologists (ICP), International Association for Cross-Cultural Psychology (IACCP), European Association of Experimental Social Psychology (EAESP), International Society of Comparative Psychology (ISCP), International Society for the Study of Behavioural Development (ISSBD), European Association of Personality Psychology (EAPA), European Association of Psychological Assessment (EAPP), and the International Neurological Society (INS). In addition to these affiliates, the IUPsyS maintains special liaison exchanges with the European Association of Professional Psychologists' Associations (EFPPA) and the International Test Commission (ITC).

Current activities of the IUPsyS

As well as assuring the regular succession of international congresses of psychology, representing psychology in international organizations, maintaining relations with other international or regional psychological organizations, publishing the *International Journal of Psychology* and sponsoring other publications, the IUPsyS engages in several other important current activities, some of which the following paragraphs will describe.

Regional conferences and congresses

The IUPsyS sponsors regional international congresses designed to assist and promote psychology within low-income countries (developing countries and countries in transition). This program addresses the problem that few psychologists from developing countries participate in the major international congresses. Even though the range of countries represented among registrants has increased with each international congress, the difficulties and costs of travel, accommodation, and congress registration fees pose significant obstacles to the attendance of psychologists from developing countries. To address these problems, the IUPsyS in 1995 creatively began the practice of sponsoring international regional congresses within developing countries. This IUPsyS initiative has become a joint venture with the IAAP. Both associations contribute to the support of each regional congress with the primary sponsorship alternating in successive odd-numbered years. IUPsyS sponsored the first regional congress in Guangzhou, China (1995) and the African regional congress held in Durban, South Africa (1999). The IAAP was the primary sponsor for the Latin American regional congress in Mexico City (1997).

Codes of ethics

Although the IUPsyS had long encouraged its national members to adopt codes of ethics, a survey by the Secretary-General in the 1970s revealed that only a small number of national members had actually adopted codes and were enforcing them. A special symposium on ethics at the 1976 International Congress in Paris gave further impetus to this effort. (For more on this, see Chapter 11.)

In 1993 the Union Executive Committee instructed the then Deputy Secretary-General, Bruce Overmier, to survey the membership once again, to see whether or not each country had adopted a set of ethical guidelines or code to govern activities by psychologists. The president or executive officer of each national member was contacted to determine whether or not a formal "ethics code" had been officially adopted in their country, and, if so, was asked to provide a copy to the Union. Twenty-four countries reported having such a code and submitted copies. Four Scandinavian countries shared a single code, yielding 20 different codes. Interestingly, many of the codes were submitted in English; those that were not were translated into English to allow comparisons among the codes. (It was recognized that such English translations performed without a back-translation check may not be fully accurate representations of the original code.) Mark M. Leach and Judd J. Harbin of the University of Mississippi undertook a systematic comparison of these 20 codes for the Union. The result was published in the *International Journal of Psychology* (Leach & Harbin, 1997), highlighting similarities and differences. This paper also put their review into a context of prior smaller surveys of national codes of ethics for psychologists.

Advanced Research Training Seminars (ARTS)

Going back to the 1988 International Congress of Psychology in Australia, where the participation of psychologists from low-income countries was very poor, the idea emerged among some psychologists of the need for sponsored research/training seminars for psychologists from low-income countries that would also enable their participation in international congresses. This idea materialized in 1992 under the auspices of IUPsyS when the first Advanced Research Training Seminars (ARTS) were held in conjunction with the 25th International Congress of Psychology in Brussels. The coordinator was Ype Poortinga, and the two ARTS were organized in Tilburg and Berlin by Fons v.d. Vijver and Ute Schönpflug, respectively. The International Association for Cross-Cultural Psychology (IACCP) also collaborated in sponsoring ARTS.

Since then ARTS have been organized every 2 years in conjunction with the international congresses of psychology and of applied psychology under the auspices of IUPsyS, in collaboration with IAAP and IACCP. For two terms, in 1994 and 1996, Cigdem Kagitcibasi was the ARTS coordinator. In 1994 two ARTS were organized in conjunction with the Madrid IAAP Congress, one in Saarbrucken by Lutz Eckensberger on "Eco-Ethical Thinking from a Cross-Cultural Perspective" and the other in Istanbul by Sevda Bekman, Banu Oney and Cigdem Kagitcibasi on "Human Development and Assessment." In 1996 two more ARTS were organized in Canada, in conjunction with the 26th International Congress of Psychology, one in Ottawa by Alastair Ager, assisted by Martha Young, on "Qualitative Research Methods" and the other in Sherbrooke by Pnina Klein and Michael Boivin on "Early Intervention in Families and Other Settings for Infants and Young Children." In 1998 John Adair served as the ARTS coordinator. In conjunction with the San Francisco IAAP Congress three ARTS were organized, by Robert Serpell and Abdeljalil Akkari in Baltimore on "Qualitative Approaches in Cultural Psychology," by Martin Fishbein in Bellingham on "Developing Effective Health Behavior Interventions," and by Peter Graf in San Francisco on "Advances in Cognitive Psychology."

John Adair continues as the ARTS Coordinator for 2000. In conjunction with the 27th International Congress of Psychology in Stockholm, three ARTS are being planned by Jarl Risberg in Lund on "Imaging the Structure and Function of the Brain," by Thomas Oakland and Walter Lonner in Stockholm on "Psychological Test Adaptations to Diverse Cultures and Measuring Personality Cross-Culturally," and by Heidi Keller in Stockholm on "Pathways across Development: Cross-Cultural Perspectives."

ARTS have been very successful in fulfilling their mission, that is, providing research/training to psychologists from developing countries and from Eastern Europe, as well as supporting their participation in international congresses. Greater participation of psychologists from low-income countries in international congresses is crucial for increased internationalization of psychology. ARTS is serving this worthwhile purpose.

Publications

The IUPsyS has developed an extensive program of publications to foster communication with and among psychologists around the world. Starting with the first International Congress of Psychology in 1889, the practice arose of publishing the proceedings of each congress, often including texts of some of the main papers and abstracts of the others. When the International Union was formally organized in 1951, its statutes included the provision that proceedings of the congresses be published in a uniform manner, and the practice has been maintained to a large extent. The proceedings of the 26th International Congress of Psychology, Montréal, 1996, and of the 25th Congress, Brussels, 1992, are available from Psychology Press, UK.

In 1966 the Union founded its journal, the *International Journal of Psychology*. The *Journal* publishes scientific and theoretical papers in all fields of psychological research. Most issues of the *Journal* include a second part, the *International Platform*, which gives news of the Union and its national members, provides an opportunity to exchange views and opinions of psychological topics, and lists the *International Meeting Calendar*. The *Journal* is widely distributed to the national member organizations, to libraries, and to individual subscribers throughout the world.

To aid in contacting psychologists around the world, many in countries that do not publish directories of psychologists, the Union has published a series of volumes entitled *International Directory of Psychologists*. They appeared in 1958, 1966, 1980, and 1985. The most recent of these volumes (Pawlik, 1985) presented information on more than 32,000 psychologists from 43 countries. The international directories did not include psychologists from the USA because the American Psychological Association regularly publishes directories of its members.

The increasing number of psychologists around the world made it impractical to continue publishing directories of individual psychologists beyond 1985. The Union then tried a new form of publication, the *IUPsyS Directory of Major Research Institutes and Departments of Psychology* (d'Ydewalle, 1993). This volume listed contact information for psychological organizations in 171 countries.

A new "publication" initiative of the Union is the CD-ROM global resource file, *Psychology: IUPsyS Global Resource*, to appear in 2000. This electronically based publication is described in the *Global resource file* section, following.

Subscriptions to the *International Journal of Psychology*, the *IUPsyS Directory of Major Research Institutes and Departments of Psychology*, and to the proceedings of the 25th and 26th International Congresses of Psychology are available from

> *Psychology Press*
> 27 Church Road
> Hove, East Sussex
> BN3 2FA, UK
> (Fax: 44 1273 205612; Tel: 44 1273 207411.)

The Union has sponsored or given its auspices to a number of books intended to increase information about psychology and/or to promote communication among psychologists around the world. A complete listing will appear in the CD-ROM global resource file, *Psychology: IUPsyS Global Resource*. Some recent publications are: Jing (1991), *Chinese Concise Encyclopaedia of Psychology*; Rosenzweig (1992, 1994), *International Psychological Science: Progress, Problems and Prospects*; and Pawlik and Rosenzweig (2000), *International Handbook of Psychology*.

Global resource file

As the Union moves into the new millennium, it is launching a new "publication," *Psychology: IUPsyS Global Resource*, which is congruent with the electronic computer capabilities coming on line throughout the world. This new product is a "resource guide" in CD-ROM format. This publication product follows the tradition of—yet extends in scope and media—the Union's previous publication of the *International Directory of Psychologists* (editions published in 1958, 1966, 1980, 1985) and the *IUPsyS Directory* (published in 1993). The first issue of the CD-ROM, which will be published in 2000, will be distributed to all subscribers to the *International Journal of Psychology* and also marketed by Psychology Press as a free-standing reference tool. The *Psychology: IUPsyS Global Resource* CD-ROM will include several resource tools as separate searchable files using proprietary integrated software. These resource tools will be diverse. Among them will be brief descriptions and histories of the state of psychology in 84 countries, contact information for national psychological societies, a directory of international psychological societies, an international directory with postal and electronic addresses for scholarly institutions in 147 countries, a coded bibliography of published papers about psychology in each country, materials related to the structure, function, and members of the Union itself, and, importantly, the abstracts of all papers presented at the quadrennial International Congresses of Psychology—beginning with 1996 and continuing into the future. Links will allow the user to search from country in one resource file to research institute in a second file to a congress author from that institution in a third. The Union's new electronic resource guide will make information about psychological science and its worldwide context more readily available and will be especially helpful to those seeking international collaborations or wishing to trace the development of psychology in a country or region.

Sources of current information about the IUPsyS

For current information about the IUPsyS, see its website (http://www. IUPsyS.org) and its journal, the *International Journal of Psychology*. The *International Journal of Psychology* publishes not only research reports but also news about IUPsyS and its national members and affiliates and lists forthcoming meetings in all fields of scientific and professional psychology.

References

d'Ydewalle, G. (1993). *IUPsyS directory of major research institutes and departments of psychology*. Hove, UK: Psychology Press.

Jing, Q.C. (Ed.)(1991). *Chinese concise encyclopedia of psychology*. [In Chinese.] Changsha, China: Hunan Educational Publishers.

Leach, M.M., & Harbin, J.J. (1997). Psychological ethics codes: A comparison of 24 countries. *International Journal of Psychology, 32*(3), 181–192.

Pawlik, K. (Ed.)(1985). *International directory of psychologists* (4th ed.). Amsterdam: North-Holland.

Pawlik, K., & Rosenzweig, M.R. (Eds.)(2000). *International handbook of psychology*. London: Sage.

Rosenzweig, M.R. (1992). *International psychological science: Progress, problems, and prospects*. Washington, DC: American Psychological Association.

Rosenzweig, M.R. (1994). *International psychological science: Progress, problems, and prospects*. [Chinese translation.] Beijing: China Science and Technology Publishers.

The origins of scientific organizations: Historical context

2

The formation of the International Union of Psychological Science (IUPsyS) is part of a larger history of development of formal scientific organizations that began in the 17th century. In this chapter, as well as sketching the history of the IUPsyS, we will relate it to the development of scientific associations, especially those with which the IUPsyS has active relations, as shown in Figure 1.1. Because each of these kinds of organization interacts with each of the others, information about each helps to understand the others. The story shows increasing communication and cooperation among psychologists at national, regional, and international levels, and also among the different scientific disciplines. After presenting this background, we will proceed in the next chapter to a more detailed account of the 1st International Congress of Psychology, held in Paris in 1889, and the creation there of the standing International Congress of Psychology Committee, which evolved after 62 years into the IUPsyS.

A brief sketch of the origins of the International Union of Psychological Science

At the Paris International Congress of Psychology in 1889, a permanent international congress committee was formed to assure the succession of International Congresses of Psychology and to provide organization for international psychology. The IUPsyS was foreshadowed in a project adopted in principle at the 1889 Paris Congress to form an international association of psychological societies.

Once formed, the international committee was called the International Congress of Psychology; it functioned effectively and organized congresses over a 60-year period through the 12th International Congress of Psychology in Edinburgh (1948) and the 13th International Congress of Psychology in Stockholm (1951). From its start the committee grew in size and in number of countries represented. At the 5th International Congress of Psychology (Rome, 1905), the membership of the committee had grown to 76, with 16 countries represented. At the 10th congress (Copenhagen, 1932) the congress committee established an Executive Committee of seven members and chose Swiss psychologist Edouard Claparède as its Executive Secretary. After Claparède's death in 1940, American psychologist Herbert S. Langfeld became Executive Secretary of the International Committee.

At the 12th congress (Edinburgh, 1948) it was finally decided to accomplish the long-desired goal and establish an international union of psychology. Langfeld played the major role in organizing the formation of the International Union of Psychological Science, as reported by Henri Piéron, the first President of IUPsyS (Piéron, 1954, p. 404). The Union was originally named the International Union of Scientific Psychology (IUSP); changes in the name and acronym have been described in Chapter 1. The planning for the Union coincided with an initiative of UNESCO in the late 1940s to promote the establishment of international unions in sciences which did not already have such a formal organization. With the encouragement of UNESCO, the International Union of Psychological Science was established formally at the Stockholm Congress on July 15, 1951. National psychological associations from 11 countries were charter members, and psychological associations from 9 other countries promptly joined the Union, for a total of 20 national members in 1951.

Continuity between the International Committee and IUPsyS was maintained by their overlapping personnel: Langfeld was the last Secretary-General of the committee and the first Secretary-General of IUPsyS; Piéron and other officers and members of the first Executive Committee of IUPsyS had been members of the committee.

Some background: Formation of scientific associations; organization of scientific congresses

Now let us sketch some of the broader background of the formation of the IUPsyS. Formation of scientific associations proceeded historically in several stages: (1) formation of national academies of science, beginning in the 17th century; (2) organization of the early international scientific congresses, beginning in the 19th century; (3) formation of national organizations devoted to specific fields of science, also beginning in the 19th century; (4) formation of international unions devoted to specific fields of science, and founding of umbrella councils to group together international scientific unions and other international organizations, mainly in the 20th century.

Formation of scientific academies

The word academy, and its equivalents in modern languages, came from the Greek name of the garden where Plato gathered friends to discuss common philosophical interests. This term became a label for gatherings in which groups of people with enquiring minds began to form around many centers in Europe from the Middle Ages on. As well as local academies, in some larger countries national academies developed in the 17th century, such as the Accademia des Lincei (those who were as keen-sighted as a lynx) in Rome, dating from 1603. Although the Accademia dei Lincei later dissolved, to be reestablished in the 19th century, some national academies founded in the 17th century continue to this day, such as the Royal Society of London (1660) and the Académie des Sciences in France (1666), and they have served as models for other national societies. Whereas some of these academies are devoted strictly to the sciences, others are learned societies that include the arts and letters as well as the sciences; examples of such inclusive academies are the Académie Royale des Sciences et des Beaux Arts de Belgique (1772), the Royal Danish Academy of Sciences and Letters (1742), and the Royal Irish Academy (1785).

Organization of international congresses

The middle of the 19th century saw the development of scientific congresses, some being meetings of groups devoted to a particular field of study and some being devoted to a particular problem. As Montoro González (1982, pp. 23-24) points out, several international congresses were held in conjunction with the Universal Expositions in London, 1851, and in Paris, 1855. The 1st International Congress of Statistics was held in 1853, and the 1st International Congress of Medicine in 1867. The 1st International Congress of Criminal Anthropology took place in Rome, 1885; several psychologists participated in the congress of anthropology and some were encouraged to plan a similar international congress for psychology.

Some international congresses were organized by existing groups, whereas other groups grew out of congresses. Thus in 1862 some German states organized the Mittleuropaische Gradmessung (Central European Geodetic Association), whose first conference attracted participants from 13 countries, most of which were German. (Germany had not yet united at that time.) The growing European character of the geodetic association was reflected by the change of name in 1867 to the European Geodetic Association. A still wider scope was indicated by invitations to scientists from Great Britain and the United States to participate in the 1883 meeting. In 1886 the name was changed to the International Geodetic Association. Finally, this led to the International Union of Geodesy and Geophysics, founded in 1919.

The 1st International Congress of Psychology took place in Paris in 1889, in the context of congresses of other sciences. This occurred just 10 years after the first formal laboratory of psychology was founded by Wilhelm Wundt at the University of Leipzig. The International Congress of Psychology was held in conjunction with the Paris International Exposition, as was the first International Congress of Physiology. Both congresses fostered further development of their fields. As mentioned earlier, a permanent international committee was formed at the Paris International Congress of Psychology to assure the succession of International Congresses of Psychology and to provide organization for international psychology. The IUPsyS was foreshadowed in a project adopted in principle at the 1889 Paris Congress to form an international association of psychological societies, and the IUPsyS was founded in 1951. In the case of physiology, a permanent committee was established in 1929 to organize the International Congresses of Physiology, and this evolved into the International Union of Physiological Sciences in 1952.

The 1st International Congress of Psychology clearly met a need, and successive congresses were held every 3 to 5 years, with gaps caused by the two World Wars. A history of the first 16 International Congresses of Psychology (1889–1960) was prepared by Montoro González (1982); a history of the 14th–23rd congresses (1963–1984) was presented in a dissertation by González Solaz (1998).

Formation of national and international organizations devoted to specific fields of science

A side effect of the 1st International Congress of Psychology in 1889 was to encourage the formation of the American Psychological Association (APA) in 1892. The APA is the world's oldest continuously existing national psychological association. When European psychologists who were organizing the International Congress tried to identify a national organization of psychologists in the United States, they could find only the American Society for Psychical Research (ASPR). Two Americans who attended the 1st International Congress of Psychology, William James and Joseph Jastrow, disparaged the ASPR and its interests, and they probably reported these events to their American colleagues, including G. Stanley Hall who led the movement to found the APA. Some historians claim that a major factor in the establishment of the APA was G. Stanley Hall's strong ambition to be the leader of American psychology (Cadwallader, 1992). Perhaps Hall's drive hastened the founding of the APA by a few years, but conditions were clearly ripe for the APA. When other psychologists reacted to Hall's authoritarian leadership and effectively sidetracked him in the 1890s, the APA continued well without Hall.

By 1910, a few other national psychological associations had been formed—in France and in the United Kingdom, in 1901; Germany, 1904; Argentina, 1908; and Italy, 1910.

The founding of the APA in 1892 was part of the movement to establish disciplinary societies in the USA, starting with the American Chemical Society in 1876. A major influence that favored the founding of the APA was the policy of the American Society of Naturalists, established in 1883, to encourage and foster the formation of disciplinary societies. One of the resultant societies was the American Physiological Society (APS), founded in 1887. Psychologists G. Stanley Hall and Joseph Jastrow were among the original members of the APS, and some physiologists were among the original members of the APA.

The psychologists at the Paris Congress in 1889 adopted in principle a project to form an international association of psychological societies, but this was clearly premature because no national psychological societies yet existed, and there were only a few local societies, in London, Moscow, Munich, New York, and Paris. By 1948, at least 19 national psychological societies had been formed, and at the 12th International Congress at Edinburgh that year, an ad hoc committee was appointed to draw up the statutes for an international union of psychology.

The United Nations Educational, Scientific and Cultural Organization (UNESCO), founded in 1946, also fostered the formation of the IUPsyS and of other international scientific unions. UNESCO wanted to have international scientific organizations with which to deal, and it offered financial subventions to such organizations. The end of World War II saw renewed scientific communication among the former foes, and this also favored the formation of new international unions. Among those formed at that time were the International Union of Theoretical and Applied Mechanics (1946), International Union of Crystallography (1947), International Union of the History of Science (1947), International Union of Anthropological and Ethnographical Societies (1948), International Union of the Philosophy of Science (1949), International Union of Psychological Science (1951), and the International Union of Physiological Sciences (1952). Brief histories and descriptions of the international scientific unions that are either scientific union members or scientific associates of ICSU are found in the *ICSU Year Book* (International Council for Science, 2000).

From the International Association of Academies to the International Council for Science

From the start, national academies of science corresponded with each other, and many elected foreign associates, so it was natural to institute an international organization that would group together the national academies to facilitate communication and joint activities. In 1900 the first meeting of the Council of the International Association of Academies (IAA) took place in Paris. At the start, the IAA included mainly European academies of science but also the Royal Society of London and the National Academy of Sciences, USA (Greenaway, 1996, pp. 8 et seq.). The main purpose of the IAA was stated as follows:

> The object of the Association shall be to initiate and
> otherwise to promote scientific undertakings of general
> interest, proposed by one or more of the associated
> Academies, and to facilitate scientific intercourse between
> different countries.

Regular meetings of the General Assembly of the IAA continued through 1913, but the coming of the World War interrupted its activities.

After the war a successor organization was established in 1919, the International Research Council (IRC), Conseil International de Recherches (Greenaway, 1996, pp. 21 et seq.). The initial members were all national academies of science, but in the first year of the IRC a few international scientific unions were also created and made members of the IRC. (Table 2.1 lists the scientific unions now in the ICSU, the date of founding of each, and the year in which each joined the IRC or ICSU.) The IRC remained chiefly a body of national members; the few scientific unions that became associated with it had only limited powers in the IRC and were not represented on its Executive Committee.

TABLE 2.1

Scientific Unions in ICSU

Scientific Unions in order of founding	Year Founded	Year admitted to IRC/ICSU
International Astronomical Union	1919	1919
International Union of Pure and Applied Chemistry	1919	1919
International Union of Geodesy and Geophysics	1919	1919
International Union of Biological Sciences	1919	1923
Union Radio Scientifique Internationale	1919	1919
International Union of Pure and Applied Physics	1922	1922
International Geographical Union	1922	1923
International Society of Soil Science	1924	1993
International Mathematical Union	1925	1925
International Union of Theoretical and Applied Mechanics	1946	1947
International Union of Crystallography	1947	1947
International Union of the History and Philosophy of Science		
International Union of the History of Science	1947	1947
International Union of the Philosophy of Science	1949	1956
International Union of Anthropological and		
Ethnographical Societies	1948	1993
International Union of Nutritional Sciences	1948	1968
International Union of Psychological Science	1951	1982
International Union of Physiological Sciences	1952	1955
International Union of Biochemistry and Molecular Biology	1955	1955
International Brain Research Organization	1960	1993
International Union for Pure and Applied Biophysics	1961	1966
International Union of Geological Sciences	1961	1961
International Union of Pharmacology	1965	1972
(Separated from International Union of Physiological Sciences in 1965)		
International Union of Immunological Societies	1969	1976
International Union of Food Science and Technology	1970	1996
International Union of Microbiological Societies	1980	1982
(Founded 1927, but a division of IUPS until 1980)		
International Union of Toxicology	1980	1996

In 1931 the 5th General Assembly of the IRC converted itself into the 5th General Assembly of a new body, the International Council of Scientific Unions (ICSU). The membership of the ICSU was dual, in that scientific unions had equal status with the national members. Nevertheless, no new scientific union members were added until after the end of World War II. Some of the new scientific unions that entered the ICSU in the 1940s–1960s represented new sciences (e.g., the International Union of Crystallography, 1947); some were initiated by fractionation of the biological sciences (e.g., the International Union of Biochemistry and Molecular Biology, formed in 1955 and admitted to ICSU the same year; the International Union for Pure and Applied Biophysics, formed in 1961 and admitted to ICSU in 1966).

Although the IUPsyS was founded in 1951, it was admitted to ICSU only in 1982, whereas the International Union of Physiological Sciences, founded in 1952, was promptly admitted to ICSU in 1955. The IUPsyS had applied shortly after its formation for membership in ICSU, but was told repeatedly that the time was not appropriate for consideration of its application. A 30-year delay occurred before its application was accepted. Similarly, the International Union of Anthropological and Ethnographical Societies (IUAES), founded in 1948, was admitted to ICSU only in 1993. ICSU was reluctant for many years to admit international unions such as the IUPsyS and the IUAES, whose discipline was in part in the social sciences. That does not, however, explain other delays: The International Brain Research Organization was founded in 1960 but admitted as a Scientific Union Member of ICSU only in 1993, after having been a Scientific Associate since 1976; the International Union of Food Science and Technology was founded in 1970 but admitted as a Scientific Union Member only in 1996.

References

Cadwallader, T.C. (1992). The historical roots of the American Psychological Association. In R.B. Evans & V.S. Sexton (Eds.), *The American Psychological Association: A historical perspective*. Washington, DC : American Psychological Association.

González Solaz, M.J. (1998). *Los congresos internacionales de psicologia (1963–1984)*. Unpublished doctoral dissertation, Valencia, Spain.

Greenaway, F. (1996). *Science International: A history of the International Council of Scientific Unions*. Cambridge & New York: Cambridge University Press.

International Council for Science. (2000). *Year book 2000*. Paris: International Council for Science.

Montoro González, L. (1982). *Los congresos internacionales de psicologia (1889–1960)*. Unpublished doctoral dissertation, Valencia, Spain.

Piéron, H. (1954). Histoire succincte des congrès internationaux de psychologie. *L'Année Psychologique, 54*, 397–405.

The 1st International Congress of Psychology: Assuring the continuity of congresses

3

The 1st International Congress of Psychology was immediately recognized as such a great success that the participants drew up plans for the 2nd congress and for a standing committee to assure the succession of congresses. In view of the success, it is puzzling to consider in retrospect the doubts that preceded the initial meeting.

The initial proposal for an international congress of psychology was published in 1881 by a visionary young Polish psychologist who also called for an international organization of psychologists. This imaginative psychologist was Julian Ochorowicz (1850–1917), Privatdocent in psychology at the Polish University of Lemburg. (Lemburg was then in the Austro-Hungarian empire and is now the Ukrainian city of Lvov.) Ochorowicz convinced the French psychologist Théodule Ribot to publish in his journal, the *Revue Philosophique*, an article entitled "Projet pour un congrès international de psychologie" (Ochorowicz, 1881). Ribot (1890, pp. 29–30), in his presidential address at the 1st congress, confessed that when he received Ochorowicz's manuscript he found the project attractive but fanciful and published it in the hope that it might bear fruit in the distant future, never expecting Ochorowicz's vision to be realized so rapidly.

As a contemporary visionary, engineer Gustave Eiffel promised the French authorities in 1886 that he could build the tallest structure in the world and have it ready in time for the celebrations of the centenary of the French revolution. In spite of widespread skepticism, Eiffel carried out his promise. The project for the international congress of psychology and the completion of the Eiffel Tower converged in 1889, when the psychologists who attended the 1st congress held their closing banquet on the Tower.

The full name of the 1st congress was the International Congress of Physiological Psychology, and it was organized by the French Society of Physiological Psychology. This society was founded in 1885, on the initiative of professor of medicine Charles Richet; it lasted only a few years, but long enough to organize the 1st International Congress of Physiological Psychology (Piéron, 1938, p. 508. "Physiological" was used in the sense of "scientific," just as Wundt entitled his text of 1873–74 *Grundzüge der*

Julian Ochorowicz (1850–1917): First to suggest holding International Congress of Psychology and forming international organization of psychological societies. (Courtesy of Archiwum Ilustracji Wydawnictwa Naukowego PWN S.A., Warsaw)

physiologische Psychologie, meaning a psychology intended to be as scientific as physiology.

The 1st International Congress of Psychology

Organizers, sponsors, registrants, and participants

The International Congress of Physiological Psychology took place on August 6–10, 1889, during the Universal Exposition in Paris. It was Ribot who took the initiative to organize the congress on behalf of the French Society of Physiological Psychology. Other officers and members of the organizing committee included not only psychologists and philosophers but also psychiatrists and other physicians;

Théodule A. Ribot (1839–1916): Acting President of the 1st International Congress of Psychology, Paris 1889, and later President of the 4th International Congress of Psychology, Paris 1900.

psychology was interpreted more broadly then than now, and there were only a few psychologists at the time. The prominent neurologist Jean-Martin Charcot was named President of the congress, but it appears that he did not attend any of its sessions (Claparède, 1930, p.36; James, 1889), and Ribot was effectively the President; Ribot is listed as Acting President in publications of the IUPsyS, and Charcot is named as Honorary President. Ribot had just left the chair of Experimental and Comparative Psychology at the Collège de France, moving to a professorship at the Sorbonne. Technically, Ribot was one of three Vice-Presidents of the congress, the other two being the eminent psychiatrist Valentin Magnan and the philosopher and member of the Académie Française, Hippolyte Taine. The Secretary-General of the congress was Charles Richet, professor of medicine in Paris; he was a physiologist concerned with psychological and parapsychological questions, and he had helped to give scientific status to studies of hypnotism. Other members of the Organizing Committee included Edouard Brissaud, professor of medicine; Julian Ochorowicz, listed as a member of the French Society of Physiological Psychology, and René Sully-Prudhomme of the Académie Française.

The committee of sponsors of the congress included prominent psychologists and members of related disciplines from 13 different countries. Among the sponsors were several whose names many readers will still recognize: Alexander Bain of the University of Aberdeen, well known for his textbooks of psychology (Great Britain); Henri Beaunis, professor of physiology, who had just founded at the Sorbonne the first French laboratory of psychology, the Laboratory of Physiological Psychology; Francis Galton, a scientist-at-large and member of the Royal Society of London, well known for his work in heredity and in statistics (Great Britain); Hermann von Helmholtz, a physicist, neuro-physiologist, and investigator of the senses (Germany); Ewald Hering, a neuro-physiologist and investigator of vision (Czechoslovakia); John Hughlings

Jackson, a neurologist and student of brain organization (Great Britain); William James, the leading American psychologist (USA); Pierre Janet, a systematic psychopathologist and psychotherapist, who was to be an officer of later international congresses of psychology (France); M. Lange (Denmark); Cesare Lomboroso, a psychiatrist and anthropologist who studied hereditary factors in criminality (Italy); Ivan Mikhailovich Sechenov, a prominent physiologist who maintained that psychological questions should be studied by physiologists through investigation of reflexes (Russia); Wilhelm Wundt, the founder of experimental psychology (Germany).

The Organizing Committee mailed out invitations to the congress on July 1, 1889, accompanied by a preliminary program. Two hundred and four registrants came from 21 countries, paying a registration fee of 10 francs. The majority, 128, came from France; Russia had the next highest delegation, 19, and both Germany and Great Britain had 10 registrants each; only 3 came from the United States. Of the 204 registrants, only about 50 participated by giving a presentation or taking part in a symposium (Montoro González, 1982, Figure 1, p. 300). Furthermore, many of those registered did not actually attend the congress. James (1889) reported that the number at sessions varied from 60 to 120. Claparède wrote that it was a really small congress with no more than half the number of registrants present at sessions (1929, p. 36).

Program of the congress

Four main themes were discussed at the congress: hallucinations, which was understood to include also mental telepathy; hypnotism; heredity; and muscular sensations. Limitations of time and disagreements about appropriate subject matter led to elimination of some of the topics listed in the preliminary program. Unlike most of the following congresses, there were no parallel sessions.

The content of the program revealed ongoing controversies about the proper nature of psychology. One controversy concerned the role of hypnotism. A large group of physicians who practised hypnotism submitted papers on this topic. When the program committee did not accept many of these, the physicians organized their own congress, Le Premier Congrès International d'Hypnotisme, which overlapped with the Congrès International de Psychologie Physiologique. The published proceedings of the Congress of Hypnotism (Premier Congrès International d'Hypnotisme, 1890) were more than twice as long as the proceedings of the Congress of Psychology.

Another controversy concerned the role of experimental research versus investigations of metapsychology, that is, psychological events that could not be understood by conventional science. Ribot, in his address opening the congress, related the congress to the introduction of psychology among the sciences. He stressed that the congress showed how research and cooperative relations among psychologists could develop and benefit when objective methods replaced introspection (Ribot, 1890, p. 30; Piéron, 1954, p. 398). In concluding his address, Ribot called for further international congresses of psychology to succeed the opening one in Paris.

Charles Richet, the Secretary-General, had placed on the congress program the question of hallucinations in the sense of mental telepathy, and in his opening address, he called for study of metapsychology. According to Henri Piéron, Richet welcomed to the congress colleagues who shared his interest in metapsychology—not only Ochorowicz, who had stimulated the organization of the 1st International Congress of Psychology, but also Henry Sidgwick, the English philosopher who was to be president of the 2nd congress, and Baron Albert von Schrenck-Notzing, who was to be Secretary-General of the 3rd congress (Piéron, 1954, p. 399); this welcome does not, however, appear in the opening address of Richet as Secretary-General of the congress, as reported in the proceedings (Richet, 1890, pp. 32-38). In his brief history of the international congresses of psychology, Piéron (1954) characterized Richet as an eminent disciple of Claude Bernard, a poet, a dramatist, a fabulist, an inventor, a future aviator, and first among the metapsychologists. Curiously, Piéron did not mention that Richet was awarded the Nobel Prize in Medicine or Physiology in 1913 for his discovery of and research on anaphylaxis; this is a term Richet coined for the sensitivity that develops to various substances after they are placed within the body. Although in the long run Richet was not able to interest many psychologists in metapsychology, he participated in several international congresses of psychology, and served on successive International Congress Committees until his death in 1935.

The first session of the congress, on hallucinations, was chaired by Henry Sidgwick, professor of philosophy at Cambridge and president (1882-85, 1888-93) of the Society for Psychical Research of London. A committee was established to collect examples of occurrence of hallucinations, especially the perception of a distant person at the moment of his death, and to perform a statistical analysis of them.

The second session of the congress was devoted to hypnotism; it was chaired by Joseph Rémi Léopold Delboeuf, professor of psychology at the University of Liège (Belgium) and the founder of its psychological laboratory. The presentations and debate opposed the positions of the Nancy school and of the Salpêtrière hospital in Paris. According to the Nancy school, headed by physician Hippolyte Bernheim, hypnotism was a phenomenon of normal behavior related to suggestion and sleep. The Salpêtrière group, headed by the neurologist Jean-Martin Charcot, maintained that hypnotism is a pathological condition, related to hysteria. Sigmund Freud had visited both the Nancy and the Salpêtrière groups in France and attended the congresses of hypnotism and psychology to witness more of their presentations. (Freud was listed among the registrants of the congress of psychology as "Freund, Sigm., Université de Vienne.")

According to the report of William James, "The partisans of the Nancy school were decidedly in the majority at the meetings; and everyone seemed to think that the original Salpêtrière doctrine of hypnotism, as a definite pathological condition with its three stages and somatic causes, was a thing of the past" (James, 1889, pp. 614–615). Bernheim took an active part in the discussion, but as noted earlier, Charcot, although Honorary President of the congress, did not attend its sessions. James commented that the great diversity of views on hypnotism showed how much more work still had to be done in this field. He also noted that an overlapping medical congress devoted mainly to hypnotism drew off attendance from the last few days of the psychology congress.

Francis Galton presided over the third session, on heredity. He advocated performing animal research to determine whether acquired habits may be inherited, and for research on human heredity he advocated studying relatives of different degrees of relationship. Charles Richet (1890, p. 35) remarked that the subject of heredity evoked little interest among the public, and he remarked that livestock breeders pay more attention to the heredity of their animals than scholars do to that of humans. It should be recognized that the 1st International Congress of Psychology took place before the laws of heredity, published in an obscure journal by Gregor Mendel in 1866, were rediscovered and made widely known in 1900.

William James presided over the fourth session, devoted to muscular and other sensations. This session was introduced to give more weight to conventional experimental psychology and physiology in the congress. Several investigators discussed whether muscular sensations are purely afferent, like touch and other sensations, or whether they reflect in part motor innervation. Charles Richet reported that after removal of occipital cortex of a dog, the animal still detected objects as obstacles but no longer as prey.

In addition to the 4 main themes, there were 21 individual reports. These could be divided into two major areas, one revolving around hypnotism and the other around aspects of physiology related to behavior (Montoro González, 1982, p. 86). Physiology was to remain a major theme in the succeeding congresses. No reports dealt with applications of psychology. Apparently all of the reports were presented in French.

James emphasized that the formal discussions at the congress were secondary in importance to the social consequences: "the friendships made, the intimacies deepened, and the encouragement and inspiration which came to everyone from seeing before them in flesh and blood so large a part of that little army of fellow-students, from whom and for whom all contemporary psychology exists. The individual worker feels much less isolated in the world after such an experience" (James, 1889, p. 615).

The closing banquet of the congress took place in a restaurant on the first platform of the Eiffel Tower, which had been completed and inaugurated earlier that year. As Claparède wrote, the Tower, like the

International Congress of Psychology, had seemed a fantastic project when it was first proposed a few years earlier (1930, p. 36). William James (1889, p. 615) wrote enthusiastically about the final banquet and the nighttime view from the Eiffel Tower with "the wonderfully illuminated landscape of exhibition grounds, palaces and fountains spread out below, with all the lights and shadows of nocturnal Paris framing it in."

Assuring the continuity of international congresses of psychology

The participants in the International Congress of Physiological Psychology in 1889 agreed that an International Committee should be established to assure the continuity of international congresses of psychology (Claparède, 1929; James, 1889, p. 615; Nuttin, 1992, pp. 30-31). Ochorowicz (1881) had seen the necessity for such a committee. As well as setting up a permanent committee under the name of the International Congress of Psychology, the participants of the 1889 congress also decided the dates, host country, and name of the next congress, and they named the officers of the 2nd congress. The International Committee was also charged with the responsibility of organizing the 2nd congress. In the future, there would be two separate committees, the permanent International Committee and a local Organizing Committee. The permanent International Committee was to be known by several different names over the course of time: Comité Permanent des Congrès, Comité International Permanent des Congrès de Psychologie, Comité International de Propagande, International Congress of Psychology. Over the years, 12 successive International Committees were to be appointed, the last of them in 1948 (Appendix A). This last committee was also to serve as the Assembly of the first of the International Congress of Psychology to be held under the auspices of the new International Union of Scientific Psychology in 1951.

Representatives of Belgium, Great Britain, and Switzerland offered to play host to the next congress. Great Britain obtained the majority of the votes, and the congress was set for London in August 1892.

What to call the 2nd congress aroused considerable discussion. Some urged retaining the name International Congress of Physiological Psychology, stating that psychology is a branch of physiology. Others proposed using the term "Experimental Psychology," noting that in Germany and Great Britain it meant a psychology that abstained from metaphysical questions. Some wanted to use the term "Psychology" without any qualification. Finally it was decided to use the title International Congress of Experimental Psychology.

As President of the 2nd congress, the participants chose Henry Sidgwick, professor of philosophy at Cambridge and a member of the Society for Psychical Research of London. He had interacted with French investigators of hypnotism, which was a reason that they urged his election to ensure that this topic would be included at the second congress. The first Secretary was Frederick W.H. Myers, who shared interests with Sidgwick; he also was a member of the Society for Psychical Research, and he was a co-author of a widely noted book on psychic research, *Phantasms of the Living* (Gurney, Myers, & Podmore, 1886). The second Secretary was James Sully, prominent as a writer of textbooks of psychology and named professor of mind and logic at the University of London in 1892.

An international and interdisciplinary list of 11 Vice-Presidents was named, including Alexander Bain, mentioned earlier as a sponsor of the 1st congress (Great Britain); James M. Baldwin, who founded the psychological laboratory at the University of Toronto in 1889 and at Princeton in 1893 (Canada and USA); Hippolyte Bernheim, a physician expert in hypnotism (France); Hermann Ebbinghaus, whose pioneer experimental research on memory appeared in his 1885 book, *Uber das Gedächtnis* (On memory) (Germany); Joseph Rémi Léopold Delboeuf, a psychologist who investigated visual psychophysics, and a founder of the psychological laboratory at the University of Liège (Belgium); David Ferrier, a neurophysiologist who mapped sensory regions of the cortex in animals (Great Britain); Eduard Hitzig, a psychiatrist who demonstrated the electrical excitability of the brain in 1870 (Germany); Jules Liegeois, professor of law at the University of Nancy (France); Wilhelm Preyer, a physiologist, known especially for his book *Die Seele des Kindes* (1882, English translation, *The Mind of the Child*, 1888) (Germany); Charles Richet, a physiologist interested in psychological questions, including hypnotism and telepathy, and who had served as Secretary-General of the first congress (France); E.A. Schäfer, a neurophysiologist who investigated localization of brain functions (Germany).

The members of the permanent International Congress of Psychology committee, chosen by the participants of the 1st congress, were meant not only to ensure the continuation of the congresses but also to facilitate international correspondence among psychologists working on different topics in psychology. The *compte rendu* of the congress (Congrès International de Psychologie Physiologique, 1890, p. 145) and William James, in his account of the congress (1889, p. 615), provided only the surnames of most members of the International Committee, but we list full names when possible (see Appendix A1). Nine of the 27 members came from France: Henri Beaunis, Hippolyte Bernheim, Bertrand, Alfred Espinas, H. Ferrari, Eugène Gley, Léon Marillier, Théodule Ribot, and Charles Richet; 3 came from England: Francis Galton, Frederick W.H. Myers, and Henry Sidgwick; 4 from Germany: Eduard Hitzig, Hugo Münsterberg, Albert von Schrenck-Notzing, and Arthur Sperling; 3 from Russia: Danilewski, N. Grote, Julian Ochorowicz (it is not clear why the compte rendu listed Ochorowicz as Russian since we know he was Austro-Hungarian); 2 from

Switzerland: August Henri Forel, Pierre Herzen; and 1 each from 6 other countries: Benedikt (Austria), Joseph Rémi Léopold Delboeuf (Belgium), Neiglick (Finland), Cesare Lomboroso (Italy), Edouard Grüber (Romania), and William James (United States).

The lists of members of the successive international committees, named from 1889 to 1948, contained the names of many well-known contributors to psychology and related fields. Here are some examples:

Alfred Adler, Frederic Bartlett, Alfred Binet, Edwin G. Boring, Charlotte Bühler, Karl Bühler, James McKeen Cattell, James Drever Sr., Hermann Ebbinghaus, Paul Fraisse, Francis Galton, G. Stanley Hall, William James, Pierre Janet, David Katz, Otto Klineberg, Kurt Koffka, Wolfgang Köhler, Serge Korsakoff, Karl S. Lashley, Kurt Lewin, Albert Michotte, Joseph Nuttin, Ivan P. Pavlov, Jean Piaget, Henri Piéron, Mario Ponzo, Morton Prince, Burrhus Frederick Skinner, Charles Spearman, Santiago Ramon y Cajal, Théodule Ribot, Edgar Rubin, Edward L. Thorndike, Louis Thurstone, Edward B. Titchener, Margaret F. Washburn, Max Wertheimer, Robert S. Woodworth, and Wilhelm Wundt.

After the formation of the Union in 1951, the officers and members of the Executive Committee began to become more representative in terms of gender and geography, as we will see in later chapters of this history.

The participants of the 1st congress also agreed in principle that an international association of societies of psychology should be formed (Congrès International de Psychologie Physiologique, 1890, pp. 126-129). This foreshadowed the IUPsyS, but such an association was obviously premature, because there were only a few local societies at the time. These included the French Society of Physiological Psychology, the Berlin and Munich Psychological Societies, the Moscow Psychological Society, and the Boston and London Societies for Psychical Research.

Changes over the course of the international congresses of psychology

Now that we have reviewed the 1st International Congress of Psychology, it will be worthwhile to anticipate briefly some of the changes that would take place in the congresses over the next century.

Growth in numbers of congress registrants

One major change is that the congresses attracted increasing numbers of psychologists, growing from 204 in Paris, 1889, to reach about 4000 registrants for the most recent congresses (Brussels, 1992; Montréal, 1996). There were gaps in the succession of congresses caused by the two World

Wars, and there were dips in the numbers registered for the two congresses after World War I and for the three congresses after World War II. Then the growth resumed. The small numbers of participants registered for the 7th congress (Oxford, 1923) and the 8th congress (Groningen, 1926) were caused by a decision of the International Congress Committee to limit attendance at each of these congresses to about 200 well-known psychologists plus a few others. No other congress had such a limit imposed.

Although only about one quarter of the registrants at the 1st congress participated by giving a presentation or taking part in a symposium, the great majority of registrants at the recent congresses have participated actively in events on the program. This reflects the fact that since World War II, many registrants have all or part of their congress expenses reimbursed by university or governmental funds if they take an active part in the program.

Increase in numbers of women registrants

Only three women were listed among the 204 registrants at the 1st congress, but the number of women rose rapidly by the 3rd congress. At least two of the women registered at the 1st congress also participated in the 2nd congress. The report of the 2nd congress did not include a list of registrants but it showed papers presented by Mrs Christine Ladd-Franklin and by Mrs

Sidgwick (International Congress of Experimental Psychology, 1892, pp. 103–108, pp. 168–169, Notes, pp. 582 & 586). The announcements for the 3rd and 4th congresses stated that women would be accorded the same rights and privileges as men (e.g., *Psychological Review*, 1896, p. 240). The report of the 3rd congress listed at least 51 women registrants among the 453 total registrants (Dritter Internationaler Congress für Psychologie, 1897). Several of these were listed as professors' wives, but one was listed as doctor, one as professor, a few as doctoral candidates, and several without any qualification.

The first woman was named to the International Congress Committee in 1909 at the 6th congress in Geneva. This was "Mlle Dr" I. Ioteyko, a Polish physician who was head of the laboratory of psychology at the University of Brussels (VIME Congrès International de Psychologie, 1910, p. 34). Dr Ioteyko (later spelt Joteyko) was one of eight Polish psychologists, five of them women, to propose at the 1909 congress that the next international congress be held in Warsaw.

Christine Ladd-Franklin, USA (1847–1930): One of the first women to participate in International Congresses of Psychology, giving reports on color-vision.

Increase in diversity of congress sites

The origins of modern psychological science in Western Europe, its early spread to North America, and then its development around the world are

*Jozefa Joteyko
(1866–1928):
The first woman to be
appointed to the
International
Congress Committee.
(Courtesy of
Archiwum Ilustracji
Wydawnictwa
Naukowego PWN
S.A., Warsaw,)*

reflected in the sites and dates of the international congresses of psychology, as shown in Appendix D. The first eight congresses all took place in six countries of Western Europe. Successive plans to hold congresses in the United States as early as 1893 failed to materialize until the 9th congress was held at Yale University in 1929. Congresses 9–18 included two in the United States, one in Canada, and six in Western Europe. Then, in the last third of the 20th century, more varied sites began to be chosen to reflect and encourage the spread of psychology around the world. The 18th congress took place in Moscow (1966); the 20th congress, in Tokyo (1972); the 22nd congress, in Leipzig, German Democratic Republic (1980); the 23rd in Acapulco (1984); the 24th in Sydney (1988); the 25th in Brussels (1992); the 26th returned to Montréal (1996); and the 27th congress returns to Stockholm in 2000, almost a half century after the IUPsyS was founded there in 1951.

Increased geographical diversity of congress registrants

The number of countries sending participants to the congresses has increased greatly and the proportions of registrants coming from different countries have changed markedly over the history of the International Congress of Psychology. Whereas only 21 countries were represented at the 1st congress, during the first 16 congresses (1889–1960), citizens of 71 different countries registered in at least 1 congress (Montoro González, 1982, pp. 303–305). During the period 1963–1980, citizens of 88 different countries registered (González Solaz, 1998, Table 2.1.A., pp. 531–533).

Of course, each country's representation shows a peak when it is the host country. Overall, however, for the first 16 congresses, the representation of the United States came to predominate, with 27% of the total, followed by those of Germany (13%), Great Britain (12%), France (11%), Italy (5%), Belgium (4.5%), and Switzerland (4%) (Montoro González, 1982, pp. 292 et seq.). The next six congresses (1963–1980) showed rather similar results: United States (28%), Germany (German Federal Republic plus German Democratic Republic) (15%), Japan (10%), USSR (10%), France (6%), Great Britain (5%) (González Solaz, 1998, pp. 531–533). Each of the six leading countries hosted a congress during the period concerned, increasing their attendance over other countries. If one eliminates, for each of these countries, the congress in which it played host during this period, then the United States still has the greatest total attendance (23%), followed by Germany (5%), Japan (4.1%), Great Britain (2.8%), France (2.1%), and USSR (1.8%); Canada, which did not host a congress during this period, accounted for 3% of the overall attendance.

Changes in languages employed at the congresses

The languages used for presentations at the congresses also varied over time. The 1st congress appears to have been conducted entirely in French; at least the published record is entirely in French, even for English-speaking or German-speaking participants (Congrès International de Psychologie Physiologique, 1890). At the 2nd congress in London, 1892, papers were read and discussions conducted in English, French, or German (International Congress of Experimental Psychology, 1892, p. iv). The proceedings of the 3rd congress, Munich 1896, show that papers were presented in German, French, English, and Italian (Dritter Internationaler Congress für Psychologie, 1897). At the 6th congress, Geneva 1909, in the discussion about congress procedures, a speaker referred to the five languages authorized at the congress: German, English, French, Italian, and Esperanto (Clément, 1910, p. 842); the proceedings show papers in the first four of these languages, but only some discussion in Esperanto. In contrast to the 1st congress in Paris, which was entirely in French, at the 11th International Congress in Paris, 1937, there were five official languages—English, French, German, Italian, and Spanish (Onzième Congrès International de Psychologie, 1938). From this high-water mark of linguistic diversity, the number of official languages diminished so that, until recently, the official congress languages were English and French, plus the language of the host country. (See Chapter 13, where in 1991 the Executive Committee dropped French as a required official language, leaving only English and the language of the host country.)

Analyses by Montoro González (1982, pp. 381 et seq.) show that in the first six international congresses (1889–1909), those held before World War I, French predominated, accounting for 43% of the reports; German came next, with 24%, and Italian third, with 21%; English accounted for only 11% during this period. In the next five congresses, those occurring between the two World Wars, English predominated with 66%; German was second with 17%, narrowly leading French, which had 16%. In the first five congresses that followed World War II, congresses from 1948 through 1960, English had an even more impressive lead, with 74%; French was second with 16%, and German had fallen far behind, to 9%. For the seven congresses from 1963 through 1984, González Solaz (1998, p. 592) found that 70% of the presentations were in English, 14% in French, 5% in Spanish (almost entirely because of the 23rd congress in Mexico), and 4% in German. The predominance of English and French until the end of the 20th century is explained in part by the fact that, until 1996, the international congresses had adopted the practice that presentations could be made in English, French, or the language of the host country.

Changes in topics and themes of the congresses

The topics and themes of the congress programs showed marked changes as the scope, methods, and directions of psychology developed. In this regard, as in others, the history of the congresses presents a history of modern psychology. Montoro González (1982, pp. 250–291) devised a set of headings to classify the subjects of presentations at the first 16 congresses (1889–1960). González Solaz (1998) used the same classification scheme, with minor modifications, for the next seven congresses (1963–1984). We will cite some of these analyses of topics as we review the successive international congresses of psychology in the next chapters.

References

Claparède, E. (1930). Esquisse historique des Congrès Internationaux de Psychologie. In *Ninth International Congress of Psychology* (pp. 33–47). Princeton, NJ: Psychological Review Co.

Clément, H. (1910). Discussion. *VI Congrès International de Psychologie* (p.842). Geneva: Librairie Kundig.

Congrès International de Psychologie Physiologique. (1890). Bureau des Revues.

VIME Congrès International de Psychologie. (1910). Geneva: Librairie Kündig.

Dritter Internationaler Congress für Psychologie. (1897). Munich: Verlag J.F. Lehmann.

González Solaz, M.J. (1998). *Los congresos internacionales de psicologia (1963–1984)*. Unpublished doctoral dissertation, Valencia, Spain.

Gurney, E., Myers, F.W.H. & Podmore, F. (1886). *Phantasms of the living*. London: Trubner.

International Congress of Experimental Psychology. (1892). London: Williams & Norgate.

James, W. (1889). The Congress of Physiological Psychology at Paris. *Mind, 14, 614–614*.

Montoro González, L. (1982). *Los congresos internacionales de psicologia (1889–1960)*. Unpublished doctoral dissertation, Valencia, Spain.

Nuttin, J. (1992). Les premiers congrès internationaux de psychologie. *Contributions to the history of the international congresses of psychology: A posthumous homage to J.R. Nuttin* (pp. 7–75). Valencia, Spain: Revista de Historia de la Psicologia, and Leuven: Studia Psychologica.

Ochorowicz, J. (1881). Pour un congrès international de psychologie. *Revue Philosophique, 12, 1–17*.

Onzième Congrès International de Psychologie. (1938). Paris: Félix Alcan.

Piéron, H. (1938). Discours de M. Henri Piéron, Président du Congrès. In *Onzième Congrès International de Psychologie* (pp. 507–514). Paris: Félix Alcan.

Piéron, H. (1954). Histoire succincte des congrès internationaux de psychologie. *L'Année Psychologique, 54, 397–405*.

Premier Congrès International d'Hypnotisme. (1890). Paris: Dion.

Ribot, T. (1890). Discours du président. In *Congrès International de Psychologie Physiologique* (pp. 29–32). Paris: Bureau des Revues.

Richet, C. (1890). Discours du secrétaire général. In *Congrès International de Psychologie Physiologique* (pp. 32–38). Paris: Bureau des Revues.

The International Congresses of Psychology become regularized, 1892–1909

After the success of the 1st International Congress of Psychology in Paris, 1889, five other congresses followed at intervals of 3 to 5 years, through the 6th congress at Geneva in 1909. This chapter carries the story of the international congresses of psychology and the International Congress Committee up to the eve of World War I. Several themes emerge from examination of this period. The congresses became a regular means of communication among psychologists and with members of neighboring disciplines. The growth in attendance at the successive congresses showed their popularity and effectiveness. The International Congress Committee grew in size and in number of countries represented. Although the congresses were international, a large proportion of the attendees of each congress were from the host country. This is understandable because travel was difficult and time-consuming a century ago. The definition of psychology was disputed at the early congresses, with psychical research strongly represented, but contested by experimental psychologists. After the controversy over psychical research at the 4th congress in Paris, 1900, its proponents sought other outlets than the congresses of psychology. The chapter ends with a brief account of "The American congress that wasn't" (Evans & Down Scott, 1978)—the failure of American psychologists to organize an international congress in the United States for 1913.

The 2nd International Congress of Psychology, London 1892 (International Congress of Experimental Psychology)

The International Congress of Experimental Psychology took place at University College, London, August 1–4, 1892. The president was Henry Sidgwick, professor of utilitarian philosophy at the University of Cambridge and president of the Society for Psychical Research (SPR) of London. Sidgwick was the initial president of the SPR (1882–85) and served a second term as president in 1888–93. The Honorary Secretary of the congress was Mr Frederick W.H. Myers, also a member of the SPR. Professor James Sully shared the work of Secretary and was influential in organizing the experimental aspects of the program. The proceedings did not include a list of registrants but noted that over 300 persons attended, "including nearly a hundred foreign visitors, from all parts of Europe and from America and Australia" (International Congress of Experimental Psychology, 1892a, p. iv).

Because the number of papers presented—42—seemed large to the organizers, they were divided into two concurrent sections: (a) "papers dealing with Neurology and Psycho-physics," and (b) "papers dealing with Hypnotism and phenomena akin to those of Hypnotism." The latter heading included psychic phenomena.

The inclusion of psychic or metapsychological papers was a controversial subject. The leading German psychologist Wilhelm Wundt, who had attended the 1st congress, protested against this subject by refusing to attend the 2nd congress. Professor Sidgwick regretted this in his presidential address (Sidgwick, 1892). He expressed the hope that the narrowness of his own interests:

> had no tendency to narrow the conception that I have formed of the proper work of the Congress. I observe that Professor Wundt, in a recent number of his Philosophische Studien, suggests the probability that under my influence "clairvoyance, under the innocent mask of a statistic of hallucinations", will be the chief topic at our present meeting; but this only shows that the most accomplished psychologist is liable to go rather wide of the mark, if he is determined to express his opinions on matters on which he is determined to seek no information. It has, on the contrary, been my aim — as I hope our programme shows—to avoid giving an undue place to the enquiries in which I am especially interested; to make our list of papers as adequately representative as possible of the various lines of enquiry, pursued by very diverse methods, which are included within the range of our subject (H. Sidgwick, 1892, p. 2).

In fact, Sidgwick was scrupulous in avoiding giving a major place in the congress to psychical research. He wrote in his memoirs that he had attended the Paris congress purely out of friendship for Richet and was surprised there to be elected President of the 2nd congress:

> Behold me, then, President-elect of a Congress of experimental Psychologists—most of them stubborn materialists, interested solely in psychophysical experiments on the senses; whereas I have never experimented except in telepathy. Water and fire, oil and vinegar, are too feeble to express our antagonism! What was to be done? I sought out James Sully—probably the one Englishman known to

> *German Professors as a writer on physiological Psychology—*
> *and said to him, "… be secretary: write to leading Germans:*
> *and, in short, get up the Congress so far as ordinary*
> *experimental Psychology goes; Myers and I will provide the*
> *extraordinary element; and we will trust in Providence to*
> *make the explosion when the two elements meet endurable"*
> *(A. Sidgwick & Sidgwick, 1906, pp. 515–516).*

Sidgwick took further steps to try to get German experimental psychologists and physiologists to take part in the 2nd congress. Because he had not used German in many years, he spent his Easter vacation of 1892 in Germany to revive his fluency, and he visited several German professors and encouraged them to participate in the congress.

Finally, only a few reports at the congress were on psychical research. One was an international survey of cases of hallucinations, including cases of telepathy, among the sane. This survey, planned at the 1st congress, was co-authored by Henry Sidgwick in England, William James in the United States, and Léon Marillier in France. Other reports at the congress covered a wide range of topics, including mechanisms of color vision, intersensory associations, functional attributes of regions of the cerebral cortex, development of arithmetic concepts in children, sex differences in sensory sensitivity, and relations between respiration and fluctuations of attention. Conway Lloyd Morgan discussed "The limits of animal intelligence" and made an early presentation of what later became known as Lloyd Morgan's canon: "In no case is an animal activity to be interpreted as the outcome of the exercise of a higher psychical faculty, if it can be fairly interpreted as the outcome of the exercise of one which stands lower in the psychological scale." Hypnosis was discussed extensively, as at the 1st congress. Some speakers stressed its therapeutic value. The downfall of the Salpêtrière concept of hypnosis as an abnormal phenomenon was now considered complete.

In commenting on the development of psychology in England, Professor Sidgwick confessed that England had fallen behind in converting psychology to an exact science by making precise determinations and measurements. He noted that England did not yet have a properly equipped psychological laboratory. He hoped that one of the benefits of holding the congress in England would be to stimulate development by comparing the position of England "not only with that of Germany, which originated and still leads in this movement, but also with that of our American cousins—who, with characteristic energy, have developed eight or nine psychological laboratories in the last few years ..." (H. Sidgwick, 1892, p. 3).

Professor Charles Richet, one of the Vice-Presidents of the congress, gave an address on the future of psychology. He held that a major field of psychology is "transcendental psychology," that is, the study of extraordinary powers of human intelligence which may hold the keys to clairvoyance, transmission of thought, and prevision. Richet declared that determining whether or not such powers exist would be a major accomplishment and would require great perseverance.

Decisions of the permanent International Committee

At the conclusion of the congress, the International Congress Committee accepted an invitation of German psychologists to hold the 3rd congress in Munich in the summer of 1896, with Professor Carl Stumpf as President and Baron Albert von Schrenck-Notzing as Secretary. This was to be called simply the 3rd International Congress of Psychology, without any qualification such as "physiological" or "experimental."

The permanent International Committee was given a formal name, the Permanent Committee of Organization. It was reconstituted with Professor Carl Stumpf as President and Baron Albert von Schrenck-Notzing as Secretary. Twenty-one additional members were named (International Congress of Experimental Psychology, 1892a, p. 178), and three others were named before the 3rd congress, keeping the total membership of the International Committee at 27 (Dritter Internationaler Congress für Psychologie, 1897, pp. xxi-xxii). Nine different countries were represented in the committee. Seven members of the first International Committee continued on the second: Bernheim, Hitzig, James, Richet, von Schrenck-Notzing, and Sidgwick; Delboeuf was also reappointed, but he died shortly after the congress. See Appendix A.2 for the complete list of members of the International Committee chosen at the 2nd congress.

An international congress in America?

It was also resolved to invite American psychologists to organize an extraordinary session of the congress in America in 1893. A committee of American psychologists was appointed to explore this idea: Professor James M. Baldwin, Dr Henry H. Donaldson, Professor George S. Fullerton, Professor G. Stanley Hall, Professor William James, Dr Lightner Witmer, and Dr William Romaine Newbold (International Congress of Experimental Psychology, 1892a, p. 178). A footnote to the page stated "that this Committee have decided *not* to hold an extraordinary session of the Congress in America," so their decision was reached promptly. It is possible that this decision was related to the discussion in December 1892 at the meeting of the American Psychological Association about organizing a psychological congress at the World's Columbian Exposition, Chicago 1893, but the APA decided not to do so. Nuttin (1992, p. 65) speculated that the decision of the Americans not to organize an extraordinary session of the international congresses may have reflected a desire to distance American psychology from metapsychology after the London congress.

An evaluation of the 2nd International Congress

The 2nd congress lacked the pathbreaking nature of the 1st congress. Neither did it provide the boost for development of British psychology that the 1st congress gave to French psychology. It did further the process of disengagement of psychology from metapsychology, which had begun in the 1st congress. Professor Stumpf, in his presidential address at the 3rd congress, noted that the 2nd congress took up an ensemble of themes notably broader than that of the 1st congress. The decision to hold the 3rd congress in Germany, the original and principal home of experimental psychology, was a further step in asserting the primary role of experimental psychology.

The 3rd International Congress of Psychology, Munich 1896

The 3rd International Congress of Psychology took place at the Royal University of Munich, August 4–7, 1896. The President was Professor Carl Stumpf of the University of Berlin; President II (Vice-President) was Professor Theodor Lipps of the University of Munich, and Secretary-General was Dr Albert von Schrenck-Notzing. The list of registered members showed a total of 455 (Dritter Internationaler Congress für Psychologie, 1897, pp. xxiii-xli), considerably larger than at the London congress. Of these, 268 (59%) were German, 30 (6%) Austrian, 27 (6%) from the USA, 24 (5%) French, and 19 (4%) Italian (Montoro González, 1982, p. 659). In part, the relatively large attendance was due to extensive correspondence undertaken by the German organizers; in part it was in response to announcements placed in journals. Thus, an announcement in *Mind* (1896, p. 143) stated that "All educated persons who desire to further the progress of Psychology and to foster personal relations among the students of Psychology in different nations are invited to take part in the meetings of the Congress." The announcement in the *Psychological Review* (1896, p. 240) added, "Women will have the same rights as men."

Carl Stumpf (1848–1936): President of the 3rd International Congress of Psychology, Munich, 1896.

Many more papers were presented than in London—116—so 29 sessions were scheduled. Most of the time, there were five concurrent sessions. Section I was devoted to brain anatomy and physiology; section II, to the psychology of the normal individual; section III, to psychopathology and criminal psychology; section IV, to the psychology of sleep, dreaming, hypnosis, and allied phenomena, including telepathy; and section V, to developmental and pedagogical psychology.

For the first time at an international congress of psychology, commercial firms displayed laboratory instruments and publishers displayed recent books. Such displays became a feature of subsequent congresses.

Also for the first time, a congress newspaper (*Tageblatt*) was distributed during the 4 days of meetings. It informed members about activities, changes in the program, registration of members, information about Munich, and so forth.

Four languages were used in congress presentations, discussions, and the publication of the proceedings: German, English, French, and Italian. Papers or abstracts had to be submitted in advance so they could be distributed to the members to permit better understanding of the different languages.

On the morning of the last day, the permanent International Committee met and decided to hold the 4th congress in Paris in 1900 with Professors Ribot and Richet as Presidents, and Pierre Janet as Secretary. As for the 1st congress in 1889, the 4th congress was planned to occur during an international exposition in Paris. The International Committee was reorganized and its membership enlarged to 38, including representatives from 12 countries (Dritter Internationaler Congress für Psychologie, 1897, pp. 164–165). (See Appendix A.3 for the membership of the International Committee.)

Ebbinghaus proposed that the International Committee request that the Royal Society of London include psychological publications in its catalog of scientific publications, and a committee was appointed for this purpose. Nuttin (1992, p. 65) speculated that this initiative may have led to the decision of the International Bibliographic Conference of London in 1896 to include experimental psychology among the 15 "leading sciences" to be catalogued.

Edward B. Titchener (E.B.T., 1896–97) reported that the many social occasions at the 3rd congress stimulated valuable personal exchanges among the participants. He also noted that excursions planned for the participants had to be cancelled because it rained throughout the congress.

Impacts of the 3rd International Congress

The 3rd International Congress had several favorable influences on the development of psychological science. As Nuttin noted (1992, pp. 63–65), although the congress was open to many aspects of psychology and of neighboring disciplines, it was psychological science as it existed at the end of the 19th century that was fully represented at the congress. There were still some conflicts with metapsychology, but these were muted, only to have a final outburst at the Paris congress in 1900. After that, there were to be only some rearguard skirmishes at the congresses of Rome in 1905 and Geneva in 1909. Nuttin (1992, pp. 64–65) speculated that if this change of emphasis had not occurred at Munich, German and American psychologists would have progressively abandoned the international congresses.

The congress was greeted with acclaim and hospitality by the City and University of Munich and the Kingdom of Bavaria, and a small number of members were invited to dine with the Prince-Regent. This was the first time such recognition was given to a congress of psychology.

For the first time, the permanent International Committee was named in the proceedings of the congress as the organizing committee for the congress. It was also the permanent International Committee that proposed that the next congress be held in Paris in 1900 and proposed the names of its main officers. Thus, the International Committee played a larger role in this congress than in the previous one.

The 4th International Congress of Psychology, Paris 1900

The 4th International Congress of Psychology took place in the Palais des Congrès at the Paris Exposition Universelle, August 20–25, 1900. Théodule A. Ribot was President, Charles Richet was second President, and Pierre Janet was secretary. The list of registered members showed 430 (IVE Congrès International de Psychologie, 1901, pp. 11–34); this was 25 fewer registrants than at the 3rd congress. Fifty-five per cent came from outside France; this was the first time that the majority of attendees came from outside the host country. Of these, 38 (9%) came from the USA, 35 (8%) from Germany, 32 (7%) from Great Britain, 26 (6%) from Russia, and 22 (5%) from Italy (Montoro González, 1982, p. 660).

In his presidential address, Ribot noted the impressive increase in numbers of psychological publications. The items reported in the *Psychological Index* increased from 2234 for 1896 to 2746 for 1899. Ribot foresaw the time when a single psychologist would no longer be able to review all the publications because, no sooner had he finished with those for one year, he would have to start again for the next.

Hermann Ebbinghaus reviewed the psychology of the 19th century. He stressed the differences of philosophical psychology among France, Germany, and England, whereas it seemed to him that scientific psychology was becoming a common international field, inspired by the unity of approach that characterizes science.

It seemed to some that "a large number of spiritualists, theosophists, occultists, and people interested in psychic research tried to dominate the scene" at the 4th congress (Montoro, Tortosa, Carpintero, & Peiro, 1984, p. 246). The German neurologist Oskar Vogt delivered a paper, "Contre le spiritisme," in which he strongly criticized the "spiritists" (spiritualists) as being "anti-scientifique" (Vogt, 1901). In the lively discussion that followed this paper, Ebbinghaus deplored the fact that scholars came from great distances to a congress of scientific psychology and had to hear such fanciful papers on spiritualism.

In the face of such opposition, there was a sharp decline in reports by proponents of psychical research at the international congresses of psychology after the 4th congress. An International Psychological Institute was established in 1900 for the scientific study of psychical phenomena. Piéron (1954, p. 401) reported that it was so effective in disproving claims of occult phenomena that supporters of psychical research withdrew their financial support and founded a Metapsychical Institute in Paris.

The program of the 4th congress was divided into symposia and general sessions. The six symposia were these: (1) Relations between psychology and anatomy and physiology. (2) Introspective psychology and its relations with philosophy. (3) Experimental and physiological psychology. (4) Psychopathology and psychiatry. (5) Psychology of hypnotism, suggestion, and related subjects. (6) Social and criminal psychology; this symposium also included reports on animal and comparative psychology, anthropology, and ethnography. The six general sessions were on these subjects: (1) Studies of the history of psychology. (2) Cerebral physiology. (3) Somnambulism. (4) Physiological psychology. (5) Experimental psychology. (6) Social and abnormal psychology. Of the 139 presentations at the congress, the most frequent subject was general psychology, with 21% of the total, followed by psychometrics (14%) and clinical psychology (13%) (Montoro González, 1982, p. 120).

The International Committee (called in French the Comité International de Propagande) increased its membership to 55, representing 14 countries (IVE Congrès International de Psychologie, 1901, pp. 221–225). (See Appendix A.4.) The countries with the largest representations in the International Committee were Italy and Germany with eight each, Great Britain with seven, and France, Russia, and the USA with six each. The committee decided to hold the 5th congress in Rome in 1904, with Professor Luigi Luciani, a physiologist and rector of the university of Rome, as President, and Giuseppi Sergi, professor of anthropology and psychology, as Vice-President; Sergi had founded the first laboratory of psychology in Italy in 1877. Professor Augusto Tamburini, psychiatrist and neurologist, was to be Secretary-General (IVE Congrès International de Psychologie, 1901, p. 221). The 4th congress closed, as had the first, with a banquet in a restaurant on the first platform of the Eiffel Tower.

The 5th International Congress of Psychology, Rome 1905

The 5th International Congress of Psychology took place in Rome, April 26–30, 1905. The national Organizing Committee changed the date from 1904 to 1905 to avoid a conflict in dates with the International Congress of Physiology meeting in Brussels in 1904. By the time of the congress, the Italian Organizing Committee had changed the composition of officers of the congress: Luigi Luciani, because of his many other responsibilities, gave up the presidency and became Honorary President; Giuseppi Sergi became President; Augusto Tamburini, professor of psychiatry, remained Secretary-General, and psychiatrist Sante de Sanctis was Vice Secretary-General. Thus, although the psychologist Sergi was President, two of the four principal officers were psychiatrists, and one was a physiologist. It was de Sanctis who prepared the extensive 798-page volume of proceedings for publication (Atti del V. Congresso Internazionale di Psicologia, 1906). The attendance at the 5th congress was 440, and 53% of the registrants were Italian. Of the rest, 60 (14%) were French, 32 (7%) German, 20 (5%) Austrian, 12 (3%) British, and 11 each came from Hungary and Russia; the United States, which had major representations at the 3rd and 4th congresses, had only 5 members at the 5th conference (Montoro González, 1982, p. 661).

As well as 12 addresses by major psychologists, there were 190 papers divided into 4 sessions: (I) Experimental psychology, including relations to anatomy and physiology, psychophysics, and comparative psychology. In connection with this session, there was a display of scientific instruments and of books. (II) Introspective psychology, psychology in relation to philosophy. (III) Pathological psychology, psychology in relation to hypnotism, suggestion, and related phenomena (including clairvoyance); psychotherapy. (IV) Criminal, pedagogical, and social psychology.

Of the 202 presentations, the most frequent subject was clinical psychology with 21% of the total; general psychology was second, with 14%, and physiological psychology third with 11% (Montoro González, 1982, p. 129).

At the start of the second general session, the chair gave the floor to Dr Felix Krueger, who was later to succeed Professor Wilhelm Wundt at Leipzig. Krueger greeted the congress in the name of Wundt (Krueger, 1906, pp. 72–73). After extolling the contributions of Wundt to psychology, Krueger stated that Wundt was concerned with current tendencies to apply psychological findings to practical fields such as education, jurisprudence, and social psychology, as reflected in the program of this congress. While acknowledging the extensive research that underlay these currents, Wundt was concerned about the dangers for psychology that these practical tendencies might cause, especially if they led to neglect of the theory and research that must be the basis of psychology.

An important benefit of the 5th congress for Italian psychology was that it led Leonardo Bianchi, Minister of Public Instruction and named honorary president of the congress, to create the first three professorships of experimental psychology in Italy.

At the meeting of the Comitato Internazionale di Propaganda (as the International Congress Committee was called in the proceedings of the 6th congress), invitations to host the 6th congress were presented from Boston, Geneva, Graz, and Stockholm. When William James, who had presented the proposal for Boston, found that his friend Théodore Flournoy was inviting the congress to Geneva, he withdrew his proposal, and the Congress Committee decided to hold the 6th congress in Geneva in August 1909.

The committee debated whether to increase its membership. William James held that if the membership was to be increased, an attempt be made to equalize the representation of different countries. It was decided to increase the membership to 76, and 18 different countries were represented. With the congress taking place in Italy, it is not surprising that Italy had the greatest number of committee members, 11; Germany had 10, France and the USA had 8 each, Russia had 7, and Great Britain had 6. For the first time, some members were chosen from outside Europe and North America; these were two Japanese, Yujiro Motora, professor of psychology at the Imperial University of Tokyo, and Yasusaburo Sakaki, professor of psychiatry at the University of Fukuoka (V. Congresso Internazionale di Psicologia, 1906, pp. 783–784). (For the list of members appointed or reappointed to the International Committee in 1905, see Appendix A.5.)

The 6th International Congress of Psychology, Geneva 1909

The 6th International Congress of Psychology took place in Geneva, August 2–7, 1909. Professor Théodore Flournoy of the University of Geneva was President, and Dr Edouard Claparède, director of the psychological laboratory at the University of Geneva, was Secretary-General. Both Flournoy and Claparède had doctorates in medicine, and both were members of the International Congress Committee. Flournoy had studied with Wundt and introduced experimental psychology to Switzerland.

The 6th congress attracted 582 members coming from 28 countries, a larger attendance than at any previous congress. Switzerland accounted for 42% of the members; France, 17%; Italy, 9%, Germany, 6 %, and the USA, 5% (Montoro González, 1982, p. 662).

At the opening social meeting on the evening of August 2, Professor Flournoy greeted the participants and urged them to get to know each other and to form cordial personal relations, which he said was the main purpose for international congresses. To aid in forming acquaintances, the host committee had assigned a number to each participant and placed these numbers in the congress program and on the participant's badge (Flournoy, 1910a, p. 824).

The program of the congress included 10 main themes, each with 1 or more presenters, and individual papers. In addition, there were seven sessions on unification of psychological terminology and symbols, color standards, mathematical methods, and so forth. There was also a display of books and of scientific instruments. The main themes were the following: (1) The sentiments. (2) The subconscious. (3) Measurement of attention. (4) Psychology of religious phenomena. (5) Classification of the educationally retarded. (6) Methodology of pedagogical psychology. (7) Perception of positions and movements of the body and limbs. (8) Tropisms. (9) Navigation by pigeons. (On August 6, pigeons from Versailles and two other cities in France were released in Geneva, and their success in reaching their home cities was reported in the proceedings: Thauziés, 1910, p. 834.) (10) Physical phenomena related to mediumism. (Although mediums are claimed to channel messages from the dead, no such reports were presented. In the only presentation under this heading, Professor Sydney Alrutz of the University of Upsala, Sweden, presented evidence of transfer of energy from a person to a recording instrument, apparently by nonphysical means. The discussion from the floor raised doubts about these claims.) No sessions were scheduled in parallel, so that congress members could attend all the sessions they wished. The proceedings were the fullest of any congress to date, amounting to a volume of 877 pages.

The sessions on unification and standardization of psychological terminology were reported in a lengthy section of the proceedings of the congress (VIME Congrès International de Psychologie, 1910, pp. 458–578). Professor Edouard Claparède, in introducing these sessions, pointed out that confusion reigned in psychology with regard to the use of specialized terms. He urged that it was high time for psychology to start to define and standardize its terminology, as other scientific disciplines had done or were engaged in doing. After noting desirable aims, he proposed that the congress name a special international commission to establish the bases of this work and that the commission report at the next congress. A discussion ensued about how many languages should be included in the commission, and it was decided to have one representative of each of the four official languages of the congress—English, French, German, and Italian. The artificial language Esperanto was proposed as a common language for unification of terminology, and part of the discussion was printed in that language, but the proposal was abandoned. It is not clear what happened to the special commission on unification of terminology during the long interval before the 7th congress in 1923, but no mention of that subject appears in its proceedings. The topic of terminology was taken up again vigorously, however, at the 10th and 11th congresses.

The International Committee, presided over by Professor Flournoy, added 35 new members (Flournoy, 1910b, pp. 835–836). Professor Flournoy also announced with regret the deaths of four members of the committee: Hermann Ebbinghaus (Germany), J. Mourly-Vold (Sweden), Ezio Sciamanna (Italy), and N. Vaschide (Romania). With the losses and new appointees, the International Committee now numbered 108 (Comité International de Propagande, 1910). (See the list of members in Appendix A.6.) Montoro González (1982, p. 685) stated that the committee now included members from 22 countries, but that is based on the present boundaries. At the time, Austria-Hungary was a single monarchy, the current Czechoslovakia was then part of Austria; Finland and Poland were then parts of the Russian Empire. Fifteen of the members of the committee were French (14%), 15 Italian, 13 from the USA, 12 German, and 6 each from Belgium, Great Britain, and Switzerland. A Polish psychologist at the Geneva congress urged that members of the congress be classified by nationality (e.g., Polish) rather than by country (e.g., Russia), claiming that one's nationality is a psychological reality, whereas country is only a geographical fact (Lutoslawski, 1910, p. 841). No record of discussion of this matter appears in the proceedings, but the Swiss finessed the issue by listing the participants in the proceedings volume by city rather than by country. The proceedings of some earlier congresses had already followed this practice of listing participants by their city of residence, and the following congresses continued to do so.

Not only was the representation of countries in the committee greater than ever before, but as noted in Chapter 3, the first woman was appointed to the International Committee: Polish psychologist, Dr I. Ioteyko, who was head of the laboratory of psychology at the University of Brussels (VIME Congrès International de Psychologie, 1910, p. 835). Dr Ioteyko was one of eight Polish psychologists, five of them women, to propose at the Geneva congress that the next international congress be held in Warsaw. (As also noted in Chapter 3, in the list of members of the 8th congress her name appeared as Prof Dr Jozefa Joteyko of Warsaw.)

Among those named to the International Committee in 1909 were two psychologists who were to be retained for several successive terms and then to serve on the first three Executive Committees of the International Union of Psychological Science, 1951–1960. These were Professor Henri Piéron of the University of Paris and Professor Albert Michotte of the University of Louvain. Piéron was the first President of the IUPsyS (1951–54) and Michotte was the third President (1957–60).

The final discussion about the organization of future international congresses revealed certain doubts about methods of choosing the speakers and topics, and it was also informative about the attempts of leading psychologists to make their discipline better defined and organized (VIME Congrès International de Psychologie, 1910, pp. 841–847). Some discussants were concerned that certain speakers were not well qualified. One proposal was that communications be limited to experts invited by the Organizing Committee of the congress. There was also a proposal to limit discussion to designated experts. Another was that speakers be limited to people who had an official position in a scientific organization, such as a psychological society, a scientific journal, or an educational organization. This raised objections that it might limit the participation of psychologists from some countries such as Italy, who were productive but did not have a psychological society. One couldn't force them to organize a society! Another speaker proposed limiting participation to those whose expertise gave them competence in psychology, including physicians, biologists, educators, and so forth. Finally, no action was taken to limit participation in future congresses, and the question was left up to future organizing committees. As we will see, the organizers of the 7th congress did decide to limit stringently the membership of that congress. The 6th congress did vote to request the organizers of the next congress to place on the program certain main themes for which rapporteurs would prepare papers to be circulated in advance of the congress.

The Geneva congress program included several social occasions, including the opening reception, a cruise on the lake, a dinner offered by the City of Geneva, and a farewell lunch at the Parc des Eaux-Vives.

The 1913 International Congress that never was

At the 6th congress, two petitions were put forward requesting the opportunity to host the 7th congress. One was an official petition from Polish psychologists for a congress in Warsaw. The other was a petition prepared by Morton Prince, a neurologist interested in abnormal behavior; it was not a formal invitation and no American institution offered to host the congress. Nevertheless, the International Committee, recalling that Americans had already offered in 1905 to play hosts, accepted the American proposal. It named Professor James Mark Baldwin of Johns Hopkins University as President and William James of Harvard University as Honorary President. Baldwin was empowered to choose the other members of the host committee, and difficulties in making the choices soon appeared, especially with regard to the Vice-Presidents. The story was recounted in detail by Evans and Down Scott (1978), based on their examination of the correspondence of several major American psychologists. Evans and Down Scott claimed that the story shows that the politics of science is often as important a part of its history as the concepts involved. Since their article gave the story in detail, we will not attempt to recount it here. Personal rivalries and pique prevented effective organization of a congress. Much of the controversy revolved around James McKeen Cattell. Ironically, when an international congress of psychology finally took place in the United States in 1929, Cattell, having outlived his rivals, was elected President of the congress.

By the time the American committee informed the International Congress Committee in 1912 of its decision to withdraw as host, it was too late to organize a 1913 congress elsewhere. Then World War I started in 1914, and international meetings had to be suspended. It was not until 1923 that the 7th International Congress of Psychology took place at Oxford University.

References

Comité International de Propagande. (1910). VIME Congrès International de Psychologie (p. 34). Geneva: Librairie Kündig.
IVE Congrès International de Psychologie. (1901). Paris: Félix Alcan.
V. Congresso Internazionale di Psicologia. (1906). Atti del V. Congresso Internazionale di Psicologia. Roma: Forzani e c. Tipografi del Senato.
VIME Congrès International de Psychologie. (1910). Geneva: Librairie Kündig.
Dritter Internationaler Congress für Psychologie. (1897). Munich: Verlag J.F. Lehmann.

E.B.T. [Edward B. Titchener] (1896–97). The Munich Congress. *American Journal of Psychology, 8*, 142–145.

Evans, R.B., & Down Scott, F.J. (1978). The 1913 International Congress of Psychology: The American Congress that wasn't. *American Psychologist, 33*, 711–723.

Flournoy, T. (1910a). Réunion familière. In *VIME Congrès International de Psychologie* (p. 824). Geneva: Librairie Kündig.

Flournoy, T. (1910b). Séance du Comité International. In *VIME Congrès International de Psychologie* (p. 835–863). Geneva: Librairie Kündig.

International Congress of Experimental Psychology. (1892a). London: Williams & Norgate.

The International Congress of Experimental Psychology. (1892b). *Mind, 1*, 580–588.

Krueger, F. (1906). [Remarks]. In *Atti del V. Congresso Internazionale di Psicologia* (pp. 72–73). Roma: Forzani e c. Tipografi del Senato.

Lutoslawski, W. (1910). [Discussion]. In *VIME Congrès International de Psychologie* (p. 841). Geneva: Librairie Kündig.

Montoro, L., Tortosa, F., Carpintero, H., & Peiro, J.M. (1984). A short history of the International Congresses of Psychology (1889–1960). In H. Carpintero & J. M. Peiro (Eds.). *Psychology in its historical context: Essays in honour of Prof. Joseph Brozek*. Valencia, Spain: University of Valencia.

Montoro González, L. (1982). *Los congresos internacionales de psicologia (1889–1960)*. Unpublished doctoral dissertation, Valencia, Spain.

Nuttin, J. (1992). Les premiers congrès internationaux de psychologie. In *Contributions to the history of the international congresses of psychology: A posthumous homage to J.R. Nuttin* (pp. 7–75). Valencia, Spain: Revista de Historia de la psicologia, and Leuven: Studia Psychologica.

Piéron, H. (1954). Histoire succinte des congrès internationaux de psychologie. *L'Année Psychologique, 54*, 397–405.

Sidgwick, A., & Sidgwick, E.M. (1906). *Henry Sidgwick: A memoir*. London: Macmillan.

Sidgwick, H. (1892). Presidential address. In *International Congress of Experimental Psychology* (pp. 1–8). London: Williams & Norgate.

Thauziés, M.A. (1910). Lâcher de pigeons. In *VIME Congrès International de Psychologie* (p. 834). Geneva: Librairie Kündig.

Vogt, O. (1901). Contre le spiritisme. In *IVE Congrès International de Psychologie* (pp. 656–659). Paris: Félix Alcan.

Problems and progress in the period between the two world wars 5

In the period between the two World Wars, the schedule and locations of some international congresses of psychology were perturbed by financial problems, international politics, and wars. After American psychologists failed to organize an international congress in 1913, the outbreak of World War I in 1914 and the hostile feelings that persisted for some years after the armistice in 1918 prevented the holding of the 7th International Congress of Psychology until 1923. The 8th congress was originally planned for the United States, but the grave financial situation in Europe made it unfeasible for European psychologists to travel to the USA, so the congress was shifted to the Netherlands in 1926. The following two congresses occurred on schedule in 1929 and 1932, and the 1929 congress in New Haven, Connecticut was the largest to date. In contrast, because of the depression the 1932 congress in Copenhagen was small and publication of its report was delayed. The 11th congress was scheduled for Madrid in 1936, but the outbreak of the Spanish Civil War caused it to be shifted to Paris in 1937.

The 12th congress was scheduled for Vienna in 1940, but the occupation of Austria by Nazi Germany in March 1938 caused some national psychological associations to call for a change of venue. The International Congress Committee debated a suitable choice, and German governmental agencies tried to make sure that the congress would be held in a site favorable to Germany. In a mail ballot, the committee narrowly favored Edinburgh over Stockholm for the congress in 1940. Then the outbreak of World War II in 1939 forced postponement of the 12th congress, which finally took place in Edinburgh in 1948. The increased organization and structure of the International Committee in the 1930s helped it to cope with the problems that arose.

In spite of these difficulties, a review of the congresses of the 1920s and 1930s reveals the steady progress psychology was making during this period.

The 7th International Congress of Psychology, Oxford 1923

In the autumn of 1922, some leading psychologists of France and Switzerland suggested to British colleagues that they attempt to revive the international congresses by arranging a meeting in Britain for the summer of 1923. An Organizing Committee was formed in London, and its members agreed that such a congress must be truly international. The French Société de Psychologie agreed that invitations to the congress should be issued without restriction as to nationality. The British Organizing Committee decided to hold the meeting in Oxford, July 26–August 2, 1923.

Probably influenced by the discussion at the 6th congress in Geneva on the qualification of members and on limiting the size of congresses, the British committee decided "to limit membership to trained psychologists and to restrict it to about 200 persons. Accordingly, invitations were sent out to the most distinguished psychologists throughout the world. Some refusals were received on the ground that international conditions did not yet permit of the resumption of friendly relations between members of nations so recently at war with one another; but the number of such replies was negligibly small" (VIIth International Congress of Psychology, 1924, p. v).

It seems curious that the congress was held at Oxford, "which was even more reluctant than Cambridge to move with the times" and accept modern psychology (Boring, 1950, p. 494). "It was hoped in 1923 that Oxford would be aroused by all the visiting scholars at the Congress to discover the existence of its missing field ...," but it was only in 1936 that Oxford established an Institute of Experimental Psychology and finally, in 1947, a chair of psychology (Boring, 1950, p. 494).

In accordance with the decision of the organizers, the membership of the 7th congress totalled only 239, scarcely more than at the 1st congress. Does the membership list provide a roster of "the most distinguished psychologists throughout the world," in accordance with the intentions of the Organizing Committee? Not really, because, similarly to the 1st congress, 60% of the members were from the host country. The second largest delegation came from the United States, 12%, followed by France, Germany, and the Netherlands, with 3.4% each (Montoro González, 1982, p. 663). No members came from Russia or Hungary, both of which had been well represented at the 6th congress but which were undergoing severe difficulties in the 1920s after the war and the revolution in Russia. Piéron (1954, p. 463) noted that most German psychologists refused to attend but that Wolfgang Köhler and Kurt Koffka brought a warm spirit of reconciliation. Lord Curzon, chancellor of the University of Oxford and Secretary of State for Foreign Affairs, thanked congress President Charles Myers for holding the congress: "All such meetings draw closer the bonds between the minds and spirits of nations, and make for that peace which statesmen are endeavouring, however ineffectively, to secure" (VIIth International Congress of Psychology, 1924, p. vi).

Congress President Dr Charles S. Myers was one of the founders in 1908 of the *British Journal of Psychology* and was its editor in 1913–24. He and his family subsidized the enlargement and improvement of the Cambridge

University psychological laboratory in 1913, and he was appointed its (unpaid) director. In 1922, Myers left Cambridge for London to become director of the new National Institute for Industrial Psychology, whose purpose was "the application of psychology and physiology to industry and commerce." The Institute reflected the importance that applied psychology had reached in Great Britain during the war and in the post-war period. The Secretary of the congress was Dr William Brown of Oxford. Brown was to become the first director of the Institute of Experimental Psychology at Oxford in 1936.

Each of the five weekday mornings had a symposium, and each afternoon had a session of individual papers. Because the attendance was small, all sessions were plenary and there were no parallel sessions. The languages employed at the congress and in the proceedings volume were English, French, and German.

Charles S. Myers (1873–1946): President of the 7th International Congress of Psychology, Oxford, 1923.

The first symposium, chaired by Professor Godfrey H. Thompson of the University of Newcastle, was on "The nature of general intelligence and ability." In addition to Thompson, participants in the symposium were Dr Edouard Claparède of Geneva and Dr Louis L. Thurstone of the Bureau of Public Personnel Administration, Washington, DC. The place of this symposium at the start of the congress reflects the interest in measurement of intelligence that had grown during and after the war. Further evidence of this interest was the resolution passed by the members of the congress at the closing meeting to appoint an international committee on intelligence and intelligence tests, in order to review and distribute tests, to establish a clearing house for information, and if possible to publish a yearbook and handbooks on intelligence testing.

The third symposium was entitled "The conception of nervous and mental energy" and was organized by the eminent Oxford neurophysiologist Charles S. Sherrington. Cambridge neurophysiologist Edgar D. Adrian summarized research on the nerve impulse and asked whether psychologists would be able to develop an equally useful concept of "mental energy." London neurologist Henry Head discussed concepts of vigilance.

In the fourth symposium, "The classification of the instincts," Edinburgh psychology professor James Drever urged a behavioral, biological viewpoint, whereas London psychoanalyst Ernest Jones defended the Freudian view.

The final symposium, "The principles of vocational guidance," had participants from England, Germany, the Netherlands, and the United States. Along with the first symposium and several individual papers, it reflected the emphasis of the 7th congress on applications of psychology.

Individual papers by Wolfgang Köhler and Kurt Koffka of Germany and G. Révész of the Netherlands reported on research on Gestalt psychology, the first time this topic was discussed at an international congress of psychology. Classification of the topics of communications showed physiological psychology in the lead, followed by industrial and military psychology (Montoro González, 1982, p. 149). The prominence of industrial and military psychology was understandable both because of the recency of the World War and also because of the interests of the President of the congress, Charles Myers, in this field.

As Montoro González (1982, p. 151) summarized it, the 7th congress showed psychology steadily developing its own identity and becoming more and more independent from philosophy, on the one hand, and from physiology, on the other. The general tendency was for a functional psychology, more dynamic than structural, more psychobiological than psychophysical, more empirical than logical, and moving rapidly toward applications.

At the meeting of the International Committee, 24 new members were elected. With the continuing members, this brought the total to 105 (VIIth International Congress of Psychology, 1924, p. xx). (See Appendix A.7.) Sixteen of the members were from the USA, 14 from France, 10 each from Germany and Italy, and 9 each from Great Britain and the USSR (Montoro González, 1982, p. 688).

For the next congress, both American psychologists and Dutch psychologists offered to play host. The American offer was accepted provisionally, but a small committee was established to determine whether the precarious financial situation in Europe made it feasible to hold a congress in the United States. This committee consisted of Edouard Claparède (Switzerland), Charles Myers (England), and Henri Piéron (France) (Montoro González, 1982, p. 153). In February 1924, Dr Claparède, writing for the committee, invited the Dutch to organize the 8th congress, and they accepted to do so for September, 1926.

The 8th International Congress of Psychology, Groningen 1926

The 8th International Congress of Psychology took place at the University of Groningen, September 6–11 1926. Following the precedent of the 7th congress, the Organizing Committee of the 8th congress limited its invitations "to about 200 well-known psychologists and a few others." Actually, 241 members were registered (VIIIth International Congress of Psychology, 1927, pp. 57–67). The largest number of these, 71 (29%), came from the host country. Next in order of registration was Germany with 52; note the large increase from the German attendance of only 8 at the 7th congress in Oxford. Then followed Great Britain with 25, USA with 24, and France with 11 (Montoro González, 1982, p. 664).

The President of the congress was Gerardus Heymans, who had been professor of philosophy and psychology at the University of Groningen since 1890. Vice-President was Enno Dirk Wiersma, professor of psychiatry at the University of Groningen. Secretary was F. Roels, professor at the University of Utrecht.

The languages used at the congress were English, French, and German. President Heymans gave his address in English but asked the indulgence of the congress members to use Dutch to thank the representatives of the national government, the province, the city and the university for their warm interest in the success of the congress.

The program included five symposia on the following topics: (1) The intensity of sensations. (2) The psychology of religion. (3) Understanding and explaining. (4) Form perception. (5) The psychology of primitive races. There were also about 60 individual papers.

The terminology and content of the symposium on the psychology of primitive races stands in marked contrast with contributions on cross-cultural psychology in more recent congresses of psychology. F.C. Bartlett of Cambridge University entitled his paper "The psychology of the lower races."

Classification of the topics of the presentations shows that sensation and perception led with 29.8%, followed by general psychology with 17.5%, psychometrics with 9.5%, and physiological psychology with 7.1% (Montoro González, 1982, p. 157).

Gerardus Heymans (1857–1930): President of the 8th International Congress of Psychology, Groningen, 1926.

The International Committee for the first time appointed a Permanent Secretary, Dr Edouard Claparède of Geneva. It also appointed 11 new members, bringing the total to 110 (VIIIth International Congress of Psychology, 1927, pp. 19–20). (See Appendix A.8.) Sixteen of the members were from France, 15 from the USA, 13 from Germany, 11 each from Great Britain and Italy, and 9 from the USSR (Montoro González, 1982, p. 691). It might be noted that members from the USSR were retained on the International Committee although no USSR citizen attended either the 7th or 8th congress. At its closing session, the congress resolved unanimously that the next session be held in America. The improved financial situation in Europe made this feasible.

The International Committee approved four languages for official use at the congresses: English, French, German, and Italian.

The 9th International Congress of Psychology, Yale 1929

The 9th International Congress of Psychology took place at Yale University, New Haven, Connecticut, September 1–7, 1929. Early in the program of the

Edouard Claparède (1873–1940): Named Permanent Secretary of the International Congress Committee in 1926; served until his death in 1940.

9th congress, Edouard Claparède, Permanent Secretary of the International Committee, gave a brief account of past congresses in which he recalled the long history of disappointed hopes to meet in the United States before this congress fortunately came about. Claparède thanked the Carnegie Foundation for having aided psychologists from outside the United States to attend the congress (Claparède, 1930, p. 34).

The American Organizing Committee did not maintain the limitation of invitations practised at the two previous congresses; on the contrary, they adopted measures to ensure a large attendance. One was to hold the congress jointly with the annual meeting of the American Psychological Association (APA), which then had about 1000 members. The APA agreed to cover the expenses of the congress and to publish its proceedings. More difficult was the problem of attracting participants from outside the United States. One measure taken was to reduce the registration fee to $5 for attendees from outside the United States, versus $10 for Americans. A more important step was to pay the travel and lodging of some important European psychologists— including Bühler, Köhler, Michotte, and Mira— and arrange for them to give lectures at some American universities (Piéron, 1929; Woodworth & Boring, 1930). These measures were relatively successful with regard to American participation, but only moderately successful with regard to attracting others. There were 826 regular members

registered; 722 Americans but only 104 "foreign members." In addition, over 200 persons were registered who would have been counted as members at previous congresses—106 wives of members and 129 other guests—making a total registration of 1051. This was by far the largest international congress of psychology to date.

The President of the 9th congress was Professor James McKeen Cattell. This is ironic because conflicts over Cattell's role were mainly responsible for the failure of American psychologists to organize an international congress in 1913. But by 1929 Cattell had outlived most of his rivals, and had become a major spokesman for psychological science. Cattell was the first American to obtain a doctorate with Wundt in 1886. At the University of Pennsylvania he occupied the world's first chair in psychology in 1887. He was the first

James McKeen Cattell (1860–1944): President of the 9th International Congress of Psychology, Yale University (New Haven, Connecticut) 1929.

psychologist to be elected to the National Academy of Sciences, USA, in 1901.

The Vice-President of the congress was James R. Angell, a prominent functionalist psychologist, who at the time of the congress was rector of Yale University. The Secretary was Professor Edwin G. Boring of Harvard University; in the year of the congress he published the first edition of his *History of Experimental Psychology*.

Cattell devoted his presidential address to the history and present state of psychology in America, which of course derived from psychology in

Europe and also from the progress of related sciences and technologies. Cattell noted that 1929 marked the 50th anniversary of Wundt's founding the first formal laboratory of psychology in Leipzig and also the 40th anniversary of the 1st International Congress of Psychology. He recounted the rapid increase in professorships of psychology and laboratories of psychology in America, and also the founding in 1892 and rapid growth of the American Psychological Association, the first national society of psychology. Cattell extolled international congresses for advancing scientific research and for promoting international cooperation and goodwill. He welcomed psychologists from around the world "and with special pleasure psychologists from Soviet Russia."

In the scientific program of the congress, two or three parallel sessions were held each morning. Each afternoon, there were informal symposia or round tables, 38 in all. The evenings saw formal addresses by major investigators including Ivan P. Pavlov, Wolfgang Köhler, Albert Michotte, Henri Piéron, Carl Spearman, and Edward L. Thorndike; Karl S. Lashley gave the presidential address of the APA. Altogether, 424 papers were presented, and many of them were published in the proceedings (Ninth International Congress of Psychology, 1930).

The topics treated covered a wide range. Psychometrics was the most frequent, with 16.7% of the reports. This reflected mainly the study of intelligence in school settings. In second place came physiological psychology, with 11.7%. The addresses of Pavlov and Lashley also reflected this emphasis on this topic. Third place was held by clinical psychology, with 10.6%, reflecting in part the influence of child guidance clinics (Montoro González, 1982, pp. 166–167).

Most of the papers were in English, but French, German, and Italian were also used. In his address as Secretary-General of the International Committee, Claparède took up the question of use of different languages at the different congresses. Recalling that the International Committee had decided at the 8th congress that four languages be accepted officially—English, French, German, and Italian—Claparède said he looked forward to the day when Esperanto would be sufficiently widespread to be the general language at congresses. Meanwhile he advocated that each speaker be allowed to use whatever language he wished, thus making the choice of limiting his audience (Claparède, 1930, p. 40).

The International Committee voted to add 28 persons to its membership, bringing the total to 122 (see Appendix A.9). The only woman member of the committee was Margaret F. Washburn, USA. Four of the new members were from the USSR and three of these were present at the 9th congress, including Ivan P. Pavlov.

Although some members of the International Congress Committee attended congresses and committee meetings regularly, many people who had been appointed to the committee did not attend International

Congresses of Psychology. Therefore the committee adopted the following policy:

> It was voted that members of the International Committee who have been absent from three consecutive Congresses be automatically relieved as members of the Committee unless re-elected.

This new provision was first put into effect with the appointment of the International Committee at the 10th congress in 1932, and it led to a sharp reduction in the number of members of the next committees (see Appendix A.10). The congress voted to accept the invitation to meet in Copenhagen in 1932; thanks were expressed for other invitations from Gothenburg and Poland (Ninth International Congress of Psychology, 1930, pp. 6–7).

The 10th International Congress of Psychology, Copenhagen 1932

The 10th congress took place August 22–27, 1932, at the University of Copenhagen with the King of Denmark as patron. The eminent psychologist Harald Höffding had been designated to be President of the congress, but he died the year before the congress, so the Chair of the Organizing Committee, Professor Edgar Rubin, became President of the congress. Rubin was director of the Laboratory of Psychology at the University of Copenhagen and a well-known investigator of perception.

The records of the 10th congress are less readily available than those of the other International Congresses of Psychology, so relatively little has been written about it. In fact, Montoro González, in his detailed description of the first 16 congresses, states that the usual proceedings do not exist for this congress, so it is not possible to see the list of members, the members of the International Committee, and so on (Montoro González, 1982, p. 174). Actually, the proceedings were published, but with more than the usual delay and in two parts instead of the usual single volume. One part was a 53-page paper-bound report, which gives the formal proceedings and lists of members of the International Committee and Organizing Committee, the members of the congress, and the papers submitted for presentation (Tenth International Congress of Psychology, 1935). The report notes that the national committee regretted having to send out the following letter a year after the congress took place:

> During the Congress we requested the members to send in copies of their lectures or synopses thereof, as we thought we had every reason to believe that the finances of the Congress would permit of the publication of a report containing this material. Partly due to the general depression we have,

however, met with unexpected difficulties, and ... we have
now seen ourselves reluctantly compelled to return the
manuscripts without having been able to make use of them
(Tenth International Congress of Psychology, 1935, pp.
14–15).

Twenty-six of the papers and addresses delivered at the congress were, however, gathered together as the first number of the journal *Acta Psychologica* (Papers read at the X International Congress of Psychology at Copenhagen, 1932 [1935]).

The report of the congress listed 288 active members registered, 74 accompanying ladies, and 106 passive members, but this somewhat overstated the actual attendance. The numbers stated those registered for the congress, but several of these did not attend. Of the 150 members listed as submitting papers, 26 (17%) were noted as "absent," and at least as large a percentage of the total list of members probably did not attend. Thus, the congress report noted that the entire Brazilian delegation "was prevented from attending" (Tenth International Congress of Psychology, 1935, p. 11), although the list of active members of the congress included 11 from Brazil. The largest number of listed active members came from the United States (71), followed by the delegations of Germany (43), Denmark (35), Great Britain (24), and Sweden (14).

The Danish Organizing Committee received financial support from the Danish government and major breweries, among others. The University of Copenhagen placed its Festival Hall and lecture halls at the disposal of the congress. The municipality of Copenhagen invited the congress members to a reception at the town hall, and there was a closing banquet on the final evening. After the close of the congress, some of the members went on a circular tour of German and Austrian institutes arranged by Professor David Katz on behalf of the Deutsche Geselleschaft für Psychologie.

Among the invited speakers at general sessions of the congress and their topics were Edouard Claparède, Geneva, "La psychologie fonctionelle" (Functional psychology); Augustino Gemelli, Milan, "Nuove richerche sulla strutturazione della parole e della frase" (New research on the structure of words and phrases); Arnold Gesell, Yale, "The growth of infant behavior patterns studied by cinematography"; Walter Hunter, Clark University, "Voluntary activity from the standpoint of behaviorism"; Arthur Kronfeld, Berlin, "Die Bedeutung Soren Kierkegaards für die Psychologie der Person" (The meaning of Soren Kierkegaard for the psychology of the person); Charles S. Myers, London, "Recent evidence of the value of vocational guidance"; Ivan P. Pavlov, Leningrad, "Das dynamische Stereotyp der Grosshirnhemisphären" (The dynamic stereotype of the cerebral hemispheres); Henri Piéron, Paris, "L'intégration du temps dans la notion du seuil et le problème des mécanismes d'excitation sensorielles" (The integration of time in the concept of threshold and the problem of mechanisms of sensory excitation); Carl E. Seashore, University of Iowa, "The psychology of the vibrato in music and speech"; and William Stern, Hamburg, "Raum und Zeit als personale Dimensionen" (Space and time as personal dimensions). In addition to these papers, the program lists about 140 individual papers. English, French, German, and Italian were the official languages.

Claparède, as Chair of the section on terminology, proposed a resolution to the International Committee, which passed it unanimously, for increased efforts to standardize psychological terminology within and among languages. This effort was continued at the 11th congress.

The International Committee decided to elect an Advisory Committee (Executive Committee) in addition to its Permanent Secretary, Edouard Claparède, who had been appointed at the 8th congress in 1926. This was to consist of the present congress President and the incoming President, together with the Permanent Secretary and five members to be elected by the International Committee at its closing meeting during the congress. The members elected to the Advisory Committee were Herbert S. Langfeld (USA), Charles S. Myers (UK), Henri Piéron (France), and Mario Ponzo (Rome). Edgar Rubin (Denmark) and Emilio Mira (Spain) were members as current and incoming congress Presidents, respectively. Herbert S. Langfeld (USA) was elected Associate Secretary. The records do not indicate why the International Committee decided to appoint the Advisory Committee, but this proved to be a wise decision to help the committee confront problems that were to arise in the latter part of the 1930s.

The list of members of the International Committee was revised in accordance with the resolution adopted at the 1929 congress to drop members who had been absent from three successive congresses. This action, coupled with the election of 7 new members, brought the committee to a total of 84 members (Appendix A.10), whereas the membership had been over 100 for the previous 4 terms. With further eliminations and new appointments, it was to remain around 80 at the next 2 congresses (see Appendix A).

The International Committee received several invitations to hold the 11th congress—in Germany, Spain, Japan, the USA, and Austria. It chose Spain as the site of the congress in 1936. The invitation to hold a congress in Japan was the first for a site outside of Europe or North America; a congress was finally held in Japan in 1972.

The Spanish Civil War causes the congress planned for Madrid in 1936 to be shifted to Paris in 1937

The International Committee had decided at the 10th congress to hold the 11th congress in Madrid in September 1936. Santiago Ramon y Cajal, famous neuroanatomist and Nobel Prize laureate, was designated as honorary

President; he had been a long-time member of the International Committee and had attended some of the early congresses. Emilio Mira was designated to be President and José Germain as Secretary-General. A productive planning meeting took place in 1935, attended by the Spanish Organizing Committee and some members of the international Executive Committee (Michotte, 1938, p. 520). Then politics and warfare intervened.

In the Spanish elections of February 1936, the Popular Front (left coalition) won. Then in the summer of 1936, generals led a revolt against the government and the Spanish Civil War broke out. The Spanish Organizing Committee informed the International Committee of the necessity to hold the congress outside of Spain. The Permanent Secretary of the International Committee consulted the members of its Executive Committee, which had been created at the 10th congress in Copenhagen. At that time, the ideological office of the Nazi party was attempting to bring the 11th congress to Germany (Geuter, 1984, pp. 128–129). It had learned that France was trying to secure the congress but preferred to have the congress represent German rather than Western psychology. The executive board of the German Psychological Society supported the proposal to bring the congress to Germany. The Executive Committee decided to request Professor Henri Piéron, one of its members, to arrange for the organization of the 11th congress in Paris in July 1937, and this was done.

The 11th International Congress of Psychology, Paris 1937

Although organized in haste because of the shift from Madrid to Paris, the 11th congress attracted a reasonably good attendance—586 members were registered from 36 countries. Montoro González (1982, p. 184) suggested that part of the reason for the success of the congress, which took place on July 25–31, 1937, was that it again coincided with a World's Fair and it also overlapped with meetings of related groups, including the International Neurological Meeting, the 2nd International Congress of Mental Hygiene, the International Congress of Primary Education, the second International Congress of Esthetics, and the International Congress of Child Psychiatry. It was at the 1937 Paris World's Fair that the public first saw Picasso's painting Guernica, protesting the bombing of that city in the Spanish Civil War.

The President of the congress, Professor Henri Piéron, was the director of the Laboratory of Physiological Psychology at the Sorbonne and editor of l'Année psychologique; he had served on the International Committee since 1909. The Honorary President was Pierre Janet, well known psychiatrist and long-time member of the International Psychology Committee. As he mentioned in his presidential address (Piéron, 1938, p. 507), Piéron had been planning to propose a congress in Paris in 1939 to commemorate several events: the 50th anniversary of the 1st International

Henri Piéron (1881–1964): President of the 11th International Congress of Psychology, Paris, 1937. Later became first President of the International Union of Scientific Psychology (IUSP), 1951–1954.

Congress of Psychology; the centenary of the birth of pioneer French psychologist Théodule A. Ribot, acting President of the 1st International Congress of Psychology and President of the 4th International Congress of Psychology, and the 50th anniversary of the founding of the Laboratory of Physiological Psychology. The registration fee for the congress was 100 francs, ten times the amount for the first congress in 1889, an indication of the inflation in Europe during the half century that separated the two congresses.

Piéron gave credit for the efficient organization of the congress to the Secretary-General, Professor Ignace Meyerson. Instead of the extensive program planned for the congress at Madrid, the French organizers decided on a more focused congress on the overall theme "Du movement à la conduite" (From movement to conduct). Under this theme, five symposia were organized: (1) Morphology of movement. (2) The law of effect in learning and its interpretation. (3) The acquisition of habits. (4) Motor and mental development in children. (5) Animal behavior and human conduct. In addition to the symposia, there were major lectures by such well-known investigators as Pierre Janet, Edgar Adrian, William McDougall, Jean Piaget, Karl Bühler, and Edouard Claparède. There were also nine round tables. The first of these, on psychological terminology, was chaired by Claparède; it continued the effort to regularize psychological terminology that was undertaken at the 6th congress and which the 10th congress had recommended be continued. Finally, there were 115 individual papers. Classification of the topics of the presentations showed sensation and perception in the lead with 15%, followed closely by physiological psychology with 13.4%; psychometrics was the subject of 10.2% of the papers (Montoro González, 1982, p. 188).

The languages of the congress were English, French, German, Italian, and Spanish. For the opening session, simultaneous translations from French to English and German, and from English to French and German, was available through earphones. All communications were to be sent to the secretariat in advance of the congress; they were printed and given out to the members on their arrival.

The congress opened with a reception at the Foreign Ministry, the Quai d'Orsay, and the proceedings volume included several photographs of congress members there. The opening ceremonies included a speech by a representative of the foreign minister, and the French government was active in recognizing the congress. The President of the Republic received a delegation of congress members at his office in the Elysée Palace. The government named Professor James McKeen Cattell, who had presided over the 9th congress in Yale, Commander of the Legion of Honor. Official delegations to the congress included representatives of many scientific organizations, including the French Académie des Sciences, the Royal Society, the National Academy of Sciences USA, and representatives of 20 universities from around the world.

The International Committee named new members to replace members who had died since the last congress and dropped four members because they had not attended the last three congresses. This brought the International Committee to 84 members, as shown in Appendix A.11; they represented 21 different countries. The largest number, 24 (29%) came from the USA; the next largest came from Great Britain, 12 (14%), followed by France, 10 (12%), and Germany, 7 (8%); Italy and the USSR each had 4 (Montoro González, 1982, p. 688). Four members of the International Committee were women: Hélène Antipoff (Brazil), Charlotte Bühler (Austria), Beatrice Edgell (UK), and Margaret F. Washburn (USA). Professor William Stern had resigned from the Executive Committee, under pressure from German authorities, but he remained on the International Committee. Stern was replaced on the Executive Committee by Professor Otto Klemm, who was favored by the German government (Geuter, 1984, p. 129). At the meeting of the International Committee in Paris, Klemm presented an invitation to hold the next congress in Leipzig, but then deferred to the invitation of Karl Bühler to hold the congress in Vienna. Klemm explained that an invitation for Vienna had already been made at the 9th congress and therefore had priority, and also that no congress of psychology had yet taken place in Austria. It was decided unanimously to accept the invitation to hold the next congress in Vienna in 1940, under the presidency of Professor Karl Bühler.

World War II causes postponement of the 12th congress

The 12th congress was scheduled for Vienna in 1940, after maneuvering to bring the previous congress to Germany. Some of the behind-the-scenes political attempts by Germany to influence the site of the congresses in the period 1936–1940 are recounted by Geuter (1984), and we review them briefly here. When at the 1937 Paris congress Otto Klemm withdrew his invitation to hold the 12th congress in Leipzig in favor of Vienna, this was more than a polite gesture. Klemm was acting on instructions from the German government to withdraw in favor of Austria or Italy, if it appeared that Germany would not receive a majority vote (Geuter, 1984, p. 130). Also, Klemm had spoken with Karl Bühler, the head of the Austrian delegation, who assured him that if Klemm supported Vienna for the 12th congress, then Bühler would support Germany as the site of the 13th congress.

Then, in March 1938 Germany occupied Austria. Karl Bühler, the designated President of the next congress, was immediately imprisoned and released only in the autumn. Several psychological organizations reacted with resolutions against holding the 1940 congress in Austria; these included the American Psychological Association and the British Psychological Society. At its meeting in September 1938 the Council of the APA considered resolutions adopted by several American groups against holding the congress in Vienna and drafted the following resolution which was adopted by the Association:

> Be it resolved, *That the American Psychological Association request the Committee in charge of arrangements for the Twelfth International Congress of Psychology to terminate, if it has not already done so, the tentative plan to hold this congress in Vienna in 1940; and that it request the Committee to arrange for the Congress in some country where the progress of psychology as a branch of science is not hindered by a government hostile to the tradition of free and unimpeded scholarship (Olson, 1939, p. 129).*

The international Executive Committee was faced with the difficult problem of finding a new site for the 12th congress. If Vienna was now impossible, the standing invitation from Leipzig would have to be considered again, but there was a consensus that Germany was no longer a possible site. Belgium, Poland, Romania, the UK (Edinburgh), and Sweden were considered as alternatives. Italian psychologists proposed that the meeting take place in Rome in 1942, at the time when a World's Fair was scheduled there. Michotte declined for Belgium, and the executive committee narrowed the choice to Edinburgh or Stockholm. They called for a mail vote by members of the International Committee.

This choice had political aspects. The well-known perception psychologist David Katz had been expelled from his professorship at the State University of Mecklenburg when the Nazis came to power in 1933, and had gone to Sweden where he became the leading professor of psychology at the University of Stockholm. The council of the British Psychological Society urged the choice of Edinburgh, suggesting that choosing Stockholm would be a violent rebuff to Germany (Geuter, 1984, p. 134). Forty-three members of the International Committee cast ballots. Six did not make a choice, 19 voted for Edinburgh, and 18 for Stockholm. Claparède then asked James Drever to organize a congress in Edinburgh in 1940, but the outbreak of World War II in 1939 resulted in postponing the 12th congress, which was finally held in 1948. At that congress, Stockholm was chosen as the site of the 13th congress in 1951, with David Katz as President.

The next chapter takes up the 12th and 13th congresses and the formal founding of the International Union of Scientific Psychology, as it was originally named.

References

Boring, E.G. (1950). *A history of experimental psychology* (2nd ed.). New York: Appleton-Century-Crofts.

Claparède, E. (1930). Esquisse historique des Congrès Internationaux de Psychologie. In *Ninth International Congress of Psychology* (pp. 33–47). Princeton, NJ: Psychological Review Co.

Geuter, U. (1984). The eleventh and twelfth international congresses of psychology. A note on politics and science between 1936 and 1940. In H. Carpintero & J.M. Peiro (Eds.), *Psychology in its historical context. Monografias de la revista de historia de la psicologia*. Valencia, Spain: University of Valencia.

VIIth International Congress of Psychology. (1924). Cambridge: Cambridge University Press.

VIIIth International Congress of Psychology. (1927). Groningen, The Netherlands: P. Noordhoff.

Michotte, A. (1938). Discours de M. A. Michotte. In *Onzième Congrès International de Psychologie* (pp. 516–521). Paris: Félix Alcan.

Montoro González, L. (1982). *Los congresos internacionales de psicologia (1889–1960)*. Unpublished doctoral dissertation, Valencia, Spain.

Ninth International Congress of Psychology. (1930). Princeton, NJ: Psychological Review Co.

Olson, W.C. (1939). The forty-sixth annual meeting of the American Psychological Association. *American Journal of Psychology, 52*, 127–130.

Onzième Congrès International de Psychologie. (1938). Paris: Félix Alcan.

Papers read at the X International Congress of Psychology at Copenhagen, 1932. (1935). *Acta Psychologica, 1*(1), 1–230.

Piéron, H. (1929). Le congrès de psychologie de Yale. *L'Année Psychologique, 29*, 924–926.

Piéron, H. (1938). Discours de M. H. Piéron, Président du Congrès. In *Onzième Congrès International de Psychologie* (pp. 507–514). Paris: Félix Alcan.

Tenth International Congress of Psychology. (1935). Copenhagen: Levin & Munksgaard.

Woodworth, R.S., & Boring, E.G. (1930). Ninth International Congress of Psychology. *Psychological Bulletin, 27*, 565–566.

Creation of the International Union of Scientific Psychology

International Congresses of Psychology 12–13

After the end of World War II in 1945, a consensus emerged that the time had come to organize an international union of psychology. The idea of such a union had been broached at the 1st International Congress of Psychology in 1889, but it was clearly premature then, as we noted in Chapter 3. Now several factors converged to make the union timely. The end of the war inaugurated a major period of growth and development of psychology and its spread around the world. Among the features of this growth were increasingly large international congresses and the formation of many national psychological associations. UNESCO was also fostering the formation of international unions, as we saw in Chapter 2.

The minutes of the International Committee, meeting at the 12th International Congress of Psychology at Edinburgh in 1948, state the matter tersely:

> *It was voted to present the question of an International Scientific Union of Psychologists to the psychological organizations of the various countries by the respective representatives on the Committee and to report the result to the Executive Committee (Twelfth International Congress of Psychology, 1950, p. xiii).*

Professor Herbert S. Langfeld of Princeton University, New Jersey, was now Permanent Secretary of the International Committee, having succeeded Edouard Claparède who had died in 1940. Langfeld organized the planning for the Union. As Henri Piéron, first President of the Union, stated, it was at the Edinburgh congress that, thanks to the activity of Herbert Langfeld, it was possible to create the International Union of Scientific Psychology within the framework of UNESCO (Piéron, 1954, p. 404). "Create" may overstate the matter, but draft statutes for the Union were discussed at the Edinburgh congress.

Initial national members of the Union

By early 1950, the following seven national societies had stated their decision to join the Union: the psychological societies of Belgium, France,

Germany, Great Britain, Italy, and Sweden, and the American Psychological Association (Piéron, 1948, p. 685—The volume of *l'Année Psychologique* for this reference is designated 1948, but it was printed in 1950, and Piéron must have added this information in 1950). By the time of the 1951 congress, 11 national psychological societies were original members of the Union, the seven just named plus psychological societies of the Netherlands, Japan, Norway, and Switzerland. As is the rule for international unions, only one psychological society or association per country could join. Over the years, there has been a steady growth in membership of the Union, as can be seen in Appendix E.

The name of the Union

At the discussions at the congress in 1948 at Edinburgh that led to the formation of the Union, one subject was the name to give it. Obvious possibilities were the International Union of Psychology, to correspond with the international congresses of psychology, or the International Psychological Union, which is how Langfeld referred to it before the Edinburgh congress (Langfeld, 1948a, p. 497). No contemporary accounts of the discussion seem to exist, but as Joseph Nuttin, a member of the international committee in 1948, later recalled, three eminent French-speaking psychologists dominated the discussion and insisted that the term psychology be qualified (Nuttin, 1992, pp. 39–40). These were Henri Piéron of France, Albert Michotte of Belgium, and Jean Piaget of Switzerland. Concerned about the scientific status of psychology in their countries, all three felt the need to separate the Union from two tendencies that still threatened scientific psychology in some European countries: (1) certain literary or philosophical forms of psychology, and (2) certain psychotherapeutic practices. English-speaking psychologists allowed themselves to be persuaded, and the Union was formed with the name International Union of Scientific Psychology/Union Internationale de la Psychologie Scientifique. By 1960 American and English psychologists were to change their minds and call for a modification in name, as we will see in Chapter 8.

Adoption of the Statutes

At the 13th International Congress of Psychology, Stockholm, 1951, the Executive Committee discussed the proposed Statutes of the Union, which had been circulated in advance (Piéron, 1948, p. 685), and adopted them without major change. The Statutes were then referred to the newly formed Assembly of the Union, which "ratified this action and commended the Committee for its excellent work" (Thirteenth International Congress of Psychology, 1952, p. 9). The Assembly consisted of 78 members, almost all of whom had been members of the 12th International Committee chosen at the Edinburgh congress in 1948 (see Appendix A.12). The largest number of Assembly members was from the USA (23); the next largest delegations were from Great Britain (11) and France (9), and Germany and Italy had 4 each. Four of the Assembly members were women. At the 14th and later congresses, in conformity with the statutes, each national member of the Union named one or two delegates to the Assembly.

The Statutes adopted in 1951 are reproduced in Appendix C1. The Statutes were to be changed from time to time to adapt them to changing circumstances, and Rules of Procedure were added in 1960. The current Statutes, most recently modified in 1996, are given in Appendix C2. Here we give the first two articles of the 1951 Statutes, which state the nature and aims of the Union:

> *Article 1—The International Union of Scientific Psychology is a group uniting the national Societies and Associations of the adhering countries, having for their aim the development of studies and scientific researches in psychology, whether biological or social, normal or pathological, pure or applied.*
>
> *Article 2—The aims and objects of the Union are as follows:*
>
> *(a) To contribute to the development of intellectual exchange and scientific relations between psychologists of different countries and in particular the organization of Congresses whether general or specialized on definite subjects to be determined.*
> *(b) To contribute to scientific documentation by fostering international exchange of publications, of books, and of reviews, of film and of bibliographies.*
> *(c) To aid scholars of different countries to go abroad to universities, laboratories and libraries, etc.*
> *(d) To foster the exchange of students and of young research workers. (Thirteenth International Congress of Psychology, 1952, p. 14).*

Herbert Langfeld (1879–1958): First Secretary-General of the International Union of Scientific Psychology, 1951–1954.

Administration of the Union

The administrative seat of the Union was located at Princeton University, NJ, that is, at the office of the Secretary-General, Herbert Langfeld (Piéron, 1948, p. 685). The statutes of the Union stated "The Central Headquarters of the Union will be fixed by a decision of the General assembly." For most of the life of the Union, the location of its secretary-general has served as its administrative seat, and only in 1992 did the Union fix a legal venue. The limitations of financial resources for administrative and other purposes has been an ongoing problem.

From the founding of the Union, its Assembly determined the sites and dates of future international congresses of psychology, and its Executive Committee consulted with the local Organizing Committees of the successive congresses. The International Congress Committee, which had been responsible for the continuity of the 2nd through the 11th congresses, dissolved or, more accurately, metamorphosed into the administrative bodies of the Union. Herbert Langfeld, who as Permanent Secretary was the chief administrative officer of the International Committee, became Secretary-General of the Union. Eleven of the 15 officers and members of the first Executive Committee of the Union had been members of the Executive Committee of the International Committee, and two others had been members of the International Committee. (See Appendix B for all officers and members of the Executive Committee, 1951–2000).

The Subcommittee on Social Research

The first Executive Committee of the Union established a Subcommittee on Social Research, consisting of two of its members, Jean Piaget and Otto Klineberg, to "represent the Union in all contacts with the Department of Social Sciences of UNESCO and with other international organizations in the field of the social sciences" (Thirteenth International Congress of Psychology, 1952, p. 10). Over time, the Union developed formal links with several other international organizations and agencies, including the International Social Science Council, the International Council for Science (ICSU), the United Nations (UN), and the World Health Organization (WHO). These links have helped the Union to create opportunities for psychologists to participate in international projects and to inform international bodies about the contributions and expertise of psychologists and psychological research.

The 12th International Congress of Psychology, Edinburgh 1948

The 12th International Congress of Psychology took place after a change of site and years of delay. As described in Chapter 5, it was originally planned for Vienna in 1940 but then the Nazis took over Austria in 1938, and in 1939 the International Committee decided to move the congress to Edinburgh for 1940. The outbreak of World War II in 1939 caused an indefinite postponement of the congress. Psychologists of countries that were still non-belligerents early in the war, the USA and Italy, proposed to organize the 12th congress, but the complicated political and military situation prevented this (Piéron, 1938, p. 982). The 12th congress finally took place in Edinburgh, on July 23–29, 1948.

Professor Emeritus James Drever Sr of the University of Edinburgh had been designated President of the congress, and he played an active role in the Organizing Committee, but ill health prevented him from attending the congress. The presidential address, which he had prepared, was presented by his son and successor as professor of psychology at Edinburgh, James Drever Jr. The General Secretary of the congress was Professor Godfrey Thompson of the University of Edinburgh. Dr Mary Collins of the University of Edinburgh was an assistant secretary and editor of the proceedings. Herbert Langfeld, Secretary-General of the International Committee, paid tribute to the organizers of the congress:

> The task of organizing an International Congress is not an easy one. It was particularly difficult in this period of world confusion. That the congress was a success is due to the self-sacrificing efforts of a small group of men: Professor Godfrey Thompson, James Drever, James Drever Jr, and their local committee (Langfeld, 1948b, p. 579).

James Drever Sr (1873–1950): President of the 12th International Congress of Psychology, Edinburgh, 1948.

Registration at the congress

The congress attracted 688 registrants. The largest number, 393 (57%), came from Great Britain. Other major representations were from the USA (10%) and France (5%). Belgium, Egypt, the Netherlands, and India and Pakistan (the latter two listed as a single entry) each accounted for about 3% of the members. There were, however, few delegates from Eastern Europe and none from the USSR.

The widespread international attendance, with members from 35 countries, was aided by a fund to assist delegates from countries with economic difficulties to attend. This fund originated with a sum of £823 received from the American Psychological Association, a balance from the Yale Congress of 1929. The APA stipulated that none of the fund was to go to American delegates, and the British similarly restricted it to non-British delegates. Most of the fund was expended to assist delegates, and the remaining £211 was retained, with agreement of the APA, to assist attendance at future congresses. The next congress and several later congresses also allotted funds to aid attendance from countries with financial problems.

Program of the congress

The presidential address of James Drever Sr, entitled "Scottish psychology since Hume," took up the philosophical background of psychology, discussing the work of such eminent Scottish philosophers as David Hume, Thomas Reid, Thomas Brown, and Alexander Bain. In contrast was Herbert Langfeld's lecture, "Psychology in America today." Langfeld noted that, "Psychology has come a long way from mental philosophy. In America it is now firmly established among the biological sciences, and, like the other sciences, should look back with sympathy and understanding upon its place of origin" (Langfeld, 1950, p. 11). Langfeld also commented on the growing importance of social psychology, clinical psychology, assessment, and human engineering. He noted the growing support of industry and of several agencies of the US government for psychological research. In response to the "violent" growth of psychology since the end of the war, the APA has "enlarged into a super-organization principally to meet the needs of the rapidly expanding group of professional psychologists" (Langfeld, 1950, p. 18); it established its central office in Washington where the Executive Secretary could be in touch with government agencies, and recruited a full-time staff of 10.

The two other major addresses were given by Albert Michotte of Belgium and Sir Frederic Bartlett. Michotte's presentation consisted of a series of film presentations of phenomena of visual perception with commentaries. These had to do with concepts of the physical world such as maintenance of identity of objects in spite of modifications, continuity of object existence despite discontinuities of their presence, and kinds of actions that objects exert on others. Copies of the film were offered to those interested. Bartlett's address was entitled "Challenge to experimental psychology." Bartlett noted that whereas in the past critics challenged the idea of controlled studies of human action and thought, at present many groups were urging psychology to take on various intractable problems. For example, during the war the armed services had set up Personnel Research Committees, and these committees were continued after the end of the war. Even in peacetime, nearly all the main departments of organized human activity were looking for help from psychology. Bartlett urged that in trying to help solve these problems, strict adherence to the standards of experimental psychology must be maintained.

The remainder of the program consisted of discussions of 5 themes and 130 individual papers. The five themes were the following: (1) Prefrontal leucotomy. (2) Tension among groups. (3) Influence of parental unconscious. (4) Psychology in government services. (5) Primary social attitudes. The most frequent topic of communications was psychometrics, with 17% of the papers; other frequent topics were clinical psychology (10%), and general psychology (10%), and personality, social psychology, and sensation and perception, with 9% each (Montoro González, 1984, pp. 198–199). Except for the main addresses, the papers were published in the proceedings in the form of abstracts of about one page each. Papers were published in English, French, and German.

The small size and tardy appearance of the proceedings reflected post-war conditions in the UK. The 152-page proceedings volume was less than one third of the size of the volumes for the two preceding congresses. The Secretary-General of the congress regretted that the proceedings appeared 2 years after the congress, the delay caused by shortage of paper and lack of skilled printers (Thompson, 1952, p. 292).

Social occasions

On the first evening of the congress, the delegates were welcomed at a reception offered by the university. The next evening there was a party for the congress members. At this time, as Godfrey Thompson stated in his résumé of the congress, the Secretary of State for Scotland, Arthur Woodburn,

> entertained to dinner in the banqueting hall of the Castle some fifty senior members of the Congress and some twenty representatives of the public life of Scotland. This dinner will live in the memory of those privileged to attend. Mr. Woodburn's speech, at once learned, witty, and charming; the austere vaulted room with its historic memories; the stroll in the starlight on the battlements before coffee; the visit to the specially opened shrine which is Scotland's memorial to her fallen in war, these made a deep impression on all.

Limitations of accommodation perforce restricted the castle dinner to a small number, and to men only. Simultaneously, however, Mrs Godfrey Thompson gave a dinner in Mackie's Restaurant, Princes Street, to a similar number of wives and women members ...

> The final social event ... was the City reception on the last evening in the spacious Assembly Halls ... We were received by a long line of ballies and councillors in their robes, flanked by halberdiers, and the Lord and Lady Provost in the centre. There was Scottish dancing, the singing of Scottish songs, and other enjoyable entertainment. ... And at the end a warm-hearted parting speech from the Lord Provost, three cheers led by the gigantic City Officer, and Auld Lang Syne (Twelfth International Congress of Psychology, 1950, p. xvii).

David Katz (1884–1953): President of the 13th International Congress of Psychology, Stockholm 1951. Became first Treasurer of the IUSP, 1951–1953.

Decision on the site of the 13th congress

At the meeting of the International Committee, invitations were received to hold the 13th congress in Stockholm and in the United States. In offering the invitation from Sweden, Professor David Katz stated that the crown prince was willing to serve as patron and the Swedish government offered the sum of 14,000 crowns toward the organization of the congress (Katz, 1950). It was voted unanimously to hold the congress in Stockholm in the summer of 1951.

The 13th International Congress of Psychology, Stockholm 1951

The 13th congress was held in Stockholm on July 16–21, 1951 with Professor David Katz as President. Katz had been the first to hold the chair of psychology and education at the University of Stockholm, and he was a past president of the Swedish Psychological Association. The King of Sweden, who had been crown prince in 1948 when he expressed his willingness to serve as patron, renewed his acceptance. The Secretary-General of the congress was Professor Gösta Eckman, director of the Institute of Psychology at the University of Stockholm and secretary of the Swedish Psychological Association. The inaugural meeting took place in the Building of Parliament, and so did three main evening lectures.

Attendance at the 13th congress

The registration included 658 members and associates, coming from 30 countries (Thirteenth International Congress of Psychology, 1952, p. 286). Twenty per cent came from Sweden, 14% from Great Britain, 10% from the USA, 8% each from Denmark and Norway, and about 6% each from Finland, France, and Germany. Members from the Northern Psychological Cooperation Committee (Denmark, Finland, Norway, and Sweden) together accounted for 40% of the total attendance. Brazil showed a greater attendance than at any previous congress with 5%. As at the previous congress, India and Pakistan (counted together) and Egypt each accounted for about 3% of the delegates. And also as at the previous congress, there were few delegates from eastern Europe and none from the USSR.

Program of the congress

Three prominent psychologists gave plenary lectures on three evenings. Professor Godfrey Thompson, of Edinburgh, gave the first evening lecture, entitled "Factor analysis, its hope and dangers." Professor Burrhus Frederick Skinner, of Harvard University, gave the second plenary lecture, entitled "The experimental analysis of behavior." Professor Henri Piéron of Paris gave the final plenary lecture, entitled "La psychophysiologie générale de la douleur" (General psychophysiology of pain).

In addition to the lectures, there were 149 individual papers, which required parallel sessions. According to Montoro González (1982, p, 211) the distribution of topics was rather similar to that of the previous congress: the largest number of papers concerned psychometrics (17%); next came clinical psychology (13%), sensation and perception (11%), and general psychology (11%). Langfeld (1951, p. 662), using a somewhat different system of categorization, gave the following analysis, and added some interesting information:

One hundred and sixty-one papers were presented during the six days. A breakdown into topics shows the following figures: Clinical and abnormal—39 papers; social, personality, and language—28; educational and child—19; general and theory—15; perception—14; learning—13; sensory—11; tests and measurement—10; comparative—5; applied—4; physiological—3. There were few applied papers, probably because the International Congress of Psychotechnics followed directly after this Congress. The room was generally full for papers on clinical and social psychology, while those persons presenting papers on sensory psychology were left with few listeners.

The individual papers were presented in the proceedings in the form of abstracts of about a page in length. Papers were given at the congress in English, French, and German. The assembly voted to include Spanish as one of the official languages at future congresses.

Social occasions

As at other congresses, there were several social occasions. After the first plenary lecture on Monday, the city of Stockholm offered a reception in the Town Hall. On Wednesday evening, there was a boat trip to the 18th-century Drottningholm Castle where the delegates attended an 18th-century theatrical presentation. Nearly 300 delegates participated in the general dinner on Friday.

Financial results

The congress fared well economically. As mentioned previously, the Swedish government provided a grant of 14,000 crowns. Membership fees amounted to 27,000 crowns. The previous congress had provided a surplus of 11,000 crowns which, together with private gifts, was used to aid foreign delegates. It was hoped that after final expenses and printing of the proceedings there would be some surplus to carry over to the next congress.

Decision on the site of the 14th congress

The proceedings stated the decision briefly in a way that requires further explanation:

The Assembly accepted the invitation of the Canadian Psychological Association for 1954 provided that the American Psychological Association became a joint sponsor of the Congress (Twelfth International Congress of Psychology, 1950, p. 9).

Normally the United States would have been the host for the 14th congress, because the USA as well as Sweden had offered to host the 13th congress.

In fact, the Council of the APA had voted in 1951 to invite the International Congress of Psychology and the CPA to meet with the APA in 1954 in New York, just as the International Congress had met with the APA in 1929. But the motion of the Council had a proviso attached: "if the McCarran Act is modified in such a way as to avoid embarrassment to APA guests." The McCarran Act forbad entrance to the USA to members of the communist party. By 1952 the McCarran Act had not been modified and there was no indication that it soon would be, so the APA Board of Directors voted to join the CPA in a plan, initiated earlier by the CPA, whereby the CPA and APA would be joint hosts in Montréal for the 1954 congress; it also voted to inform New York hotels with which it had previously corresponded that it would not need rooms for a meeting in 1954 (Adkins, 1952, p. 664).

The formation of the International Union inaugurated a new era for psychology

The formation of the International Union gave psychology a recognized international voice, for the first time. At the 13th congress, the executive committee of the Union established a subcommittee on Social Research to "represent the Union in all contacts with the Department of Social Sciences of UNESCO and with other international organizations in the field of the social sciences." Gradually, the Union became recognized by international agencies as the representative body of international psychology.

Under the auspices of the Union, the timing of international congresses became more regular, the congresses became larger and more international in participation, and a systematic way was developed for the national psychological communities to participate in devising the program of the next congress.

The formation of the Union was one of the factors that led to a rapid increase in the number of national psychological organizations beginning in the 1950s. In some cases the Union gave guidance in formulating the statutes of a national society in a way that made it eligible for membership in the Union.

Soon after the formation of the Union, it participated with four other non-governmental social science organizations in the founding of the International Social Science Council (ISSC) in October 1952, following a Resolution adopted at the VI UNESCO General Conference in 1951. Jean Piaget and Otto Klineberg—both members of the Executive Committee of the International Union of Psychological Science—were elected President and Vice-President, respectively. Otto Klineberg had just finished an assignment in Paris with UNESCO to help establish its Social Science Department. During 1948–49, Klineberg was acting head of the new department until a permanent head could be appointed, allowing Klineberg to return to Columbia University. He served again at UNESCO in 1953–55 as Head of UNESCO's Division of Applied Social Sciences. On both occasions, he promoted the development of ISSC and the critical involvement of the Union as a leading member. As of 1999, ISSC includes 14 international organizations representing social science disciplines. In 1992 a new ISSC constitution was adopted which provides for national and regional member organizations such as national academies of science and similar bodies; there are now 16 such member organizations plus 16 associate member organizations.

In countries or regions that were not yet prepared to host an international congress, the Union has fostered national and regional development of psychology by holding regional psychological meetings.

References

Adkins, D.C. (1952). Proceedings of the sixteenth annual business meeting of the American Psychological Association, Inc., Washington, DC. *American Psychologist, 7*, 645–670.

Katz, D. (1950). XIII Congresso International de Psicologia. *Revista de Psicologia General y Aplicada,* 5:14, 422.

Langfeld, H.S. (1948a). Report of the Committee on International Planning in Psychology. *American Psychologist, 3*, 497.

Langfeld, H.S. (1948b). Twelfth International Congress of Psychology. *American Journal of Psychology, 61*, 576–579.

Langfeld, H.S. (1950). Psychology in America today. *Twelfth International Congress of Psychology* (pp. 9–22). Edinburgh, UK: Oliver & Boyd.

Langfeld, H.S. (1951). Thirteenth International Congress of Psychology. *American Psychologist, 6*, 662–663.

Montoro González, L. (1982). *Los congresos internacionales de psicologia (1889–1960).* Unpublished doctoral dissertation, Valencia, Spain.

Nuttin, J. (1992). Les premiers congrès internationaux de psychologie. *Contributions to the history of the international congresses of psychology: A posthumous homage to J.R. Nuttin* (pp. 7–75). Valencia, Spain: Revista de Historia de la psicologia, and Leuven: Studia Psychologica.

Piéron, H. (1929). Le congrès de psychologie de Yale. *L'Année Psychologique, 29*, 924–926.

Piéron, H. (1938). Note sur le XII congrès. *L'Année Psychologique, 32*, 982.

Piéron, H. (1948). L'Union Internationale de la Psychologie Scientifique. *L'Année Psychologique, 49*, 685–686.

Piéron, H. (1954). Histoire succincte des congrès internationaux de psychologie. *L'Année Psychologique, 54*, 397–405.

Thirteenth International Congress of Psychology .(1952). Stockholm: Bröderna Lagerström.

Thompson, G. (1952). Godfrey Thompson. In E.G. Boring, H.S. Langfeld, H. Werner, & R.M. Yerkes (Eds.). *A history of psychology in autobiography. Vol. IV* (pp. 279–294). Worcester, MA: Clark University Press.

Twelfth International Congress of Psychology. (1950). Edinburgh, UK: Oliver & Boyd.

The formative years of the Union

7

The shaping of an organization (1954–1960)

Since 1889, international congresses were the only means psychologists in various countries had at their disposal to coordinate their efforts toward international recognition and promotion of their incipient scientific knowledge. The need for central direction and a systematic deployment of energies had been recognized at several meetings and finally led to the creation of the International Union of Scientific Psychology in Stockholm in 1951, as presented in the previous chapter.

In the years that followed, psychologists made good use of this new structure to build an organization capable of coordinating the efforts of individual national societies, of establishing useful relations with other international scientific groups, and of providing guidelines for the rapid expansion of psychological knowledge.

The creation of the Union provided psychologists with new tools for the nurturing of international interaction and the accelerated development of the organization of psychology. Congresses remained important for the exchange of information and the stimulation of research, as well as providing a milieu for the encouragement of young scientists, needed in these initial years. The regular meeting of national member representatives and the work done between congresses by the Executive Committee contributed greatly to the improvement of structures and the development of relations with other scientific bodies, which were essential to the consolidation of psychology. This is evident in the report of the actions taken during and between congresses and in the increasing recruitment of national members, which characterize this period.

The 14th International Congress of Psychology, Montréal, Canada, 1954

In 1929, the United States had been the host of the first international congress of psychology to be held outside of Europe. Therefore, the North American psychologists were quite pleased to be asked, 25 years later, to assume the responsibility of organizing the 1954 international meeting of the newly founded International Union of Scientific Psychology (IUSP).

Edward A. Bott (1887–1974):
Co-president of the 14th International Congress of Psychology, Montréal, 1954.

It must be said that the participation in the 1929 meeting, which was held in New Haven, Connecticut, had been considerably limited due to the high cost of travel and the unfavorable rate of exchange of the US dollar, which had proved to be a deterrent even for Canadian psychologists (Pratt, 1954). It was felt that conditions overall had improved sufficiently to ensure a much larger participation in the 1954 congress.

It was therefore decided at the 1951 congress in Stockholm that the first congress following the creation of the IUSP would be held in Montréal under the joint sponsorship of the Canadian and American Psychological Associations with two Co-presidents, Edward C. Tolman, an American, and Edward Bott, a Canadian. Montoro González (1982, p.214) wrote that Tolman was appointed initially and that Bott was added as an honorary appointment.

The congress actually took place on June 7–12, 1954, in two main venues: the Université de Montréal and McGill University. At the opening session at the Université de Montréal, the welcoming addresses were given by the Hon. Brooke Claxton representing the Government of Canada, the Hon. Daniel Johnson for the Government of Quebec, and Léon Lortie representing the Mayor of Montréal. Other speakers were: F. Cyril James, Principal of McGill University, Georges Deniger, Vice-Rector of the Université de Montréal, O. Herbert Mowrer, representing the American Psychological Association (APA), and Noël Mailloux for the Canadian Psychological Association (CPA). As President of the IUSP, Henri Piéron gave his presidential address.

Edward C. Tolman (1886–1959):
Co-president of the 14th International Congress of Psychology, Montréal, 1954.

Organization of the congress

The 14th congress was the first to be organized under the responsibility of the new IUSP. An interim committee of the Union appointed in March 1952 received nominations from the APA and the CPA, and named an Executive Committee for the organization of the congress. The Presidency of the Organizing Committee was held by Donald G. Marquis of the University of Michigan, while Noël Mailloux of the Université de Montréal was appointed Secretary and George A. Ferguson of McGill University was named Treasurer (see Table 7.1 for a complete listing of the members of the Organizing Committee).

The Organizing Committee met in Cambridge, Massachusetts, on January 24, 1953, where they created four subcommittees, that is (1) Scientific Program (chaired by Robert B. MacLeod), (2) Local Arrangements (chaired by Donald O. Hebb), (3) Placement (chaired by Edwin B. Newman) and (4) Procurement (chaired by Nelson W. Morton).

TABLE 7.1

Organizational structure of the 14th International Congress of
Psychology (Montréal, 1954)

Organizing Committee

D.G. Marquis (Chair)	D.O. Hebb	E.B. Newman
N. Mailloux (Secretary)	G.W. Kisker	C.C. Pratt
G.A. Ferguson (Treasurer)	H.S. Langfeld	R.W. Russell
G. Barbeau	R.B. MacLeod	F.H. Sanford
E.A. Bott	N.W. Morton	D.C. Williams

Program Committee

R.B. MacLeod (Chair)	C.H. Graham	G. Murphy
R.B. Ammons	E.R. Hilgard	J. Nuttin
F. Beach	G.W. Kisker	C.C. Pratt
A.L. Benton	J.C.R. Licklider	R.N. Sanford
H. von Bracken	D.C. McClelland	M.B. Smith
R.W. Burnham	D.G. Marquis	D.C. Williams
C. Coombs	A.W. Melton	A.T.M. Wilson
H.C.J. Duijker	D.A.R. Moffatt	D. Wolfle
J.J. Gibson	C.T. Morgan	C.F. Wrigley

Local Arrangements Committee

D.O. Hebb (Chair)	J.W. Bridges	W.N. McBain
N. Mailloux (Secretary)	T. Décarie	W.R. Thompson
G.A. Ferguson (Treasurer)	A. Lussier	E.C. Webster
G. Barbeau	L. Malmo	
D. Bélanger	R.B. Malmo	
D. Bindra	A. Pinard	

A contribution of US$10,000 was offered by the APA as seed money to help in the preparation of the meeting: the Canadian contribution was almost symbolic (US$750). The revenues from the registration fees and the commercial exhibition amounted to US$12,740, for a total budget of US$23,495 (Montoro González, 1982, p.212). Registration fees had been set at US$15 for active members of US and Canadian psychological associations and at US$5 for active members from other countries, associate members, and students.

Despite a well-done promotional campaign, registrations came in very slowly. As the date of the meeting approached, there was a general apprehension that the number of participants would indeed be very low, possibly due to the length and cost of travel to North America and the fact that the complete scientific program of the congress had not been distributed in advance. To avoid the possibility of a serious under-representation of psychologists from outside North America, and especially from Europe, financial support was obtained from foundations, commercial enterprises, and private individuals in order to support, at least partially, the travel costs of eminent representatives of European psychology

(Montoro González, 1982, p.215). Travel grants were awarded to 59 persons from 19 countries, for a total of US$18,370. Several summer appointments and lectureships in the United States and Canada were arranged to provide small stipends to overseas psychologists, which stipends were often matched by the universities or governments of the appointees.

The deadline for advanced registration was also postponed and special notices were sent to members of the American Psychological Association, the Canadian Psychological Association, and the Eastern Psychological Association, with the hope of enhancing the local participation of North American psychologists.

In spite of all these efforts, only 1020 persons registered (876 members and 144 associate members and students), whereas preparation had been made for an attendance of 2500. Needless to say, this lower than expected registration gave rise to serious financial difficulties. Out of the 1020 participants, 54% were from the USA, while 33% were from Canada, for a total of 87%; the remaining 13% came from 31 countries (Proceedings of the XIVth International Congress of Psychology, 1955). Despite the weak representation from outside North America, it is interesting to note that a delegation of five eminent Soviet psychologists, A. Leontiev, E.N. Sokolov, E.A. Asratyan, B.M. Teplov, and A.B. Zaporozhets, attended.

Scientific program

A new program structure, which departed from that used previously, was introduced by the Scientific Program Committee. There was no general call for papers; only suggestions for session topics were solicited. To avoid the problems encountered in previous congresses, where the number of papers presented was often deemed excessive and to ensure the best possible scientific quality, the number of oral presentations was limited (Montoro González, 1982, p.216). For the sake of unity and coherence, only invited papers were presented during the congress. Two criteria were used in the selection of invited papers: on the one hand, the committee relied on the suggestion of IUSP members and, on the other hand, made their own choices based on their knowledge of the specialized areas and the quality of the work of different colleagues, as well as their ability to make a significant contribution to the thematic sessions that had been identified. There were actually two types of sessions where oral presentations could be made: the general sessions and the symposia. The general sessions were limited to keynote addresses by five eminent scholars:

- *Edward A. Bott*, "Influences of organization on psychology as a science"
- *Albert Michotte*, "Perception and cognition"
- *Wilder Penfield*, "The permanent record of the stream of consciousness"

- *Jean Piaget*, " Perceptual and cognitive (or operational) structures in the development of the concept of space in the child"
- *Edward Tolman*, "Performance vectors and the unconscious"

The symposia were designed to be accompanied by active discussions and the themes were chosen to be representative of the current fields of interest in psychology. As noted by Montoro González (1982, p. 217), many of the symposia titles contained adjectives such as "present," "recent," "new," to clearly indicate this desire to reflect current interests. Finally, the program included some special sessions, a commercial exhibition, and the projection of specialized films mostly concerned with methodological issues in psychology.

In their content analysis of the material presented based on Montoro González (1982), Montoro González, Tortosa, and Carpintero (1992) note that the following domains of psychology were best represented: psychometry, sensation and perception, as well as general psychology. But the fields of learning and social psychology were also among the major areas under discussion; they note that learning was especially popular with Soviet and American colleagues. Moderately popular in the program were physiological psychology and animal psychology, the latter in relation to the numerous studies on learning.

The two Montréal universities seized this occasion to honor renowned psychologists who were major figures of the 14th congress, by awarding doctorates "honoris causa." Such degrees were awarded to Herbert S. Langfeld, Albert Michotte, and Henri Piéron by the Université de Montréal, and to Edward Bott, Jean Piaget, and Edward Tolman by McGill University.

From left to right: Noël Mailloux (Montréal), Edward A. Bott (Toronto), Herbert S. Langfeld (Harvard), Henri Piéron (Paris), and Jean Piaget (Geneva) at the 14th International Congress of Psychology, Montréal, 1954.

The last event associated with the 14th congress was the special UNESCO symposium held on Saturday morning, June 13, 1954, on "The evaluation of international action programs."

The general feeling of the participants was that the organization of the congress had been rigorous and innovative (Montoro González, 1982, p.213). The weak participation was probably due, at least in part, to the absence of a general call for papers. It should also be mentioned that participants to the congress had been greatly impressed and pleased by the sumptuous reception hosted by the Mayor of Montréal at the "Chalet de la Montagne."

General Assembly, Montréal 1954

During the Montréal congress, on June 6, 1954, the General Assembly of the newly created IUSP met for the first time since its foundation in 1951 at Stockholm. The IUSP President, French psychologist Henri Piéron, chaired the meeting, with participants from 14 countries, as well as 5 observers (including Otto Klineberg representing UNESCO). At the request of Secretary-General Langfeld, the minutes of the Assembly held in Stockholm, previously printed and circulated, were approved. In his report, Langfeld noted that at the General Assembly held in 1951, the IUSP represented 19 countries. At the 1954 Assembly meeting the Yugoslavian Psychological Society was admitted to the Union, bringing the total to 20.

Membership issues

Since the Union was just at its beginnings, membership issues were of paramount importance. Discussions were held concerning the admission criteria; while some members felt that they needed to have as much information as possible on a potential member society for their evaluation of the candidate, others, such as Fraisse, thought that a psychological association of a given country should be admitted as long as it was legitimate and representative. However, in certain countries, such as Brazil for instance, there were many psychological societies, and it was feared that "the Union might recognize a society which did not bear the stamp of national character" (General Assembly Minutes, June 6, 1954). It was suggested that in some cases the problem could be resolved by asking different societies to get together and form a national society, which would be truly representative. It was noted that Article 6 of the Statutes did in fact include this possibility: "The members of the Union shall be national societies of scientific psychology, regularly established, or where there is more than one society in one country, a federation or association which includes all of them." This point having been satisfactorily clarified, the Yugoslavian Psychological Society was unanimously accepted as a new member of the Union.

Relations with UNESCO

After the Stockholm meeting, the relations with UNESCO developed rapidly, especially within its Department of Social Sciences, and were very profitable to the Union. In fact, the Union had been officially granted a consultative status with UNESCO. This meant that UNESCO could refer to the Union for the purpose of obtaining the information it needed, and that it could also entrust the Union with specific projects and allocate funds for their realization. In fact, UNESCO had already sponsored a meeting of social psychologists from various countries in Paris, during the summer of 1952, to explore various problems and potential research projects, as well as a meeting of the Executive Committee of the IUSP, in 1953, in preparation of the present meeting and essentially for the purpose of revising the Statutes. Grants had also been made available for two specific projects: (1) "The study of social psychology throughout the world" (under the direction of Jacobson and Nuttin), and (2) "Centers for research in social psychology" (undertaken by Duijker).

Research projects

Secretary-General Langfeld reported on a survey he had conducted at the request of the Executive Committee, asking the members of the Union to rank order different potential research projects and symposia. Two topics tied for first place: psychological techniques for the study of national characteristics, and the socialization of the child. Other topics, by order of importance, were (1) information and attitude change, (2) national stereotypes: their origin, character and effects, (3) international contacts and attitude change, (4) the teaching of social psychology, (5) attitudes toward productivity in various countries, and (6) technological change.

Admission to the International Council of Scientific Unions

Also discussed during this meeting was the relationship between the newly founded IUSP and the International Council of Scientific Unions (ICSU). Although the Union had already applied four times for admission, without success, a fifth application had been filed. It was decided to solicit the comments of various distinguished scientific bodies, such as the British Royal Society and the US National Academy of Science, regarding this application; Secretary-General Langfeld was asked to prepare a report for the latter, while Sir Frederic Bartlett would supply information to the Royal Society. Both agreed that the actual prospects of being admitted were rather tenuous, but that "perhaps, some day, they would be admitted…" (Executive Committee Minutes, 1954). It was noted that, unless the Union became a member of ICSU, it could not expect to get much support from the Scientific Division of UNESCO. The absence of a formal recognition of psychology in many countries, as well as the fact that the scientific character of psychology was not universally recognized, were regarded as the probable main reasons why the Union applications were repeatedly turned down. It also seemed that ICSU did not want to expand its membership to any great extent. In any case, if psychology were to be included in a group known as the Biological Associations, such a group would have only one representative on the ICSU Executive Committee. Such a solution, which would weaken psychology and jeopardize its autonomy, was deemed unacceptable. Some members expressed concerns about meeting with a fifth refusal; they preferred to wait until the Union was reasonably certain of being accepted. Langfeld indicated that, in view of certain changes in the leadership of ICSU, he was optimistic about the Union's chances regarding the fact that previous votes had been very close. He further added that "the pleasant side to the story was that the biologists and the physiologists were heartily in favor of the Union being admitted," as were scientists in both England and the USA.

Relations with the International Social Science Council

Regarding the affiliation of the Union with the International Social Science Council (ISSC), one of its representatives, Klineberg (the other being Piaget), noted that the ISSC, contrary to the practices reinforced by ICSU, did not want to allocate research funds to its various constituent societies, but preferred instead that each society make its own arrangements with UNESCO. In addition, he mentioned that the relationship between the UNESCO Department of Social Sciences and IUSP could not be limited to social psychologists, but applied to psychologists as a whole. This could mean that in the future, the Union could not make its own arrangements with the UNESCO Department of Natural Sciences.

International Directory of Psychologists

The possibility of establishing an *International Directory of Psychologists* was raised by Secretary-General Langfeld. It was deemed that only a small amount of money would be needed to work on such an appealing proposition and to obtain the collaboration of key people in different member countries in providing the Union with the list of their members. The name, degree, position held, type of research done, etc. would be listed. Since many countries did not have such a list, but were contemplating its establishment, it was felt that the Union should go along with the project, provided there was financial assistance.

Financial matters

The Secretary-General presented the Treasurer's report in replacement of David Katz, who had been appointed Treasurer in Stockholm, but who had passed away during the preceding year. This report covered the whole period between the Stockholm meeting and the opening of the congress. For these 3 years, the total expenditures were of US$ 1786.31. With regard to income, it was noted that the UNESCO funds had just been made available the previous March, so that the Union had to rely on its own funds for the expenses of the preceding months. Other income included the surpluses (in kroner) from the 12th and 13th International Congresses, as well as the 1951–52 membership dues for the USA and Japan, which had been paid in dollars. It was mentioned that, in fact, most of the expenses incurred by the Union were actually being met by the USA, UK, Canada and Japan, since the other member countries were paying very small dues, and some countries had not paid their dues for the past 3 years. Secretary-General Langfeld suggested to overlook the past and to begin collecting dues with a clean slate. In view of the financial difficulties incurred by some countries, the minimum dues payment was reduced to US$10. A budget of US$ 2400 (US$ 400 coming from the Union funds and US$ 2000 from UNESCO) was proposed and adopted unanimously for the next calendar year starting on January 1, 1955. It was deemed important eventually to allocate a stipend to the Secretary-General when the budget would permit and to enhance the research efforts.

A motion was then approved to change the fiscal year of the Union, from July 1–June 30, to the calendar year, in order to fall in line with UNESCO practices. It was proposed to start collecting the new dues on January 1, 1955. It was also deemed appropriate to have the present Secretary-General and also acting Treasurer, Langfeld, step down at this same date in order to allow them sufficient time to bring all material up to date and to prepare the report for 1954.

Revision of the 1951 Statutes

A revision of the original 1951 Statutes was undertaken. To prevent a potential time-consuming discussion of amendments examined article by article, these were adopted as a whole, considering the fact that the changes had been discussed for 3 days by the Executive Committee. Article 11, giving two votes to certain countries on the basis of their membership (one vote: less than 500 members, two votes: more than 500), and also giving two votes to "A society in existence for at least 50 years at the time of the establishment of the Union and whose membership is limited by its statutes…" was discussed. This latter provision, which had been added specifically to take into consideration the special case of France, was questioned. Arguments were raised in support of the important role played by the French society, as well as the fact that the problem might disappear with the reorganization of French psychology. The article was finally accepted, with only one negative vote. The suggestion was made to Mr. Queiroz, the observer from Brazil, to examine the possibility of forming a national Brazilian society representative of the many organizations currently grouping psychologists in his country.

Elections of the Executive Committee

During the afternoon session of the General Assembly, the first item on the agenda was the election of a President and a Vice-President. Three names

had been put forward for the presidency: Bartlett, Michotte, and Piaget. Since the two first nominees declined, Piaget from Switzerland was elected President by acclamation. For the vice-presidential position, there were two candidates, Rasmussen (Denmark) and Germain (Spain); Rasmussen was elected by majority vote. The results of the election to the Executive Committee (10 positions) were as follows: Klineberg (USA), Bartlett (UK), Piéron (France), Mailloux (Canada), Drever (UK), Germain (Spain), Langfeld (USA), Michotte (Belgium), Elmgren (Sweden), and Duijker (the Netherlands).

It was agreed that the new Secretary-General and the new Treasurer be appointed at a meeting of the incoming Executive Committee immediately after the congress.

Choice of the next congress venue

The selection of the venue for the next International Congress of Psychology was debated. Many candidates were suggested—Montevideo, Rome, Amsterdam—although members felt that they were unable to commit themselves before returning to their home country and considering the matter. It was decided that the Executive Committee would look into this matter and consult with the member countries at a later date.

Executive Committee meeting, Montréal 1954

On June 12, the incoming Executive Committee, chaired by Piaget, met for the first time. It was first decided that, as a general rule, observers should not attend the meetings of the Executive Committee, but could occasionally be allowed to do so when discussions on special local problems made it necessary.

Klineberg was elected Secretary-General, and Germain, Deputy Secretary-General. Mailloux was elected Treasurer. It was decided to leave the task of appointing an Executive Secretary to help the officers of the Union in their functions to the Secretary-General and the Treasurer.

The question of allowing Executive Committee members to appoint substitutes to the meetings of the committee with the right to vote led to a long discussion. Although some strongly favored this option, others were strongly opposed. It was finally decided unanimously that since a statute change would be required, the question would be submitted to the next General Assembly.

The Secretary-General proposed that *Acta Psychologica* be asked to publish the proceedings of the congress as a special issue, and that therefore this journal be published under the auspices of the Union. The Union might publish notices in *Acta Psychologica* from time to time, without precluding publications in other journals. There would be no financial obligations on the part of the Union, but the proceedings should probably be financed from outside sources. It was also suggested that a member of the Union be appointed on the editorial staff to act as its representative. It was agreed that the Secretary-General should approach *Acta Psychologica* and seek an agreement on these issues.

The question of asking the editorial board of the *Psychological Abstracts* to enlarge its scope was also raised. It was thought that they might, at some time in the near future, be published in languages other than English. But no action was taken.

Executive Committee meeting, Paris 1955

A special meeting of the Executive Committee of the IUSP was held, on August 2 and 3, 1955, at the UNESCO House in Paris. The President of the Union, Jean Piaget, opened this meeting, which was attended by Secretary-General Klineberg and Treasurer Mailloux, as well as by the following members of the Committee: Piéron, Elmgren, Duijker, Germain, and Rasmussen. K. Szczerba, of UNESCO, as well as George Ferguson, of McGill University (Canada), who had been Treasurer of the Montréal 1954 congress, attended as observers.

Venue of the 15th congress

After the adoption of the agenda, the discussion centered on the major issue to be dealt with at this meeting: the choice of the venue for the next International Congress of Psychology.

Although a suggestion had been made to hold the forthcoming congress in Belgium, Michotte had not, by then, been able to secure appropriate subsidies from the Belgian Government. Other possible candidates were Spain, Italy, and Yugoslavia. The committee decided to ask Germain to examine the possibility of a congress in Madrid, Spain, if the Belgium venue proved to be impossible. Unless the financial difficulties proved to be unsolvable, the 1957 congress would be held in Belgium.

Organization of congresses

A discussion followed on the nature of the problems raised by the organization of a congress. Szczerba indicated that UNESCO might be able to help, perhaps by having their Director-General send a circular letter to all member states asking governments to subsidize the travel expenses of their national participants.

Ferguson gave a brief account of the financial involvement of the Montréal congress, which had a total budget of approximately US$50,000, much of which went to pay for the travel of delegates. However, most of the work done in preparation of the congress relied on voluntary labor at no cost to the congress budget. It was noted by Piéron that the financial requirements depended heavily on the type of congress and what needed to be prepared for the delegates in the way of entertainment, etc. The difficulties associated with the date chosen for this event were considered; it was recognized that whatever dates selected, the decision could not please everyone. Both Ferguson and Mailloux insisted on the necessity of advance publicity and a very early planning of the budget in order to help the coordination of efforts and to avoid the possibility of two congresses of this nature being held in the same area within a brief interval.

The problem of having open sessions, at which papers without mutual relevance would be presented, was raised and it was decided to inform the organizers of the next congress that the Executive Committee would be ready, if they so wished, to nominate a group of their own to help with the planning of the scientific program. It was also suggested that the three following points be taken into consideration: (1) to have invited lecturers; (2) to program several symposia in the "Montréal style," and (3) to offer several open sessions, but on predetermined subjects.

Relations with the International Council of Scientific Unions

The next item on the agenda was the Union's application for membership of the International Council of Scientific Unions (ICSU). It was agreed that Piéron, who was to attend the next ICSU meeting in Oslo during the following week, would be the best advocate for this task. It was recalled that, at the last General Assembly meeting of the Union, both the Canadian and British delegates (the latter being at that time the Secretary-General of the Union) had voted against the motion to apply for membership in ICSU. President Piaget noted that the existence of a Section on Experimental Psychology within ICSU was not an obstacle to full membership of the Union; he also remarked that, since the Union was receiving grants from UNESCO, the issue was not of a financial nature, but one of principle. Klineberg, however, did not think that this application should be maintained indefinitely and made the suggestion that, were it not to be accepted this time, the whole issue should be reexamined before putting forward another such request.

A letter dated June 22, in which Langfeld asked the Executive Committee to establish a "Bureau" for the Section on Experimental Psychology that belonged to the International Union of Biological Sciences (IUBS), was read to those present. Member associations from seven countries had endorsed this petition. After discussion, it was resolved that, in spite of the absence of any official connection between the Union and this section, the following tentative list of names could be proposed: Piéron as President, Donald Hebb as Secretary-General, Graham, Piaget, and Bartlett as Vice-Presidents, Ubeda as Executive Secretary, and Buytendijk and Murinaka as substitutes.

International Directory of Psychologists

Duijker informed the Executive Committee that he had received an invitation to assume the European editorship for an *International Directory of Psychologists* and requested the recommendations of the committee. The Washington-based International Council of Research, of which Klineberg was a member, had adopted this project. Duijker indicated that the project raised a number of problems, including that related to the question "What is a psychologist?," as well as the criteria for the definition of a psychologist and the question as to whom to send the questionnaire necessary to obtain the information required to establish such a directory. The Union had no official information which could be used. It was generally agreed that in addition to local recognition as a psychologist, the only possible criterion for the inclusion in the list was the publication of scientific works.

Membership issues

Questions related to the actual membership of the newly founded Union were examined. It was felt that in some countries the member associations were not representative at all of the psychologists in those countries; Brazil and Uruguay were given as examples. It was felt that some countries should be told that they would not be able to adhere to the IUSP unless they established a truly representative psychological society in their country. Although no Soviet society existed as yet, it was mentioned that it had been decided to constitute one. Piéron also mentioned that the necessary modifications to widen the scope of the French Society had been made. A certain number of countries were to be solicited by the Secretary-General for membership in the Union: India, Australia, Portugal, Austria, and Turkey. With regard to East Germany, it was agreed that as long as Germany was not reunited, there were no reasons why two societies should not coexist, and invitations should be received and accepted from either.

Publication program

The decision was made to collaborate with UNESCO on the drafting of textbooks to be used for advanced training courses in psychology in various developing countries. It was also decided to prepare a work plan, with the help of UNESCO, for the international study of the origin and development of national images or stereotypes. A commission, composed of Klineberg, Duijker, and Mailloux, was formed to work out the details of this project, and it was agreed that the Union should subsidize such a study. The same group was also asked to prepare a project to foster the contribution of psychologists to the problem of "peaceful cooperation and/or coexistence" among the nations, following a recommendation made at the UNESCO General Conference. Mailloux was asked to represent the Union at a meeting of non-governmental organizations (NGOs) in Paris to discuss UNESCO's future program.

On the matter of publications, Klineberg proposed the creation of a quarterly *International Newsletter* providing details of international activities, new research, the organization of institutes of research, programs for the teaching of psychology in various universities, etc. The project received the approval of the committee. The publication of the first issue was planned for October 1955 and would be sent to all members of the Assembly. It was also noted that the *Psychological Abstracts* should present a wider international coverage of reviews and books. The proposition was made to reconstitute the International Committee, which could make an effort to remedy this type of situation.

Administrative and financial issues

Relations with other international organizations in psychology were also a subject of discussion. It was decided that certain associations should be represented as observers (without voting rights) at the Assembly and it was suggested that the Statutes of the Union be amended to reflect this "Associated Organizations" category.

Concerning financial matters, Treasurer Mailloux summarized the financial situation of the Union and produced a financial statement. Mention was made of the request made by Michotte for a loan to help the organization of the next congress in Belgium, but no decision was taken.

The 15th International Congress of Psychology, Brussels, Belgium, 1957

As decided at the 1955 meeting of the Executive Committee of the Union, the 15th International Congress of Psychology was held in Brussels, Belgium, from July 28 to August 3, 1957. The venue of the meeting was the Université Libre de Bruxelles. The congress was held under the auspices of the IUSP and the Belgian Society of Psychology, under the patronage of the King of Belgium, His Majesty Baudoin I. Financial support was provided not only by the IUSP, but also by the Belgian government. The Ford Foundation provided travel grants to enable the participation of over 25 Americans. Table 7.2 presents the organizational structure of the congress.

The presidency of the congress was assumed by Baron Albert Michotte van den Berck, Director of the Experimental Psychology Laboratory of the Université de Louvain and Member of the Royal Academy of Belgium, an internationally renowned scholar in the area of perception. René Nyssen of the Université de Bruxelles and Past President of the Belgian Society of Psychology, was appointed President of the General Organization Committee, whereas Joseph Nuttin of the Université de Louvain presided over the Scientific Program Committee. The Secretary-General of the congress was Louis Delys, and the Treasurer, Gérard Goosens. Meetings of the Organization and Program Committees were held periodically from the beginning of 1956 to the time of the congress (Proceedings of the Vth International Congress of Psychology, 1959, p. xv).

A record attendance

A record number of 1256 psychologists (including 951 regular members) coming from 47 different countries registered for the congress (Proceedings of the XVth International Congress of Psychology, 1959, p. XVI). The largest national delegation came from the USA (28%) and was even superior to the local Belgian participation (20%). Definitely an international event, this congress attracted delegations from Poland (headed by Blakowski of the University of Poznan) as well as from the USSR (conducted by Smirnov, President of the newly founded Russian Psychological Society, and Leontiev). Also present, right beside the delegation of the Federal Republic of Germany, was the East German delegation headed by Gottschaldt,

Albert Michotte (1881–1965):
President of the 15th International
Congress of Psychology, Brussels, 1957;
later President of the IUSP,
1957–1960.

TABLE 7.2

Organizational structure of the 15th International Congress of Psychology (Brussels, 1957)

General Organizing Committee

President: René Nyssen (Université de Bruxelles)

a. Members appointed by the IUSP

Jean Piaget (Switzerland)   Noël Mailloux (Canada)
Otto Klineberg (USA)   Henri Piéron (France)

b. Members appointed by the Belgian Society of Psychology

R. Buyse (Université de Louvain)   J. Kriekemans (Université de Louvain)
L. Coetsier (University of Ghent)   J. Ley (Université libre de Bruxelles)
J. De Busscher (Université libre de Bruxelles)   A. Michotte (Université de Louvain)
—. De Clerck (Belgian Society of Psychology)   J. Nuttin (Université de Louvain)
W. De Coster (Université libre de Bruxelles)   A. Ombredane (Université libre de
L. Delys (Université libre de Bruxelles)   Bruxelles)
G. de Montpellier (Université de Louvain)   P. Osterrieth (Université libre de
A. Fauville (Université de Louvain)   Bruxelles)
F. Fransen (University of Ghent)   N. Paulus (Université de Liège)
L. Knops (Université de Louvain)   R. Piret (Université de Liège)

Program Committee

J. Nuttin (Chair)   A. Michotte
L. Coetsier   R. Nyssen
L. Delys   A. Ombredane
G. de Montpellier   P. Osterrieth
A. Fauville   N. Paulus

Jean Piaget (1896–1980): President of the IUSP, 1954–1957.

director of the Institute of Psychology at Humboldt University. Egyptian psychologists were also seated adjacent to their Israeli colleagues (Piéron, 1957, pp. 625–626).

Registration was 500 Belgian francs for regular members (psychologists and other related professionals), and 250 Belgian francs for associate members (students and accompanying persons).

The opening ceremony was held in the Grand Hall of the Université Libre de Bruxelles. On this occasion, welcome speeches were made by W. Vermeylen, the Belgian Minister of the Interior, as well as by Jean Piaget and Otto Klineberg, respectively President and Secretary-General of the Union, by the President of the congress, Albert Michotte, and by Henri Piéron, in the name of the foreign participants.

Michotte then gave the inaugural address ("Réflexions sur le rôle du language dans l'analyse des structures perceptives"). Other evening lectures were given during the following days by Wolfgang Köhler ("Psychologie und Naturwissenschaft"), Jean Piaget ("Le rôle des modèles d'équilibre dans l'explication en psychologie: rétroactions, anticipations et opérations") and by Clyde Kluckhohn, of Harvard University, USA ("Anthropology and psychology").

Scientific program

The Program Committee had made a special effort to regroup the presentations into thematic sessions. In fact, to better identify the current themes of the sessions, a survey had been previously conducted with researchers in different areas and with the different psychological societies

15th Congress— Brussels, 1957: Congress participants outside the venue.

in the IUSP. The presentation of the 26 various themes that were retained was through (1) general conferences (opening lectures and keynote addresses), (2) symposia, (3) individual presentations, and (4) colloquia. Twenty four themes were retained for the symposia (see Table 7.3).

Individual papers were regarded as the prolongation of the different themes, adding more flexibility to the presentations of the symposia. Finally, the colloquia consisted of round-table discussions with a limited number of specialists. These colloquia dealt with practical issues : (1) the training of psychologists, (2) psychological terminology, and (3) cooperation between psychologists and neuro-psychiatrists.

Classifying the 329 presentations at the congress by subject, 16% were in the area of sensation and perception, 15% in the area of psychometry,

TABLE 7.3

Themes of the symposia: 15th International Congress of Psychology
(Brussels, 1957)

1. Interdisciplinary approach: values (Chair: Clyde Kluckhohn)
2. The problem of measurement with respect to intensity of sensation
   (Chair: Henri Piéron)
3. Information theory and its applications in psychology (Chair: Sir Frederic
   Bartlett)
4. Non-parametric structural analysis (Chair: Benoit Mandelbrot)
5. The phenomenology of behavior (Chair: Robert MacLeod)
6. Methodological problems in the psychological study of indigenous black
   populations of Africa (Chair: S. Biesheuvel)
7. Biochemical processes and behavior (Chair: Roger W. Russell)
8. Brain and behavior (Chair: Ward C. Halstead)
9. The neurological basis of perception (Chair: O.L. Zangwill)
10. Space perception (Chair: R.C. Oldfield)
11. Psychology of time (Chair: Henri Piéron)
12. From perception to thought (Chair: Martin Scheerer)
13. Dynamic factors in perception (Chair: Jerome S. Bruner)
14. Human motivation (Chair: Joseph Nuttin)
15. Conflict, decision and post-decision phenomena
    (Chair: Sir Frederic Bartlett)
16. Current approaches to the theory of emotion (Chair: J. Paulus)
17. Longitudinal studies in personality (Chair: A.G. Skard)
18. Early childhood experiences and personality development, psychoanalytic
    concepts and experimental findings (Chair: Robert R. Sears)
19. The theoretical bases of projective techniques and assessment procedures
    (Chair: Gardner Murphy)
20. Problems of religious psychology (Chairs: Robert H. Thouless, A.T. Welford)
21. Interpersonal perception (Chair: Urie Bronfenbrenner)
22. National characteristics and stereotypes (Chair: Otto Klineberg)
23. Psychological and social aspects of automation (Chair: James Drever Jr)
24. Psychological and social aspects of the cinema (Chair: Robert Zazzo)

The two other themes suggested (language and learning) were not the object of symposia.

12% in social psychology, 9% in physiological psychology, 6% each in general psychology and evolutionary psychology (Montoro González, 1982, p.229).

The Proceedings of the 15th Congress (1959) were published by North-Holland, and also as a special issue of *Acta Psychologica*.

On Tuesday, July 29, a luncheon was offered by the Belgian Society of Psychology to the following foreign participants who were elected Honorary Members of the Society: Bartlett, Klineberg, Kluckhohn, Köhler, Langfeld, Piaget, and Piéron. The traditional closing banquet was held on Friday, August 2. Visits to the laboratories and facilities of the Université Libre de Bruxelles and of the Université de Louvain were arranged for August 3.

The congress organizers generally considered, on the basis of the good atmosphere encountered, the broad participation, and the positive opinions expressed by experienced as well as less experienced participants, that the Brussels congress definitely reached the goal it had set itself: an occasion of intellectual confrontation and scientific exchange.

General Assembly, Brussels 1957

The General Assembly of the IUSP was held in Brussels on the Sundays that preceded (July 28) and that followed (August 4) the congress. Nineteen of the 21 member societies of IUSP were represented by delegates.

After introductory remarks by Piaget, President of IUSP, the Secretary-General and the Treasurer presented their reports, which were commended and approved. The Assembly then proceeded to elect, as new members, the psychological societies of New Zealand and Australia (even though these were branches of the British Psychological Society), Poland, USSR, and Turkey. Counting these new admissions, the membership of IUSP now reached 26 countries.

From left to right: Henri Piéron, Jean Piaget, and Wolfgang Köhler at the 15th International Congress of Psychology, Brussels, 1957.

By virtue of an addition to the Statutes that had been voted by mail ballot, it was announced that the following international organizations in psychology were granted "Associate" status in the Union: the International Association of Applied Psychology, l'Association de psychologie scientifique de langue française, and the Interamerican Society of Psychology.

In his report, Secretary-General Klineberg mentioned the success of the book entitled *Perspective in Personality Theory* (H. David & H. von Bracken, Eds.) which was published under the auspices of the Union after the Montréal congress. He further added that the Union was considering the financial support of a psychological lexicon in three languages (French, English and German) and that it would also continue to collaborate with the editors of the *International Directory of Psychologists*, looking into the possibility of periodically reviewing this directory. The possibility of periodically making available English translations of major psychology papers published in a foreign language would also be considered by the Executive Committee; a group of psychologists met during the Brussels congress to consider this issue more in depth. Secretary-General Klineberg ended his report by listing the different grants received by the Union. He mentioned the financial support provided by the Research Institute for the Study of Man to extend the pilot study originally funded through UNESCO on "The origins and developments of national stereotypes in children."

Treasurer Mailloux's report on the finances of the Union for the 1955, 1956, and 1957 period was approved unanimously.

Following the request of some Scandinavian countries to eliminate the possibility of voting by mail ballot, the Executive Committee approved an amendment to the Statutes that specifies that in such cases, a 2/3 majority of voters would be required.

In the absence of applications to host the next congress, the Executive Committee was once again charged to take a decision concerning the venue and time of the 16th congress that would, in principle, be held in 1960.

The results of the elections of the Executive Committee conducted during the second (August 3) General Assembly meeting were the following: Michotte (Belgium) (President), Drever (UK) (Vice-President). The following members of the Executive Committee were re-elected: Bartlett (UK), Duijker (Netherlands), Klineberg (USA), Mailloux (Canada), and Piéron (France). New members were: Mäki (Finland), Nuttin (Belgium), Piaget (Switzerland), Russell (USA), and Mrs. A. Skard (Norway).

Executive Committee meeting, Brussels 1957

On August 3, at the end of the second General Assembly meeting, the newly elected Executive Committee met for the first time and Klineberg, Duijker, and Mailloux were appointed Secretary-General, Deputy Secretary-General, and Treasurer, respectively, of IUSP.

Among the decisions taken was the appointment of two commissions, one to revise further the Statutes of the Union with a particular emphasis on the establishment of working relations between the Union and a national society for the purpose of organizing an international congress, and the other to examine ways to enhance cooperation with *Psychological Abstracts*. It was also decided to provide funds for an English-German-French lexicon of psychology to be prepared by Wolfgang Luthe, as well as to support an Inter-Union Symposium on Chromatic Discrimination (organized by the Experimental Psychology Section of the International Union of Biological Sciences).

References

González Solaz, J. (1998). *Los Congresos Internacionales de Psicologia (1963–1984)*. Unpublished doctoral dissertation, University of Valencia, Spain.

Montoro González, L. (1982). *Los Congresos Internacionales de Psicologia (1889–1960)*. Unpublished doctoral dissertation, University of Valencia, Spain.

Montoro González, L., Tortosa, F.M., & Carpintero, H. (1992). Brief history of the international congresses of psychology. In M. Richelle & H. Carpintero (Eds.), *Contributions to the history of the international congresses of psychology. Revista de la Historia de la Psicologia Monograph and Studia Psychologica*. Leuven, Belgium: Leuven University Press.

Piéron, H. (1957). Chronique: le XVième Congrès International de Psychologie. *Année Psychologique, 57*, 625–626.

Pratt, C.C. (1954). The XIVth International Congress of Psychology. *American Journal of Psychology, 67*, 551–553.

Proceedings of the XIVth International Congress of Psychology, Montréal, Canada, 1954. (1955). Amsterdam: North-Holland.

Proceedings of the XVth International Congress of Psychology, Brussels, Belgium, 1957. (1959). Amsterdam: North-Holland.

Expansion and international collaboration (1960–1965)

The creation of the Union, the improved organization of international congresses, the larger international participation, and the enthusiasm of the participants of the 14th and 15th congresses, particularly the one in Brussels, all contributed to the enhancement of psychologists' confidence in the scientific character of their discipline. In spite of poor financial means at their disposal, the elected officials of the Union succeeded in gradually expanding the collaboration of international organizations as well as of member societies. There was still a long way to go, but progress was being made. The Executive Committee started to meet regularly between congresses in view of the increasing volume of Union activities and the need to monitor many issues closely. It was also necessary to frequently amend the Statutes of the Union to adapt to changes brought about by rapid growth.

The 16th International Congress of Psychology, Bonn, Federal Republic of Germany, 1960

As noted earlier, by the end of the 15th congress the Union had not received any invitation from a member society to host the 16th congress. The Executive Committee had been instructed to come to a decision at the earliest possible time.

In September 1957, the German Society of Psychology (Deutsche Gesellschaft für Psychologie) sent an invitation to the Union to hold its forthcoming congress in the Federal Republic of Germany. Sixty-four years had passed since the last meeting had taken place in a German-speaking country. The invitation was promptly accepted and the Executive Committee proposed that the congress be held under the presidency of Professor Johannes von Allesch of Göttingen. Eventually, for health reasons, von Allesch couldn't assume the presidency (Montoro González, 1982, p. 235). The 16th congress was held in Bonn, Federal Republic of Germany, from July 31 to August 6, 1960, under the presidency of Wolfgang Metzger, and the Honorary Presidency of Karl Bühler, who would have presided at the 12th congress if it had been held in Vienna in 1940 (Piéron, 1960, p.620). Hans Thomae assumed the position of Secretary-General of the Congress, Udo Undeutsch acted as Treasurer, while Albert Wellek was in charge of the Program Committee.

Wolfgang Metzger (1899–1979): President of the 16th International Congress of Psychology, Bonn, 1960.

The sessions were held in the rooms of the Rheinische Friedrich-Wilhelms-Universität and the Beethoven-Halle, in Bonn. Official governmental support was obtained from Gerhard Schroder, the Federal Minister of the Interior, from Werner Schutz, the Minister of Culture and Education of the Nordrhein-Westfalen State, from Max Braubach, Rector of the University of Bonn, and from the Lord Mayor of the City of Bonn, Wilhelm Daniels. The Minister of the Interior of the Federal Republic of Germany and the Minister of Cultural Affairs and Education of the State of Nordrhein-Westfalen also generously accepted to assume the costs of the publication of the proceedings of the congress, in collaboration with the IUSP. These proceedings were published in 1962 by North-Holland, but also as a special issue of the journal *Acta Psychologica*, similarly to the 15th congress.

Organization of the congress

The organization fell under the joint responsibility of the IUSP and the German Society of Psychology. Therefore the General Organizing Committee was composed of members appointed by both the IUSP and the German Society of Psychology, as can be seen in Table 8.1.

The number of participants (1833, out of which 1116 were regular members) was greater than the number at the Brussels congress. For the first time in its history, the congress organization made use of modern technical facilities, such as simultaneous translation. All addresses, presentations, and discussions of the general meetings and, to some extent, of the individual meetings, were simultaneously translated into the three official languages of the congress—English, French, and German.

An informal welcoming ceremony by the Honorary President, the President, the Chair of the Program Committee, and the Secretary-General took place in the Beethoven-Halle on July 31, the night preceding the official opening, and it was followed by a reception. The opening ceremonies on the morning of August 1 began with the presentation of the well-known Toccata and Fugue in D-minor for Organ of Johann Sebastian Bach, and was followed by brief welcoming remarks from the President of the Congress, the Federal Minister of the Interior, the Minister of Cultural Affairs and Education of Nordrhein-Westfalen, the Rector of the University of Bonn, the Lord Mayor of the City of Bonn, as well as the President and the Secretary-General of the IUSP. The President of the congress, Wolfgang Metzger, then read his opening address ("Homage to Gustav Theodor Fechner") in recognition of the centennial of the publication of Fechner's well-known book "Elements of Psychophysics". He was followed by the Honorary President, Karl Bühler, who gave the presidential address ("Gestalt in the lives of men and animals").

TABLE 8.1

Organizational structure of the 16th International Congress of Psychology (Bonn, 1960)

General Organizing Committee

President: Wolfgang Metzger

a. Members appointed by the International Union of Scientific Psychology

James Drever, Jr (UK)
Hubert C.J. Duijker (Netherlands)
Otto Klineberg (USA)
Noël Mailloux (Canada)

Albert Michotte (Belgium)
Joseph Nuttin (Belgium)
Jean Piaget (Switzerland)
Henri Piéron (France)

b. Members appointed by the German Society of Psychology

W. Arnold (University of Würzburg)
E. Boesch (University of Saabrücken)
H. von Bracken (University of Marburg)
H. Düker (University of Marburg)
R. Heiss (University of Freiburg)
P.R. Hofstatter (University of Hamburg)
I. Kohler (University of Innsbruck)

K. Mierke (University of Kiel)
E. Rausch (University of Frankfurt)
J. Rudert (University of Heidelberg)
Th. Scharmann (University of Nürnberg)
K.S. Sodhi (University of Berlin)
W. Witte (University of Tübingen)

Program Committee

A. Wellek (University of Mainz) (Chair)
K. Gottschaldt (University of Berlin)
Ph. Lersch (University of München)
A. Mayer (University of Mannheim)
J. Nuttin (Université de Louvain)

H. Rohracher (University of Wien)
J. Rudert (University of Heidelberg)
H. Thomae (University of Bonn)
U. Undeutsch (University of Köln)

Scientific program

The Program Committee, under the chairmanship of Wellek, had its first preparatory meeting in Louvain in April 1959 together with some of the Brussels congress organizers. As had been done for the Brussels congress, the national psychological associations that were members of the Union, certain psychology departments and institutes of higher learning in various countries, as well as individual scholars, were asked to propose topical subjects. Out of these suggestions, 20 principal themes emerged, each to be treated in a symposium and, depending on the importance of the subject, by one or more discussion speakers (see Table 8.2). Individual presentations related to each main theme were also encouraged in order to address broader aspects. Because of the wide variety of individual papers submitted, eight more themes were added. Three public evening lectures were also added to the program, as well as four colloquia on special professional and organizational problems. There were small group discussions with invited guests. A book and equipment exhibition was arranged. The participants could take advantage of various visits, excursions, and social receptions during the congress. The traditional closing banquet was replaced by a boat trip up the Rhine river to Linz, an old wine town near Neuwied.

TABLE 8.2

Scientific program themes:
16th International Congress of Psychology (Bonn, 1960)

1. Microgenesis of perception
2. Theory and critique of projective tests
3. Problems of the aging personality
4. Instinct behavior
5. Scaling problems in psychophysics
6. The problem of the "ego" in motivation
7. Differential psychology of adolescence
8. Perceptual learning
9. Mathematical models in psychology
10. Effects of affective deprivation in children
11. Interaction processes in small groups
12. Problems of the theory of expression
13. The phenomenological approach in psychology
14. Perception and information theory
15. Problems of interpersonal perception
16. Origin and development of national stereotypes in children
17. Psychology of religion
18. Language and comprehension
19. Personality and perception
20. Drugs as research tools in psychology
21. Problems of method
22. Physiological psychology
23. Problems of perception
24. Clinical psychology
25. Social psychology
26. Behavior under stress
27. Time perspectives
28. Lectures with demonstrations

The following evening presentations were open to the general public:

- *Paul Fraisse* (France): "L'adaptation de l'homme au temps"
- *Richard C. Oldfield* (UK): "Listening, attending and speaking"
- *Alexej N. Leontiev* (USSR): "Le social et le biologique dans la mentalité de l'homme"

The colloquia dealt with the following issues:

1. Social sciences, psychology, and mental health: The role of the psychologist in World Mental Health Year.
2. Problems of cooperation between psychology and psychopathology.
3. Means of international exchange among psychologists speaking different languages.
4. The legal status and responsibility of psychologists in different countries.

In the summary account of the congress (Proceedings of the XVIth International Congress of Psychology, 1962, p. XXVIII), we find the following conclusion, which synthesizes the significant contribution of the Bonn congress:

> It is still too early to give a complete appreciation of the success of the congress or to expect immediate practical results from it, just as it was the case after the Brussels Congress. Yet, there can be no doubt that the use of the latest technical facilities, those mentioned above (i.e. simultaneous translation) and the rotaprint method—at the beginning of the Congress each participant was given two volumes containing summary accounts of the talks—as well as the record participation will be milestones in the history of the International Congress and will certainly be conducive to fruitfully shaping its progressive development, structure and organization.

General Assembly, Bonn 1960

As was the case in Brussels 3 years before, the General Assembly of IUSP met during two sessions, just before and right after the congress.

Reports of the Officers

The first meeting of the Assembly was held on July 31. After the usual roll call, which indicated that delegates from national societies from 17 countries were present (Australia, Belgium, Canada, Denmark, France, Germany, Israel, Italy, Japan, Netherlands, Norway, Spain, Sweden, Switzerland, USSR, UK, and USA) as well as an observer, Dr N. Leites, of the Social Sciences Division of UNESCO, the meeting was opened by the President of the Union. After the adoption of the provisional agenda, Secretary-General Klineberg gave his report. He first mentioned the upcoming publication in German and Spanish of *Perspectives in Personality Theory* (Eds.: H. David & H. von Bracken) and the publication in English of *Perspectives in Personality Research* (Eds.: H. David & J.C. Brengelmann). He also indicated that H.C.J. Duijker had prepared for IUSP a trend report on "National Character and National Stereotypes" that would soon be published under the auspices of the International Committee for Social Science Information and Documentation. He further mentioned that the Union would be sponsoring (1) a symposium and research project on the origins and development of national stereotypes in children (conducted in 10 different countries by W.E. Lambert from Canada), (2) an attitude survey among young people on the peaceful uses of atomic energy, (3) a meeting in New York (in collaboration with UNESCO) on the use of psychological concepts in other social sciences. In view of the expected increase of UNESCO support, the Secretary-General suggested that there should be a meeting of the Executive Committee between congresses and that larger contributions should be available for the increasing activities of the Union.

Treasurer Mailloux presented his report on the Union's financial status, which indicated a small, but favorable balance on hand, as well as a reserve fund of about US$5000 for support of international congresses. He raised the issue of nonpayment of annual dues to the Union and it was decided to consider this problem when revising the statutes. He announced an increase of the UNESCO grant to IUSP (US$6000 in 1961) and it was decided that the final general budget for 1961 should be prepared by the officers of the Union according to the following formula: approximately one third for administrative purposes, one third for activities of the Executive Committee, and one third for other activities of the Union.

Review of the Statutes

In the discussion that accompanied the presentation of a draft revision of the Statutes, the following points received particular attention: (1) it was voted to move certain items concerning ways in which the Union conducts its business to a new document entitled "Rules of Procedure"; (2) a proposal to remove the adjective "scientific" from the name of the Union was not accepted at that time, because there still remained in many countries the need to differentiate "scientific psychology" from other uses of "psychology," but it was agreed to reconsider the issue in the future; (3) a proposal to change the representation of national societies on the IUSP Assembly by allowing a maximum of four representatives based upon the size of membership of a national society was not accepted, but the Revision Committee was asked to determine what should be the precise size of membership required for an appointment of two representatives; (4) the issue of whether or not the delegates should represent their personal views or the views of their national societies was resolved by adding the provision to the statutes that at least 3 months' notice of the business to be transacted at a meeting of the General Assembly would be required in the future; all new issues, raised after this period, would be placed on the agenda only if supported by a two thirds majority vote of the delegates present; (5) in view of the fact that national societies were sometimes delinquent in the payment of their annual dues, the Ad Hoc Revision Committee was instructed to draft a statement regarding grounds for termination of membership; and (6) the Ad Hoc Committee was also instructed to draft a formal section in the Statutes recognizing the affiliations already voted upon at the last meeting.

During the next session, the Ad Hoc Committee appointed during the first session to redraft some of the revised statutes made its report. All its recommendations regarding the nature and aims of the Union, the affiliation, and its administration were approved. Questions were raised regarding the election of Executive Committee members. It was decided to fill vacancies on the Executive Committee between General Assemblies through a mail ballot vote, to have 8 of the 10 members chosen from among members of the Assembly, and that not more than 2 members of the Committee be from any one country. A draft was presented of the new Rules of Procedure for the Assembly that included three major sections, i.e. organization of international congresses, subscriptions, and nominations. While the first and last sections were adopted unanimously, the second section, particularly the requirement for a vote of a two-thirds majority to alter the rate of subscriptions, caused considerable discussion and was finally adopted by a small majority.

Establishment of a Committee on Communication and Publications

On the issue of the publication of *Psychological Abstracts* that had been raised during the Brussels meeting, and more broadly speaking on the problems of international communications in scientific psychology, Russell presented a report in which he recommended the establishment by the Union of a Committee on Communication and Publications. This was approved unanimously by the Assembly, as was a motion to have each national society nominate one of its members to serve as an advisor to the editor of *Psychological Abstracts*.

Following the establishment in Brussels of a committee to advise on the desirability of preparing future editions of the *International Directory of Psychologists*, it was decided that future editions should appear at regular intervals of 3 years, that an editorial committee be established to oversee the production of this directory, that one or more editors be appointed by the Executive Committee to assume responsibility for each new edition, and that all national societies appoint someone responsible for supplying the information on their members.

Election of the Executive Committee

As stipulated in the Statutes, the Assembly proceeded with the elections. Klineberg was elected President, and Duijker, Vice-President. Those elected to the Executive Committee were: Drever, Fraisse, Leontiev, Mailloux, Nuttin, Piaget, Russell, Sato, Skard, and Westerlund.

Membership issues

The applications of South Africa, Mexico, and Venezuela for membership in the Union were considered. Whereas South Africa was turned down because barriers prevented the participation in the South African Society of psychologists of all races, those of Mexico and Venezuela, which had been received just prior to the congress, were postponed for lack of sufficient information, especially concerning the representativeness of the societies applying. A similar request by the International Council of Psychologists for affiliation with the Union was postponed.

Relations with the International Council of Scientific Unions

The relations with the International Council of Scientific Unions (ICSU) and the difficulties encountered by the failures of applications for membership were discussed. It was believed that the two main reasons for these failures were (1) that ICSU is traditionally slow in granting approval of new memberships, and (2) that present members of ICSU were perhaps fearful that any new addition might decrease the level of funds available to ICSU members. It was nevertheless decided to reapply for admission in 1961, to ask Leonard Carmichael to represent IUSP in the formal discussion of this application, and to make clear to ICSU that IUSP would neither request financial support nor contribute financially to ICSU.

Choice of the venue for the next congress

The Assembly was pleased to accept an invitation from the American Psychological Association to hold the next International Congress of Psychology in the United States in 1963.

Executive Committee meeting, Bonn 1960

Roger Russell (1914–1998): Secretary-General of the IUSP (1960–1966); President of the IUSP (1969–1972).

The 1960 meeting of the Executive Committee was held in two sessions: one on July 31 and the second immediately following adjournment of the Assembly on August 6. The first session, termed "outgoing", was devoted principally to discussion of items to be considered during the forthcoming Assembly, especially the changes in the Statutes.

At the second session, the incoming session, all newly elected members were present and the first item of business was the appointment of Russell as Secretary-General, Westerlund as Deputy Secretary-General, and Mailloux as Treasurer.

A discussion of the ways in which IUSP might better cooperate with UNESCO was held in the presence of a UNESCO observer, Dr Szczerba-Likiernik. A certain number of specific projects involving both organizations were discussed and considered possible. Among these were the preparation of interdisciplinary trend reports, the organization of symposia or round-table conferences, technical assistance to economically underdeveloped countries, and assistance to university projects in Africa.

The discussion on the allocations of the 1961 budget for specific activities was introduced by the Treasurer and it was finally decided that the final figures would be decided by the President and the other officers of the Union.

In view of the Assembly's decision to establish a Committee on Communication and Publications, it was decided that the following persons should be invited to serve as members of this new committee: L. Ancona, H.C.J. Duijker, P. Fraisse, A. Luria, A. Melton, J. Nuttin, R.W. Russell (ex-officio), K. Sato, A. Summerfield, G. Westerlund, and W. Witte. Duijker agreed to serve as the first chairman. A subcommittee composed of Eugene H. Jacobson and Arthur Summerfield was appointed to take responsibility for the preparation of the *International Directory of Psychologists*.

The desirability of holding a meeting of the Executive Committee at some convenient time between the 1960 and 1963 congresses was discussed, but no decision was taken.

Executive Committee meeting, Paris 1962

The Executive Committee meeting was held on July 9–11, 1962. It was attended by Drever, Duijker, Fraisse, Leontiev, Mailloux, Nuttin, Piaget, Russell, Sato, Skard, and Westerlund, and chaired by the President, Otto Klineberg.

After approving the minutes of the 1960 Executive Committee meeting in Bonn and reiterating that the members of the committee were not representing particular national societies, but were acting on their own behalf, the Secretary-General, Roger Russell, made a report in which he raised the following issues: membership requirements, Union representation, affiliation with ICSU, production of a newsletter, International Congress of Applied Psychology, and a full-time Executive Secretary.

Membership requirements and issues

In the light of the new statutory membership requirements adopted at the 1960 Assembly meeting, principles of membership in the Union were discussed, taking up the case of Brazil. It appeared that, in Brazil, there was a rivalry between several psychology societies and that it was not clear what criteria were used for the admission of members. The situation was further complicated by the fact that since Brazil's election as a member in 1957, no dues had been received. It was decided to inform the Brazilian Society of the difficulties noted and to give them notice that, in accordance with the possibility of terminating their membership after nonpayment of three annual dues (Art. 9b of the Statutes), a decision to that effect would be taken at the 1963 Assembly meeting. It was also agreed that non-member national groups, and in particular India, China, Mexico, Austria, Thailand, and Romania, should be contacted by members of the Executive Committee to encourage them to apply for membership. For coordination purposes, the Secretary-General would be kept informed of all actions taken.

Two national societies, South Africa and Venezuela, which had recently applied for membership, were accepted, while the application of the Czechoslovakian Society was deferred to the 1963 Assembly meeting.

The Executive Committee approved terminating the membership of Cuba and Egypt in the Union.

Relations with other organizations

The Union was invited with increasing frequency to send a representative to various meetings of UNESCO and ISSC, as well as that of other organizations in whose activities the Union was interested. A general principle of representation was approved, whereby it was stipulated that the Union should be present at as many meetings as possible. Whenever possible, senior psychologists should be asked to serve as Union representatives. Joseph Nuttin was appointed as the new Union representative to the ISSC for a period of 3 years in place of Jean Piaget.

In the presence of Dr Szczerba-Likiernik, the Secretary-General of ISSC, Westerlund reported on his activities as representative to ISSC. The committee was pleased with the useful relations that had been established with ISSC and agreed that the relationship should be developed further. The recent changes in the ISSC statutes, which had resulted in ISSC becoming a "federation of societies in the social sciences," were presented. It was noted that ISSC was becoming more interdisciplinary and more concerned with the promotion of research.

Miss de Franz, representing UNESCO, discussed her organization's interest in projects in which the Union might be of assistance. Inter alia, UNESCO would be interested in exploring research methods and techniques applicable in demographic and statistical studies in countries that lacked such basic data, and second, it would also be interested in the development of good teaching materials for educational purposes in Africa. It was suggested that the Secretary-General should make an inventory of African psychologists involved in research or applied areas and that the Treasurer prepare a report on psychological aspects of problems of delinquency in newly developing countries.

A resolution had been circulated in advance by the Swiss Society of Psychology to all members of the committee regarding the possible role of the Union in international affairs. Comments would be requested from National Members on questions such as: (1) Should IUSP make a common approach to all governments and to the United Nations? (2) What kind of unique services can IUSP offer? (3) How should an approach to governments and the United Nations be made in order to maximize its success? (4) To what extent should IUSP consult with national societies regarding the details of their specific approaches? The Executive Committee, at its upcoming meeting in Washington in 1963, determined to examine the comments made by the members and organize a small working conference on these issues.

Concerning the ongoing efforts to have the Union admitted to ICSU, it was agreed to ask Leonard Carmichael (USA) to represent the Union in further contacts with ICSU with the assistance, if necessary, of Fraisse, Klineberg, and Piaget.

Publications

Although difficulties were experienced in receiving information from national societies, it was the view of the committee that the *Newsletter*, regardless of its completeness, should come out regularly, beginning with the 1962 Autumn issue.

Duijker reported on the activities of the Committee on Communication and Publications. The Executive Committee approved the following recommendations: (1) that an Ad Hoc International Committee should be established and composed of Piéron, Thomae, and Solman to assist with the preparation of the new *Lexicon*, and (2) that the feasibility should be explored of obtaining from national societies summaries in French or English of all articles published in psychology journals. The selection and translation of important articles from the non-English literature was also discussed. The status of the research project on "The Origin and Development of National Stereotypes" was discussed and it was expected that a final manuscript would be ready by 1963.

Planning of the next congress

Questions were raised concerning the considerable overlap between the programs of the last congresses of IUSP and IAAP, and leading to the recommendation that the possibility of coordinating the planning of both congresses should be explored.

The Executive Committee heard a report from Carl Pfaffmann on the American Psychological Association's (APA) plans for the 1963 International Congress in Washington. The committee urged the APA to send out, at its earliest convenience, the information on the general organization of the congress so that all those interested in attending could make plans well in advance. It was recommended that the working languages of the congress should be French and English and that simultaneous translation should be provided. It was also recommended that presentation of papers should be permitted in German, Italian, Russian, and Spanish. APA's novel idea of a "Young Psychologists' Program" was very well received and it was decided unanimously that IUSP should provide a sum of US$500 as a token contribution to this program.

Regarding the international exchange of psychologists, a review was presented of the project originated by APA for the collection and dissemination of information on international opportunities for advanced training and research in psychology. The cooperation of IUSP in the conduct of the project had been approved by the Executive Committee in February 1962.

Review of Statutes

Issues were raised on the interpretation to be given to certain new IUSP Statutes. Although the Executive Committee was elected by the Assembly, its members did not serve as delegates of their national societies. After the proceedings and decisions of the Executive Committee were communicated to them by the Secretary-General, they should feel free to report back to the national society to which they belonged. Regarding the issue of voting by correspondence on elections to membership in the Union, two possible rules of procedure could be considered: (1) following a discussion at the Assembly, the President may approve a final vote by mail ballot, and (2) if a question is raised regarding a vote by correspondence, the issue could go to the Assembly for its consideration. Furthermore, regarding voting by correspondence, each mail ballot should contain three options: approve, disapprove, or postpone a decision until the next Assembly meeting.

The 17th International Congress of Psychology, Washington, USA, 1963

Organization of the congress

The 17th International Congress of Psychology was organized by the American Psychological Association and took place in Washington, DC, from August 20 to 26, 1963, at the Mayflower Hotel. Otto Klineberg was President and Edwin G. Boring was Honorary President. Table 8.3 presents the main organizers of this congress.

The total registration (members and associates) reached 1902, including approximately 600 participants from abroad (Piéron, 1963, p. 597) representing 45 different countries . An innovation of particular interest at this congress was the introduction of the "Young Psychologists' Program". Twenty-two promising young psychologists, one from nearly every member society of the Union who, by and large, would have been unable to attend this meeting, were nominated by their own society and received a travel grant donated by individual American psychologists, or by professional societies and other organizations. The Union also contributed

17th Congress, Washington, 1963: Congress participants outside the venue.

TABLE 8.3

Organizational structure:
17th International Congress of Psychology (Washington, 1963)

Steering Committee
Carl Pfaffmann, *Chair*, Brown University
Eugene Jacobson, *Vice-Chair*, Michigan State University
Charles W. Bray, *Chair, Local Arrangements Committee*, Smithsonian Institution
Leonard Carmichael, Smithsonian Institution
Meredith Crawford, *Chair, Finance Committee*, Human Resources Research
    Office, Alexandria
Henry P. David, Dept of Institutions & Agencies, State of New Jersey
George Ferguson, McGill University
Robert MacLeod, Cornell University
Donald G. Marquis, Massachusetts Institute of Technology

Program Committee
Donald G. Marquis, *Chair*, Massachusetts Institute of Technology
Daniel Katz, *Vice-Chair*, University of Michigan
Clyde H. Coombs, University of Michigan
George Kelly, Ohio State University
Donald B. Lindsley, University of California, Los Angeles
Robert MacLeod, Cornell University
Noël Mailloux, Université de Montréal

to this fund. The goal of the organizers was that "both the youthful vigor of our science (as well as) international cooperation and understanding (would) be fostered" (Proceedings of the XVIIth International Congress of Psychology, 1964, p.v.).

Financial support for the congress came from multiple sources, including the American Council of Learned Societies, the National Science Foundation and the National Institute of Mental Health. The first meeting of the Steering Committee took place in Washington, on December 17, 1960. John Darley, at that time Executive Officer of APA, participated actively in the early planning, and his successor, Arthur Brayfield continued his support.

The opening session of the congress was held on Tuesday evening, August 20, followed by a reception. Dr John T. Wilson, a psychologist recently appointed Deputy Director of the National Science Foundation, brought to the congress words of greetings from the President of the United States. González Solaz (1998, pp. 105–106) notes with surprise that these presidential greetings, reproduced in the congress proceedings (Proceedings of the XVIIth International Congress of Psychology, 1964, pp. 2–3), are specifically oriented toward the field of mental retardation. After welcome addresses by Carl Pfaffmann, Leonard Carmichael, Charles Osgood (the President of APA), and Otto Klineberg, Edwin Boring gave the presidential address entitled "Eponym as placebo."

Scientific program

Thirty-three symposia constituted the core of the scientific program. They covered topics of current interest in psychology, ranging from psychophysiology to personality and social psychology. There were also 12 sessions of submitted papers. Table 8.4 lists the topics of the symposia.

Four distinguished psychologists presented evening lectures: Gordon W. Allport ("The Fruits of Eclecticism: Bitter or Sweet?"), Jerzy Konorski ("On the Mechanisms of Instrumental Conditioning"), Ivo Kohler ("The Concept of Adaptation in Perception"), and Joseph Nuttin ("Time Perspective in Human Motivation and Learning").

Many visits were arranged for the participants. They included the National Institute of Mental Health, the Walter Reed Army Institute of

---

TABLE 8.4

Symposia themes:
17th International Congress of Psychology (Washington, 1963)

1. Human motivation
2. Behavior genetics
3. Critical periods in development
4. Development of the cognitive processes
5. Regulation and control of sensory functions
6. Personality change in psychotherapy
7. Personality assessment
8. Psychophysiology of motivation
9. Language and the science of man
10. Social development of the child
11. Biochemical correlates of behavior
12. The historical background for national trends in psychology
13. Cross-cultural studies of attitude structure and dimensions
14. Temporal aspects of perception and performance
15. Psychology and the humanities
16. Choice and decision
17. Creativity and the growth of concepts
18. The body percept
19. Psychophysics and the ideal observer
20. Social psychological studies of international behavior
21. New technologies in education
22. Small groups and interpersonal process
23. Sleep and wakefulness
24. Mathematical behavior theory
25. Personality: theories and systems
26. Uses of computers in psychology
27. Brain and visual perception
28. Attitude consistency and change
29. Information processing and performance
30. Mental retardation and special defects
31. Multidimensional analysis of similarity data
32. Neurophysiology of learning
33. System theory and organization change

Research, St Elizabeth's Hospital, and the Smithsonian Institution. Social activities, such as a tour of the White House, an evening at the National Gallery of Art, a picnic at the Woodland Plantation, and a boat trip to Mount Vernon, were also arranged for the enjoyment of the congress participants. It must be noted that all participants from abroad were invited, at least once, to dinner in the home of one of their American colleagues.

General Assembly, Washington 1963

The meeting of August 20 was brought to order by President Klineberg, in the presence of representatives of the national societies of 15 countries (Australia, Belgium, Canada, Denmark, France, Finland, Germany, Italy, Japan, Netherlands, Norway, Sweden, USSR, USA) and of observers from the International Association of Applied Psychology and the International Sociological Association.

Reports of the Officers

The President reported briefly on his activities during his tour of office. The Secretary-General reviewed the accomplishments of the Union during the 1960–1963 period. He mentioned the completion of a revision of the IUSP's Statutes and the creation of "Rules of Procedure." Also of importance were the interactions of IUSP with other organizations, especially UNESCO and ISSC. During the previous 3 years, five publications had been sponsored by IUSP: (1) the *Proceedings of the Bonn Congress, 1960*, (2) a German language

THE WHITE HOUSE
WASHINGTON

August 19, 1963

Dear Mr. Klineberg:

It is a great pleasure to greet the members of the International Congress of Psychology whose work in the past and whose professional endeavors in the future represent an opportunity for man to increase his capacities through self-awareness, the expansion of his intellectual abilities and an increased understanding of human behavior and the human mind.

I note with special interest that a segment of your program deals with the subject of mental retardation. The mentally retarded--victims of both intellectual and emotional disabilities, still await major contributions that the behavioral scientists can make.

There is still a long way to go in the investigation of social and cultural factors as possible causes of mental retardation and in testing the effectiveness of special educational and vocational training programs for the mentally retarded. There is a vast need for the early identification of mental retardation and of conditions leading to it. The special training and orientation of the psychologist makes him an essential member of the clinical and research teams required for the full exploration of cause and prevention factors in mental retardation.

Your discipline encompasses a wide range, extending from the biochemical bases to the social determinants of behavior. Although progress has been made, further advances in

- 2 -

psychology and related behavioral science fields are vital to the solution of the demanding problems of mental retardation and mental health. It is my deep hope that this meeting will be fruitful and productive, not only for the period of its duration, but for the years to follow.

Sincerely,

[signature]

Mr. Otto Klineberg
17th International Congress of Psychology
American Psychological Association
1333 16th Street, NW.
Washington 6, D.C.

Letter to Otto Klineberg, President of the 19th International Congress, from President John F. Kennedy edition of *Perspectives in Personality Theory*, (3) *Perspectives in Personality Research*, (4) *National Character and National Stereotypes*, and (5) a report of the La Napoule Planning Conference of the APA. Also, six special projects had received particular attention: (1) Public opinion regarding the peaceful uses of atomic energy, (2) Research on the origins and development of national stereotypes, (3) the *Lexicon of Psychological Terms*, (4) Psychological terms used in other social sciences, (5) a revision of the *International Directory of Psychologists*, and (6) International opportunities for advanced training and research in psychology. The Secretary-General also presented basic questions that he felt the Union should consider at this point in its development: Should it continue to operate as in the past, or organize itself for an expanded program of activities? This latter alternative would require a reevaluation of the Union's present administrative structure. He also raised the need for the development of the Union's activities in the area of biological psychology.

A general discussion followed this report and it was suggested to promote biological psychology first by publishing a book on *Perspectives in Biological Psychology* and, second, by organizing colloquia or small scientific meetings to enhance more systematic development in this area. It was also suggested that the name of the Union be changed by deleting the adjective "scientific," since psychology was now firmly established as a science. Continued use of "scientific" could be perceived as a sign of insecurity in this regard. The matter was deferred to the Executive Committee. Finally, in the light of the increase in the activities of the Union, it was decided that the Executive Committee should meet more often, and at least once before the next congress.

The report of the Treasurer indicated that the general account of the Union had a small favorable balance at this point and that expenditures from funds provided by UNESCO were being made as budgeted.

Next congress venue

The Assembly was delighted to receive an invitation from the Soviet Psychological Association to hold the 1966 International Congress in Moscow and unanimously gave its approbation.

Elections of the Executive Committee

Drever was elected as President, while Fraisse was elected as Vice-President of the Executive Committee.

At the second session of the Assembly meeting, held on August 25, 1963, the first item on the agenda was the election of the Executive Committee. In view of the increasing membership in the Union, and in conformity with the statutes, it was decided to appoint the Secretary-General and the Treasurer and to elect 10 additional Executive Committee members. The tradition had been thus far to appoint the Treasurer and the Secretary-General from among the elected committee members. It was thus suggested by the Assembly that Roger W. Russell and Noël Mailloux be appointed respectively Secretary-General and Treasurer. Those elected to the new Executive Committee were: Duijker, Klineberg, Leontiev, Nuttin, O'Neil, Piaget, Sato, Summerfield, Tomaszewski, and Westerlund.

International collaborations

In the ongoing effort to obtain membership in ICSU and in view of the little progress made, Carmichael was asked to act as the IUSP's "official ambassador" and, with the help of Pfaffmann, an APA representative, to continue actively seeking membership in ICSU during the 1963–66 period.

The Assembly heard a report by Sherman Ross of APA concerning the APA-IUSP project of collecting and disseminating information on international opportunities for advanced training and research in psychology. A meeting on this project had been held in July 1962 in La Napoule, France, and a two-volume report had been published by the APA. This report contained a number of suggestions for action by the IUSP. An Ad Hoc Committee was created to review these suggestions and report back to the Assembly.

Actions taken concerning the Swiss resolution on the contributions of psychology to the reduction of international tensions were discussed and the papers prepared by some of the national members on this topic were reviewed by the ad hoc group (Fraisse, Klineberg and Piaget) appointed by the Executive Committee. Approval was granted to convene a small working conference on the issues raised.

Report on the congress

Carl Pfaffmann, Chair of the APA Steering Committee, reported on the success of the 1963 International Congress of Psychology. One of the new features deserving particular attention was the Young Psychologists' Program, which had been very successful. It was agreed that this program be continued in future years. Pfaffmann called attention to the wide range of topics covered by the congress program and emphasized the fact that contributions within each topic clearly showed psychology to be "an empirically-based science with very active and challenging frontiers of discovery which overlap both the biological and the social sciences" (IUSP Assembly Minutes, 1963). Deep appreciation was expressed to the American Psychological Association for subsidizing the attendance of so many participants from countries abroad and for the outstanding success of the Washington congress.

Membership issues

The increasing interest shown by national societies of psychology in becoming members of the Union was noted. Hence, the Czechoslovakian Society was elected to membership, and new applications from three national societies were presented: the German Democratic Republic, Peru, and the Philippines. However, the Assembly had to consider with deep regret the necessity of terminating the membership of certain national societies for nonpayment of dues. The Cuban and Egyptian societies were given until the end of the year to make their payment. If the dues were not paid by that time, it was decided that their membership would be terminated. The case for the Brazilian Society, which had not paid its dues since 1957, was further complicated by the fact that a second society of psychologists had developed in this country. It was decided to terminate the membership of the first, the Sociedade Brasileira de Psicologia, but to support the application of the second, the Associacao Brasileira de Psicologos, in view of information that the first would merge into the second. Also approved was the change of membership for Venezuela; the present member, the Associacion Venezolana de Psicologos, had been integrated into the newly founded Colegio de Psicologos de Venezuela. The request of the International Council of Psychologists for affiliation with the Union (as made possible by Article 10 of the Statutes) was approved, after reviewing the information that had been requested concerning the objectives, activities, and constitution of the council. The request for affiliation of the Madras Psychological Society in India was, however, turned down, since the term "regional" indicated in the affiliation statutes was considered to be related to groups of nations within a particular geographical area and not to provinces within a country.

Executive Committee meeting, Washington 1963

During its first session, on August 20, the Executive Committee, under the chairmanship of Otto Klineberg, reviewed the agenda of the upcoming Assembly meetings. Suggestions were made regarding the procedure for the nomination of candidates to the offices of President and Vice-President.

The budget for 1964, totaling expenses of US$6000, was examined and approved. In reply to a request from the South African Psychological Association, it was agreed that the IUSP would participate in the ICSU International Biological Program, as a means of establishing closer relations.

The rules for voting by mail ballot, discussed at the 1962 meeting, were considered and adopted. On the matter of membership issues, it was agreed to recommend to the Assembly that the membership of the Sociedade Brasileira de Psicologia, presently representing Brazil, be terminated for nonpayment of dues and that the application of the Associacao Brasileira de Psicologos be considered. It was also agreed to recommend termination of the Cuban and Egyptian societies for nonpayment of dues, with the provision that they could reapply if they so wished. The admission of the Czechoslovakian Society was approved and would be recommended to the Assembly. The Executive Committee agreed to add to the agenda the application of the International Council of Psychologists for affiliation.

At its second session, all the newly elected members of the Executive Committee were present, with Drever acting as President. The first item of business was the appointment of a Secretary-General (Roger Russell), a Deputy Secretary-General (Gunnar Westerlund), and a Treasurer (Noël Mailloux), following the recommendations of the Assembly. Hubert Duijker was reappointed Chair of the Committee on Communication and Publications.

Actions on recommendation of the Assembly

Following a recommendation from the Assembly, the committee decided unanimously that the name of the Union be changed from "International Union of Scientific Psychology" to "International Union of Psychological Sciences" (and in French, "Union internationale des sciences psychologiques"). But first, this proposal would have to be sent to Assembly members for a mail ballot vote.

As requested at the 1962 meeting, Mailloux presented a report on the psychological aspects of the problems of delinquency in newly developing countries. He was asked to examine the feasibility of a more specific project proposal for consideration by the committee.

At the suggestion of the Assembly, it was decided to hold a meeting of the Executive Committee in Europe in 1964 following the 15th International Congress of Applied Psychology, in order to take advantage of the fact that a certain number of members would already be present and would therefore be available at minimum travel cost.

Next congresses

The nomination of Moscow, USSR, as the congress venue for 1966 having received the approval of the General Assembly, Fraisse was appointed liaison to the Soviet Society's Program Committee and it was decided that the official languages of the 1966 congress would be English, French, and Russian. Since a tentative invitation had been made by the British Psychological Society (BPS) to hold the 1969 congress in the United Kingdom and by the Japanese Psychological Association to hold the 1972 congress in Japan, the Secretary-General was instructed to request a mail ballot vote from Assembly members regarding the BPS proposal; if this vote was positive, the BPS could then begin planning for the 1969 congress.

Discussion of the excessive duplication of functions and the necessary coordination of the international congresses sponsored by the Union and by the International Association of Applied Psychology led to the conclusion that, although there is some degree of overlap, there is no need for concern because the two congresses will continue to have differences in emphasis and in the interests of attendees.

International collaborations

The Union's interest in pursuing research projects in both Africa and Asia was discussed and potential sources of funding were identified.

Relations with UNESCO were reviewed and the important role that UNESCO subventions play in helping to maintain continued stability in the Union's administration and scientific activities was reiterated.

Regarding the relations with the United Nations, some uncertainty was expressed as to the role that the Union should seek to play. This issue was raised through correspondence with representatives of the Conference of Non-Governmental Organizations in Consultative Status with the United Nations Economic and Social Council (ECOSOC).

An Ad Hoc Committee composed of Fraisse, Klineberg, and Westerlund was appointed to contribute to the upcoming ISSC report on the general trends of research in the social sciences.

The idea of supporting an ISSC proposal for a "World Social Science Year" was closely examined and it was deemed premature, in view of the amount of activity and the level of efforts that such a project could require. Since the idea originated from the Australian UNESCO Committee for Social Science, O'Neil was asked to explore further this issue with his compatriots, reporting back to the Executive Committee.

To complete the review of the 1964 budget proposal presented during the first session of the Executive Committee meeting, it was agreed to specify in greater detail the support to be given to special scientific projects. The three current research projects were: "Reduction of international tensions"; the ISSC project on "Current trends in social science research"; and the preparation of a third *Perspectives* volume that would cover topics in biological psychology. Up to US$1000 of the Union funds would also be used to complete the *Lexicon of Psychological Terms* project.

Executive Committee meeting, Bellagio, Italy, 1964

The Executive Committee meeting was held July 27–29 at the Villa Serbelloni in Bellagio, Italy. The roll call indicated that all members were present, with the exception of Klineberg, who would join the meeting on July 29.

Reports of the Officers

The report of the President raised an important issue: the relations of IUSP with UNESCO. It was believed that it was not a UNESCO responsibility to support IUSP congresses, but that it should be prepared to subsidize the Union's international projects that met with its approval. The necessity of seeking and obtaining membership in ICSU was once again noted as a priority.

Duijker, Chair of the Committee on Communication and Publications, reported on the two ongoing projects. The preparation of the *International Directory of Psychologists* was progressing well, thanks to Eugene Jacobson's efforts in collecting data from countries with no psychological association. The second main project, the *Trilingual Lexicon*, was expected to be finished during the 1964–65 academic year.

The Treasurer presented his report. No changes were anticipated in the US$6000 level of UNESCO support for the 1965–66 subvention, and a provisional budget was approved.

Membership issues

After the presentation of his yearly financial statement, Mailloux opened a discussion on membership issues. He indicated that he received no replies from Cuba or Egypt regarding the termination of their membership. It was decided that the Brazilian and the Philippines memberships should be confirmed by mail vote but that the application of the Indian Psychological Association be acted upon at the next Assembly meeting. The committee was informed that an application from Romania had been made and that a request was received from West Germany for the approval of the new Federation of German Psychological Associations as representing both the Deutsche Gesellschaft für Psychologie and the Berufsverband Deutscher Psychologen. The potential memberships of Ireland, the German Democratic Republic, Hungary, Pakistan, and Peru were examined.

Recommendation for change of name

A mail ballot had given 26 votes for and 5 against the change of the name of the Union. After some discussion, it was decided to call for another mail ballot of the Assembly on the following recommendation: "that the names of the Union are the International Union of Psychological Sciences and l'Union Internationale de Psychologie Scientifique, both names being considered equivalent."

Next congresses

With regard to the preparation of the 1966 Congress in Moscow, Leontiev reported that the organization of the congress was in progress. The Program Committee was under the direction of Luria, while the Organization Committee and the Secretariat were the responsibility of Smirnov. With regard to the program, two symposia were to be held in parallel during the morning and the afternoon sessions, and there would be two series of individual communications, two plenary meetings, with opening and closing sessions. The first circular of information regarding the congress would be sent out in September 1964.

The results of a mail ballot vote indicated that 29 votes were in favor of accepting the invitation from the British Psychological Society to hold the 1969 Congress in the UK, while 1 vote asked for a postponement until the next Assembly meeting. The Executive Committee decided to accept the British invitation, thus enabling them to start working immediately. It was also decided to change the rule of procedure so that venues of future congresses should be discussed 6, rather than 3, years in advance.

International exchange program and other projects

Russell reported on the APA-IUSP project regarding the international exchange of psychologists. The discussion raised the problem of the screening of the students to be involved. It was recommended that a system equating educational systems of different countries be set up and that the decisions made at La Napoule be followed up.

Among other issues raised were: Mailloux's report on the psychological aspects of problems of delinquency in newly developing countries, Tomaszewski's proposal for an international program of psychological research, Russell's reports on the Union's interest in African studies, Mailloux's report on Asian studies, and Russell's report on the International Biological program.

Publication of a journal

A working group composed of Fraisse, Leontiev, Nuttin, Piaget, Sato, Tomaszewski, and Westerlund, chaired by Duijker, reported on the need for the development of an IUSP periodical. This journal would be the Union's "house organ" and would replace the aperiodic *Newsletter* which was no longer capable of meeting the expressed need of the national societies and of the Union for communication on the various activities in which IUSP was now engaged. It was suggested that the contents of the journal deal mainly with the following areas: (1) reports of international research, preferably of a comparative and cooperative nature, (2) information on psychological activities of an international nature and interest, including news from national societies of psychology, (3) reports on IUSP's activities and issues that concern it, (4) notices of international projects requiring personnel specialized in various areas of psychology, and (5) information to facilitate the exchange of advanced scholars and students interested in acquiring knowledge and skills in the various applied fields of psychology. It was recommended that this journal be published in both official languages of the Union: English and French. It was suggested that a name such as "The World Psychologist" or "The International Journal of Psychology" be given to this journal and that the editorial responsibility be given to an assigned editor and a Board of Consulting Editors, all elected by the IUSP's Assembly. Other publications, e.g. monographs on subjects related to projects endorsed by IUSP, should also be produced. The overall objective of IUSP publications should be to strive for the creation of a general climate in international psychology that would encourage comparative and cooperative research and facilitate a broad exchange of psychological information.

Executive Committee meeting, Royaumont, France, 1965

The Executive Committee meeting was held in Royaumont, France, from June 1 to June 3, with all members present. After approval of the minutes of the 1964 meeting in Bellagio, Italy, President Drever reported briefly on the major events arising since the last meeting and stressed the urgent need for establishing a permanent secretariat of the Union. Both the Secretary-General and the Treasurer then read their annual reports referring to documents already circulated that had been prepared in compliance with UNESCO's subvention program requirements. Satisfactory progress had been made in all the funded projects, and the Treasurer added that the Union account held a small, but favorable balance. A budget of operations amounting to US$10,500, funded mostly from UNESCO subventions, was proposed and adopted.

Publications program

The Chair of the Committee on Communication and Publications, Duijker, reported mainly on two major projects. He indicated that the first draft of the *Trilingual Lexicon of Psychological Terms* had undergone a substantial second revision and that every effort would be made to publish it as early as possible. In the case of the second project, the *International Directory of Psychologists*, questionnaires were still being received. Plans were to go to press in September or October 1965. Unfortunately, the major problem of inclusion of information about psychologists in the People's Republic of China had not been successfully resolved. Therefore, the new edition would not include information about Chinese psychologists. The possibility of employing computer procedures for future editions was discussed and it was decided to explore this option further.

In 1964, the Executive Committee allocated US$3000 to support the first year of the newly approved publication, to be called *The International Journal of Psychology*. The first issue would appear before the 1966 International Congress if possible. Fraisse agreed to serve as acting Editor, with the editorial assistance of his colleague Germaine de Montmollin. The Union's Executive Committee would constitute the first Editorial Board.

Membership issues

Membership issues were, as usual, an important part of the agenda. It was first noted that the mail vote on the admission of the Philippines was favorable and therefore the Psychological Association of the Philippines was officially accepted as a member. The applications of the Psychological Society of the German Democratic Republic, the Indian Psychological Association, the Romanian Psychological Society, the new Federation of German Psychological Associations, and the Mexican Psychological Society were deemed acceptable and referred for a vote at the 1966 meeting of the General Assembly. The committee also noted that the membership of the Australian Branch of the British Psychological Society would be changed to a membership of the Australian Psychological Society as of January, 1966.

Approval of a new name for the Union

The Executive Committee examined the returns from the mail ballot of the Assembly regarding the name of the Union and noted that the recommended change had been approved. Therefore, the new English name of the Union from now on is: "International Union of Psychological Science" (IUPS), while the French name is: "l'Union Internationale de Psychologie Scientifique" (UIPS).

Future congresses

Four items related to future congresses were considered. First, regarding the 1966 International Congress of Psychology, Leontiev reviewed the arrangements and program with the committee, which indicated its satisfaction. Second, Summerfield reported on the steps being taken by the British Psychological Society for the 1969 International Congress of Psychology; an Organizing Committee had been appointed and was already working. Third, Sato reported that the feasibility of inviting the Union to hold a future congress in Japan was to be put to a vote at the July convention of the Japanese Psychological Association. Finally, Westerlund announced that the next congress of the IAAP would be held in Amsterdam in 1968. In view of the potential difficulties related to the temporal proximity of both congresses, it was decided to propose to the 1996 Assembly to hold the IUPS congresses at 4- rather than 3-year intervals and to arrange a closer coordination with IAAP.

Relations with ISSC and UNESCO

Otto Klineberg, who represented the IUPS in ISSC, reported on the council's recent activities and plans for the future. He expressed the view that the relations between ISSC and the IUPS were excellent. At the Chairman's invitation, K. Szczerba-Likiernik, Secretary-General of ISSC, attending as an observer, reflected the view that in spite of the excellent relations among individual representatives, there was room for improvement at the organizational level. It was suggested that this could be done, inter alia, by a fuller exchange of information about decisions, plans, and activities. Klineberg, who also represented the Union on the Committee on International Social Science Documentation, called attention to the project of an international bibliography of psychology. Samy Friedman, Chief of UNESCO's Division for the International Development of the Social Sciences, also present as an observer, further added that he was expecting feedback on sample volumes of this bibliography in order to properly orient the project.

While considering the involvement of the Union in the International Biological Program, a paper prepared by Piaget and titled *Projet d'un programme de collaboration interdisciplinaire entre psychologues et biologistes* served as the basis for the discussion that led to the creation of an Ad Hoc Committee, composed of Piaget, Paillard, Leontiev, and Tomaszewski, to formulate IUPS policy regarding biological psychology. With regards to possible activities within the International Biological Program, it was decided that psychology's major contribution could be made through the project on human adaptability by working on the development of a battery of behavioral measures capable of general application in different cultural settings. It was proposed to invite Dr Simon Biesheuvel, of South Africa, to act as the Chair of this working group.

The relationship with UNESCO was examined in the presence of Friedman. It was noted that the UNESCO General Conference had approved, in 1964, the merging of the social and human sciences with the cultural activities under one administrative head, despite protests from many organizations, including IUPS. Friedman indicated that this change could be viewed constructively as a move to strengthen relations with the humanities. He added that the IUPS should look into the possibility of seeking affiliation with one of the UNESCO councils in the biological sciences. Regarding financial matters, while noting that the UNESCO yearly subvention of US$6000 would continue in 1966, he also indicated that the Union had not made sufficient use of UNESCO's sources of support for research and other activities.

Piaget reported on the UNESCO project entitled "International study on the main trends of research in the sciences of man" in which he was responsible for issues concerning psychology. He indicated that questionnaires had been developed to help assist in the data collection and that the Union's national members would be called upon to provide assistance. The success of this project seemed to be very important for the future development and support of the social sciences in the UNESCO framework.

Other issues

The working group that had been established to look into the possible contributions of psychology to the reduction of international tensions (what came to be known as the Swiss resolution) proposed two specific actions: first, that the paper they had prepared, entitled *An Appeal to Psychologists*, be sent to all IUPS members. This paper suggested two orientations: (1) the emphasis of psychological knowledge relevant to the reduction of international tensions, and (2) the conduct and encouragement of new research which can add to this knowledge. Second, that an international round-table of experts be convened on the occasion of the 1966 International Congress of Psychology in Moscow. Both proposals were accepted unanimously.

The committee was informed that 77 papers had been received regarding the project on the international exchange of psychologists proposed in the 1962 La Napoule report. These papers would be edited and returned to their authors for review. No specific date was set for publication.

Simon Biesheuvel, the President of the South African Psychological Association, presented an excellent résumé of the psychological services available in African countries. He proposed that a planning conference be held under the auspices and support of the Union. Reflecting the Union's interest in Asian studies, it was noted that more opportunities for the training of Asian psychology students beyond their first degree were needed.

A proposal to establish a regional Asian Association of Psychologists, following the model set by the Interamerican Society of Psychology, had been received by the Japanese Psychological Association from Dr Ayman, Secretary-General of the National Institute of Psychology in Teheran, Iran. The Executive Committee agreed that IUPS was interested in this idea and could provide assistance in the future.

Concerning the project on "Problems of delinquency in newly developing countries," Mailloux listed three areas in need of attention: (1) the relations between the socialization of individuals and their capability to communicate, (2) the factors affecting group dynamics in this socialization process, and (3) the central problems of the nature and cause of aggression.

References

González Solaz, J. (1998). *Los Congresos Internacionales de Psicologia (1963 1984)*. Unpublished doctoral dissertation, University of Valencia, Spain.

Montoro González, L. (1982). *Los Congresos Internacionales de Psicologia (1889–1960)*. Unpublished doctoral dissertation, University of Valencia, Spain.

Piéron, H. (1960). Chronique: le XVIième Congrès International de Psychologie. *Année Psychologique, 60*, 618–621.

Piéron, H. (1963). Chronique: le XVIIième Congrès International de Psychologie. *Année Psychologique, 63*, 596–599.

Proceedings of the XVIth International Congress of Psychology, Bonn, Federal Republic of Germany, 1960. (1962). Amsterdam: North-Holland.

Proceedings of the XVIIth International Congress of Psychology, Washington, DC, USA, 1963. (1964). Amsterdam: North-Holland.

Consolidation of the Union's progress (1966–1971)

Fifteen years after its foundation, the International Union of Scientific Psychology, renamed the International Union of Psychological Science, claimed representation from every continent. Whereas a little over 1000 participants from 31 countries attended the first congress following the creation of the Union, the 1966 Moscow Congress proudly welcomed close to 4000 psychologists representing 43 different countries.

The achievements of the last few years were numerous: the growing involvement of psychologists from all parts of the world in the administration of the Union, the ever-increasing exchange of scholars and students, the establishment of a sound publication program, the active presence of the Union in other international organizations, the tremendous improvement in the quality of the congresses' scientific programs, the launching of international research projects. These were factors that contributed to the consolidation of the Union's progress. Furthermore, the Union increasingly enjoyed the recognition by psychologists the world over that it could be their voice at an international level.

The 18th International Congress of Psychology, Moscow, USSR, 1966

The participation of a strong delegation of Soviet psychologists to the 1954 Montréal congress, the admission of the Russian Society at Brussels in 1957, and the subsequent participation of psychologists from socialist countries contributed greatly to widen the base of the Union as well as to the exchange of information and the improvement of collaboration in the development of psychology across the world. This encouraging trend reached a culmination in Moscow, from August, 4–11, 1966, when the 18th International Congress of Psychology was held at the invitation of the Soviet government.

The Moscow Congress was important in enhancing the status of Soviet/Russian psychology, both at home and abroad. Robert Solso, an American scholar of Soviet/Russian psychology, wrote about this as follows:

> The selection of Moscow for the meeting of the International
> Congress of Psychology was a major event in the history of

*Soviet/Russian psychology. The organization of the
Department of Psychology [at the University of Moscow],
independent of philosophy, in 1965 by Alexei Leontiev was
planned to coincide with the event (Solso, 1991, footnote 8,
p. 313).*

Organization of the congress

It was, to that date, the most representative congress in the history of the
Union, with a total participation of 3897 scientists from 43 countries and
approximately 1000 accompanying persons. González Solaz (1998, p. 157)
notes that the attendance was far greater than any recorded in previous
congresses during the 1960s, and that such a high number of participants
was not reached again till the Leipzig congress in 1980. Montoro, Tortosa,
and Carpintero (1992) explain this record attendance by the fact that
psychologists from the more affluent countries registered in greater
numbers.

The Vice-President of the Academy of Sciences of the USSR, P.N.
Fedosseiev, had, with the consultation of eminent Soviet psychologists,
appointed a Program Committee with A.R. Luria (Chair) and O.S.
Vinogradova (Vice-Chair). The Organizing Committee was chaired by A.A.
Smirnov, with I.V. Ravich-Scherbo acting as Vice-Chair. A.N. Leontiev had
been elected President of the congress.

Scientific program

Besides the opening and closing plenary sessions, 37
symposia and 10 thematic sessions were held during the
congress (see Table 9.1). Evening lectures were delivered by
A.A. Smirnov (USSR) "The development of Soviet
psychology," by Jean Piaget (Switzerland): "Psychology,
interdisciplinary relations and the system of sciences," and
by Neal Miller (USA): "Experimental investigation of
psychopathology and theory of learning."

Three volumes of abstracts and 37 volumes of reports
which had been chosen for discussion at symposia and
thematic sessions were published before the opening of the
congress and handed out to participants. The working
languages of the congress were Russian, English, and
French. Abstracts and the texts of the reports were published
in the language in which they were presented, but the papers
by Russian authors were also translated into English or French to facilitate
their dissemination.

The ceremonial opening of the 18th congress took place in the Kremlin's
Palace of Congresses, and was attended by more than 5000 people. The first
session of the congress was opened by the Minister of Education of the

*Alexei N. Leontiev
(1903–1979):
President of the 18th
International Congress
of Psychology,
Moscow, 1966.*

TABLE 9.1

Symposia and thematic sessions:
18th International Congress of Psychology

Symposia
- Ecology and ethology in behavioral studies (Chairs: R. Chauvin and A.D. Slonim)
- Cybernetic aspects of integrative brain activities (Chair: A. Masturzo)
- Integrative forms of conditioned reflexes (Chair: E.A. Asratyan and H.F. Harlow)
- Classical and instrumental conditioning (Chair: J.M. Konorski)
- Orienting reflex, alertness and attention (Chair: E.N. Sokolov and D.B. Lindsley)
- Electrophysiological correlates of behavior (Chair: W. Grey Walter)
- Biochemical bases of behavior (Chair: R. Russell)
- Psychopharmacology and the regulation of behavior (Chair: A. Summerfield)
- Physiological bases of individual psychological differences (Chair: A.A. Smirnov)
- Frontal lobes and the regulation of behavior (Chair: H.L. Teuber)
- Mathematical models of psychological processes (Chair: W.K. Estes)
- Motives and consciousness in man (Chair: J. Nuttin)
- Experimental studies of set (Chair: E.V. Bassina)
- Neuronal and behavioral bases of sensory processes (Chair: R. Jung, Y. Katsuri, and G.V. Gershuni)
- Detection of signals (Chair: R.J. Audly and J. Krivohlavy)
- Information theory and perception (Chair: F. Attneave)
- Organization of human information processing (Chair: F. Klix)
- Psychological problems of perception of space and time (Chair: I. Akishige and D.G. Elkin)
- Biological bases of memory traces (Chair: M.R. Rosenzweig)
- Short-term and long-term memory (Chair: K.H. Pribram)
- Memory and action (Chair: T. Tomaszewski)
- Models of speech perception (Chair: G. Fant)
- Concept formation and "inner action"(Chair: J. Bruner)
- Heuristic processes in thinking (Chair: W.R. Reitman and A.D. De Groot)
- Pathological psychology and psychological processes (Chair: O. Zangwill)
- Theoretical problems of man-machine systems (Chair: A. Chapanis)
- Psychological problems of man in space (Chair: V.V. Parin)
- Longitudinal studies in child development (Chair: R. Zazzo)
- Perception and action (Chair: J.J. Gibson)
- Speech and mental development in children (Chair: L. Bartha)
- Learning as factor in mental development (Chair: J. Bruner and N.A. Menchinskaya)
- Mental development and sensory defects (Chair: A. Roska)
- Methodological problems of social psychology (Chair: R. Abelson)
- Social factors in the development of personality (Chair: U. Bronfenbrenner)
- Cross-cultural studies in mental development (Chair: O. Klineberg)
- Psychological aspects of behavior in small groups (Chair: H. Hiebsch)
- Work and personality (Chair: A.A. Zvorykin)

continued ➡

TABLE 9.1 *continued*

Thematic sessions
- Neuropsychological studies of animal behavior (Chair: J. Bures)
- Psychological mechanisms of verbal processes (Chair: R. Jacobson and N.I. Zhinkin)
- Studies in psychology of personality (Chair: A. Lewicki)
- Problems of psychology of mentally retarded children (Chair: T.A. Vlasova and N. O'Connor)
- Historical and theoretical problems of psychology (Chair: E.V. Shorokhova and K. Sato)
- Early development of behavior (Chair: A.V. Zaporozhets and G. Pyriov)
- Factors and forms of learning in animals (Chair: R. Solomon and L.V. Krushinsky)
- Problems of speech comprehension and psycholinguistics (Chair: V.A. Artiomov and A. Mazucco-Costa)
- Problems of sensation and perception (Chair: P.A. Shevarev and R.A. Gregory)
- Psychological studies in movement and action (Chair: N.F. Dobrynin and J. Brechacek)

USSR, V.P. Elyutin. Other opening addresses were given by P.N. Fedosseiev, by M.V. Keldish, President of the Academy of Sciences, by N.T. Sizov, Assistant Chairman of the Moscow City Council, and by J. Drever, Jr, President of the International Union of Psychological Science. All other congress meetings, as well an exhibition of psychological literature and one of experimental equipment, took place at the Moscow State University on Lenin Hills. Both exhibitions (particularly the books) were very popular with participants (González Solaz, 1998, p. 155).

Over 2 days, the delegates were shown films dealing with psychology and related disciplines. At the same time as the planned sessions, small scientific conferences concerned with problems of creative activity, human engineering, social psychology, ecology, and ethology, were organized on the initiative of certain participants to discuss these branches of the discipline.

The participants and guests visited several Moscow Research Institutes: inter alia, the Institute of Psychology of the Academy of Pedagogical Sciences of the USSR, and the Psychology Department of the Moscow State University.

The closing ceremony took place on August 11, in the Assembly Hall of Moscow State University. Karl Pribram (USA), Tadeus Tomaszewski (Poland), Jean Piaget (Switzerland), Paul Fraisse (France), and Barbel Inhelder (Switzerland) gave the final speeches. Concluding remarks were made by A.R. Luria, Chair of the Program Committee and by the newly elected President of IUPS, Paul Fraisse. After the final session, there was a farewell banquet in the restaurant of the Palace of Congresses.

General Assembly meeting, Moscow 1966

Reports of the Officers

The first session, held on August 4, was called to order in the presence of representatives from the national societies of 17 countries. Drever presided. He first reported briefly on the activities during his tour of office, stressing the need to re-examine the organizational structure and the operating procedures of IUPS. Secretary-General Russell then noted that international psychology was continuing to develop at an amazingly rapid pace. He reported that the Union had member societies in all continents of the world and that it had doubled its membership during the past few years. He indicated that the extent of the Union's broadening contacts and growing commitments was evident in the business before the Assembly. He expressed hope that detailed attention would be given to the items raised in the paper he had prepared at the request of the Executive Committee and entitled "Time for decision: A self-evaluation." He called attention to the article entitled "The International Union of Psychological Science" published in the first issue of the Union's new journal, the *International Journal of Psychology*.

Treasurer Mailloux presented his general report of the Union's financial status; he was pleased to report a small favorable balance in hand. Acknowledging the continued support provided by UNESCO, he also called attention to the assistance provided during the past triennium by the Aquinas and the Rockefeller Foundations. The Union approved sponsorship of Mailloux's research project on the intellectual development of the children in Rwanda.

As Chair of the Committee on Communication and Publications, Duijker reported on activities during the previous 3 years. He mentioned the work carried out to produce the second edition of the *International Directory of Psychologists*, to be published at the end of the year. He also noted the progress that had been made in the preparation of the *Trilingual Lexicon of Psychological Terms* and called attention to a round-table scheduled during the present congress to discuss issues affecting the international flow of information in psychology.

Election of the Executive Committee

Paul Fraisse was elected President by secret ballot during the first session, on August 4. At the third session of the Assembly, on August 8, in accordance with the newly voted Statute which increased the vice-presidencies to two, both Leontiev and Russell were elected Vice-Presidents by secret ballot. After customary reception of nominations and discussion, the election to the Executive Committee led to the following result: Klineberg, Luria, Mailloux, Nuttin, Pfaffmann, Piaget, Sato, Summerfield, Tomaszewski, and Yela.

Paul Fraisse (1911–1996): President of the IUSP, 1966–1969. Also, President of the 21st International Congress of Psychology, Paris, 1976.

Membership issues

Representatives of 19 national members were present at the second session on August 6. The session opened with the presentation and approval of the resolution to change the Statutes to two vice-presidents

Membership items were then considered. The Philippines Psychological Association election to membership was confirmed. The request made by Australia to be now represented by the Australian Psychological Society was accepted. Having been dropped at the last meeting in 1963, the Cuban and Egyptian Societies could be reinstated as members conditional upon payment of arrears in annual subscriptions and the submission of their statutes or constitution. The Cuban Society, having satisfied these requirements, was unanimously re-elected to membership. No word had yet been received from the Egyptian Society. The Assembly also approved the application of the German Democratic Republic (East Germany), of the Romanian Psychological Society, of the Hungarian Psychological Scientific Association, and of the Mexican Psychological Society. The request of the Western Germany Society to be represented through the new Federation of German Psychological Associations was granted. The application of Tunisia was postponed pending receipt of information on the society's membership and assurance that membership was open to all qualified psychologists in Tunisia. Many other potential members had been contacted. Among those responding, the Greek Society had requested a meeting with the officers of the Union during the 1966 congress.

Future congresses at 4-year intervals

Three major items related to future congresses were discussed. First, Summerfield reported that the plans for the 1969 congress in the United Kingdom were already underway. Second, the Assembly expressed great pleasure in receiving a formal invitation from the Japanese Psychological Association to hold the 1972 congress in Tokyo, confirming the approbation already given. Third, regarding future congresses, the Assembly considered and approved a resolution that future congresses be held at intervals of 4 years rather than 3 and that the timing be coordinated with the IAAP meetings, instructed to begin with the 21st congress in 1976. Also, the Assembly instructed the President to draft a new Rule of Procedure to be added as Section 1, Paragraph 2, stating that "the host society or association shall take all reasonable steps to ensure that political matters are not introduced into the ceremonial and social occasions which form parts of a congress."

International exchange of students and scholars

The Joint APA-IUPS Project on the International Exchange of Psychologists had led to a meeting on August 6. Out of the several recommendations made, one appeared to have particular urgency and was therefore raised with the Assembly. It was recommended that a Standing Committee on International Exchange of Scholars and Students be immediately established; after discussion, this recommendation was adopted unanimously.

Sherman Ross, director of the Joint APA-IUPS Project on International Exchange of Psychologists, was invited to report personally on the present status of this joint effort. He informed the Assembly that a volume entitled *International Opportunities for Advanced Training and Research in Psychology* was now in press and that it contained information provided by about 90 countries. It was to be distributed, free of charge, as widely as possible. The Assembly expressed its appreciation for what was clearly a major contribution to the development of international psychology. Ross added that additional actions directed toward the major objective of fostering improved exchanges of scholars and students at the international level would now be undertaken.

The Secretary-General's "suggestions for action"

The specific proposals contained in the "Suggestions for Action"section of the report entitled *Time for Decision: A Self-Evaluation* presented by Russell as retiring Secretary-General a few days previous, were considered. This lead to the consideration of the following 12 resolutions:

1. There was an agreement in principle on the need to establish a full-time secretariat. The means by which this decision could be implemented were to be explored.
2. It was agreed that each member society should identify one of its members as the primary contact person with the Union.
3. Two suggestions concerning the *International Journal of Psychology* (IJP) were discussed and approved: (a) that free subscriptions be provided to each of the national societies and to each of their representatives at the Assembly, and (b) that a regular feature of IJP should be concerned with current plans, issues, and activities of importance to the Union.
4. It was agreed in principle that the International Congress of Psychology program include a general meeting, open to all, at which IUPS' officers would report on issues and activities. Individual psychologists would have an opportunity to comment and ask questions. The British Psychological Society was informed of this resolution so that it could be implemented at the 1969 congress.
5. It was agreed that the Executive Committee should continue to support as fully as possible the work of its Ad Hoc Working Group on the International Biological Program and seek to establish closer relations with the experimental psychology group of the International Union of Biological Sciences.

6. The Executive Committee was requested to discuss problems of a purely "professional" nature and to prepare a position paper on the role of the Union in relation to such problems.

7. The Executive Committee was asked to consider actions to enable implementation of the following suggestions:
   (a) arrange conferences for young teachers of psychology in areas where the discipline is in early stages of development,
   (b) sponsor meetings of psychologists experienced in working in developing countries to explore ways by which the Union could be of assistance in the growth of psychology,
   (c) provide assistance to new universities in developing countries by making available free subscriptions to the Union's publications,
   (d) explore with member societies the possibility that their publications could also be made available to new universities free of charge.

8 It was approved in principle that procedures should be worked out to involve more fully the representatives of national societies in the ongoing activities of IUPS.

9. The advisability of establishing a category of Associate Members for new national societies which are not yet sufficiently strong to consider application for full membership was considered and rejected.

10. It was agreed that only representatives of national members receive General Assembly and Executive Committee meeting minutes. Requests from others should be considered by the Secretary-General, in consultation with the President.

11. The Executive Committee was asked to consider three suggestions:
    (a) that an Ad Hoc Committee on Collaborative Research be established to provide full and systematic support for research projects involving collaboration among psychologists from different countries,
    (b) that a feasibility study be conducted of the means by which international "centers"or "special programs"might be established for advanced training in areas of the world where psychology is only beginning to develop,
    (c) that IUPS take action toward the encouragement of fuller use of the world literature in psychology.

12. It was agreed that steps should be taken to make use of UNESCO sources of support for research and other activities.

International Journal of Psychology

Fraisse presented his first report as acting editor of the new journal. Negotiations with Publisher Dunod (France) regarding agreements for printing and distribution of the journal were described. He made two recommendations that were approved unanimously. First, that Germaine de Montmollin be appointed executive editor of the journal, and second, that the Deputy Secretary-General serve as an associate editor, with responsibility for the sections concerned with "news" of activities of the Union and its member societies.

ISSC matters

Duijker, who represented the IUPS at ISSC, reported that the Committee on International Social Science Documentation was now interested in studying the processes underlying the communication of social science information. Since the existence of *Psychological Abstracts*, published by the APA, meets the needs of the psychological community, the committee decided not to continue publication of abstracts of current psychological literature.

Klineberg and Nuttin, both members of ISSC, reported that communication channels between IUPS and ISSC were very satisfactory. They discussed the recent symposium on methods for cross-national and cross-cultural research organized by ISSC.

Relations with UNESCO

The Secretary-General reported on the activities of the Working Group engaged in various projects designed to support UNESCO's continuing interest in the world-wide alleviation of illiteracy. The IUPS provides assistance to this program by keeping the national societies informed of the role they might play.

Klineberg, the Union's special liaison to UNESCO, reported on the possible effects of the administrative reorganization of UNESCO affecting the social sciences. He indicated that a proposal to increase the annual subvention to IUPS would be presented at the next General Conference in 1966. Such additional support would come at a most opportune time, when the Union's activities were being significantly increased. Finally, he proposed that each member of the Assembly be provided a copy of the recent UNESCO publication *Attitudes Toward Peaceful Uses of Atomic Energy*, the Union bearing any costs that might be incurred.

The Moscow congress

Two resolutions related to the 1966 Moscow congress received unanimous approval: The first expressed the Union's gratitude to the government of the USSR for their support of the 18th International Congress of Psychology, the largest ever to be held. It also thanked the Academy of Sciences of the USSR and R.N. Fedossiev, who acted as Chair of the Steering Committee for the Congress. The second resolution expressed deep appreciation to the Psychological Society of the USSR for the excellent work done in the organization and conduct of the 18th congress. Particular thanks went to Luria, who chaired the Program Committee, to Smirnov, Chair of the Organizing Committee, and to Tikhomirov, the Secretary-General.

Executive Committee meeting, Moscow 1966

The first session was held on August 4. After reviewing in detail the agenda that had been set and circulated for the 1966 Assembly meetings, the Executive Committee received the report of the Committee on Communication and Publications, chaired by Duijker. It mentioned that a collaborative study of the 1966 congress would be carried out by the Soviet Psychological Society and the American Psychological Association; the results would be very helpful in the planning of future congresses. Duijker informed the Executive Committee of his resignation. Committee members expressed deep appreciation for the very significant contribution he made over his long tenure.

The second session, held on August 11, was chaired by the new President, Paul Fraisse, and attended by all members of the Executive Committee. The first item of business was the appointment of a Secretary-General (Eugene Jacobson), a Deputy Secretary-General (G. Nielsen), and a Treasurer (Noël Mailloux). Joseph Nuttin was appointed Chair of the Committee on Communication and Publications.

Future congresses

For the next International congress, to be held in London, UK in 1969, Luria was appointed as the Union's liaison with the British Psychological Society's Program Committee. The official languages of the congress would be English and French. The committee took this occasion to have a general discussion on the form and procedures of international congresses. The Committee on Communication and Publications was asked to present a report on this issue in 1968, based on the results of a review of the 1966 congress. The Japanese invitation for the 1972 congress was accepted unanimously.

Eugene H. Jacobson (1917–1993): Secretary-General of the IUSP (1966–1972).

Appointments

Special liaison appointments were made to various organizations. Thus, Klineberg was appointed to continue to serve as the Union's representative to UNESCO, Nuttin to the International Social Science Council, Duijker to the International Committee on Social Science Documentation, and Summerfield to the International Biological Program.

Proceedings of the Moscow congress

After examining the composition of the Committee on Communication and Publications and discussing its present activities, the issue of the publication of the Moscow congress proceedings was examined. Since abstracts of the program had already been distributed to all participants, it was proposed that the proceedings of the 1966 congress include only the following: (a) presidential address, (b) the special evening lectures, and (c) a résumé of the congress, with the list of the participants from different countries.

International relations and exchanges

Two recommendations came out of the meeting of the round-table on Psychology and International Relations held on the previous day. First, that there was a need to encourage research relevant to psychology and international relations and to disseminate the information that psychology already has at its disposal in this area. And second, that IUPS should establish a Standing Committee on Psychology and International Relations to meet this need. Action on this proposal was postponed until the 1967 meeting.

A pilot project on "Visitors abroad" (communication of information about who will be visiting abroad, when and where), considered to be a significant step toward the further encouragement of the international exchange of scholars and students, was approved. The Australian Psychological Society was invited to undertake this study, which would include the development of a method for implementation, and the test of the method within a limited geographical area.

Before the meeting was adjourned, it was decided to hold the 1967 meeting of the Executive Committee in England and the meeting of 1968 in Amsterdam just after the IAAP Congress.

Executive Committee meeting, Windsor 1967

Reports of the Officers

The Executive Committee met on May 12, 1967, in Windsor, UK. President Fraisse summarized recent IUPS activities and introduced the agenda of the meeting. He commented on the publication of the first issues of the *International Journal of Psychology* and on the increase in the subvention of UNESCO to the IUPS. He also emphasized the continuing need for improvement of communication between national societies and the IUPS and the need to increase the involvement of national societies.

Secretary-General Jacobson presented his 1966 report to UNESCO on the activities of IUPS and reviewed two rosters. The first roster, entitled *A List of Members of the Assembly*, raised the issue of representation when a member of a national society was elected to the Executive Committee. Fraisse suggested that a national member should be allowed to appoint an additional representative in such a case. It was proposed to amend the Statutes to clarify this issue. The second roster, *List of National Societies with Membership in the IUPS*, raised some questions about the official contacts with member societies. The Secretary-General also reported that the IUPS had 34 member societies and that communication should be continued with Tunisia regarding its possible membership.

Publication and communication

Nuttin, as Chair of the Communication and Publications Committee, first mentioned that the second edition of the *International Directory of Psychologists* had been published in the Fall of 1966 with the financial assistance of the US National Science Foundation and UNESCO. He was pleased to report that it contained the names of approximately 8000 psychologists in countries other than the USA. Second, he indicated that tentative plans for the preparation of the third edition of the *Directory* would be postponed until the Amsterdam Executive Committee meeting in 1968, in order to have more complete information on estimated costs and chosen strategy. Third, he noted that the *Trilingual Lexicon of Psychological Terms* was in its final review phase and that potential publishers were being sought. Nuttin reported on his communication with the Editor of the *Psychological Abstracts* about increasing the role of the national societies in providing information for the *Abstracts*.

Fraisse mentioned that 1300 copies of the *International Journal of Psychology* had been printed and that the number of subscribers was increasing, although more would be needed. The contract with Dunod would end in 1969, requiring new renegotiations. It was decided that a small group of editorial consultants be selected to supplement the present editorial board. A list of possible consultants was prepared.

International exchange of students and scholars

The newly established Standing Committee on International Exchange of Scholars and Students was discussed. A consensus was reached that this committee would participate in policy formation and program planning for exchange functions of the IUPS. A task force of this committee was asked to consider the revision of the volume entitled *International Opportunities for Advanced Training and Research in Psychology* that had been published by APA in 1966, in collaboration with the IUPS.

International Biological Program

The working group on the International Biological Program had suggested that, as part of the project on human adaptability of the International Union of Biological Sciences, the IUPS should convene a Working Party on Performance Measurement in London in September 1967 under the chairmanship of Simon Biesheuvel. The plan was approved and an amount of US$1500 was allocated to this project, other costs to be borne by foundations, participants, and local sources. Summerfield agreed to present a report on this activity at the 1968 Executive Committee meeting.

Proceedings of the Moscow congress

Leontiev informed the committee that the 1966 International Congress proceedings would be published in three separate volumes, one in each of the working languages of the congress, and that free copies would be sent to all congress participants, libraries, and national societies that are members of the IUPS. Luria further indicated that negotiations had been initiated to publish seven volumes of selections from the congress symposia and papers. The volumes would include: (a) psychology and higher nervous activity, (b) electrophysiological, physiological and biochemical basis of behavior, (c) general problems of psychological processes, (d) psychology of perception, (e) psychological studies of memory, speech and thought, (f) developmental psychology and (g) social psychology.

Future congresses

The plans for the 1969 congress were introduced for discussion. Also presented was the composition of the Committee of Honor, the Organizing Committee, the Program Committee, and the Finance Committee. The Duke of Edinburgh had accepted the invitation to be the patron of the congress and G.C. Drew had been invited to be the President.

Sato reported that an Organizing Committee had been appointed by the Japanese Psychological Association for the 1972 International Congress in Tokyo.

Relations with other organizations

Klineberg reported that although the IUPS relationship with UNESCO was good, the role of their Social Sciences Program was overshadowed by other activities. There were no psychologists in the UNESCO secretariat. The project on "Main Trends in the Social Sciences" was continuing, with Piaget making a major contribution to the statement about psychology. But unfortunately, the Rwanda Child Development Project had been turned down by UNESCO.

Nuttin reported that the ISSC was undertaking studies on trends in the social sciences in France and on the relationship between social sciences and development.

The never-ending quest for membership in ICSU was once again discussed and judged to be a priority. Pfaffmann and Fraisse were authorized to continue working toward this objective. For his part, Luria was asked to represent the IUPS in relations with the International Brain Research Organization (IBRO) as another way of strengthening the IUPS relationship with the biological sciences.

Statutory and administrative matters

Changes in the Rules of Procedure were considered. The first amendment studied was to extend the interval between two international congresses to 4 years. Also, it was suggested that changes should be made to allow the retiring President of IUPS to remain an ex-officio member of the Executive Committee for 4 years.

The need to establish a full-time secretariat was reviewed briefly. Action was deferred due to the estimated cost of US$30,000 to $50,000 a year. The

Executive Committee allocated US$200 of Union funds to pay for subscriptions to the *International Journal of Psychology* for a selected group of new universities.

Finally, arrangements were made for the Executive Committee to hold its next meeting in or near Amsterdam for 3 days immediately after the International Congress of Applied Psychology in August 1968.

Executive Committee meeting, Amsterdam 1968

This meeting took place in Amsterdam, the Netherlands, on August 21–24, in conjunction with the Congress of the International Association of Applied Psychology. The IAAP is one of the four international psychological organizations affiliated with the IUPS, and this meeting provided for many of the members of the Executive Committee an opportunity to meet with colleagues attending the Applied Congress and to take part in the congress proceedings. Fraisse chaired the Executive Committee session with all members present, except Piaget and Pfaffmann who were excused.

Relations with the International Union of Biological Sciences

In the presence of Jacques Paillard (Marseille, France) and Harry Alpert (UNESCO), the first item discussed was the relation of IUPS with the International Union of Biological Sciences (IUBS), which was a member of ICSU. The IUBS was composed of divisions in Botany, General Biology, Microbiology, and Zoology. In the division of Zoology, there were a number of sections, including a Section on Experimental Psychology and Animal Behavior. Fifteen national societies members of IUPS had sent representatives to this section: Belgium (Paulus), Canada (Bindra), Denmark (Perch, Rasmussen), France (Fraisse, Francès), Germany (Metzger), Iran (Etemedian), Italy (Marzi), Japan (Matsusabura, Morinaga), Netherlands (Duijker, Stovkis), Poland (Blanchowski), Switzerland (Inhelder, Meili), USSR (Smirnov), United Kingdom (Summerfield), USA (Russell), and Yugoslavia (Bujas, Petz). The implications of this complex and indirect relationship with ICSU were discussed, and it was noted that it would become further complicated by the application for membership in the section of the newly formed International Association of Ethologists.

Consideration of alternative relationships that IUPS might have with ICSU, IUBS, and the Section on Experimental Psychology and Animal Behavior led to the following recommendations: (a) to continue this discussion during sessions next year at the London congress, and (b) to encourage the convening, during the London congress, of a meeting of the 15 national societies that were members of the Section on Experimental Psychology for the purpose of exploring alternative structural arrangements with IUBS. On another aspect of the IUPS relationship with ICSU and IUBS, Luria reported on the IUPS contributions to the scientific activities of the

International Brain Research Organization (IBRO). He mentioned that IBRO had held, in March 1968, an international conference on Brain Research and Human Behavior, where many presentations were devoted to neuropsychology.

Future congresses

R.J. Audley, Vice-Chair of the Program Committee of the 19th International Congress to be held in London in 1969, reported on the state of preparation of the congress. He indicated that two circulars announcing the congress had already been distributed. The committee discussed the need for the involvement of national societies, and for an adequate representation of younger psychologists as well as that of well-known figures on the program who could present important, basic issues in psychology.

Sato presented an outline summary of progress to date and projected plans for the 1972 congress in Tokyo, Japan. A very detailed tentative schedule of all the required preparations was presented. The three official languages were to be English, French, and Japanese. Discussion on the planning of this particular congress led to the decision that the structure and substance of future congresses, broadly speaking, be discussed at length by the Executive Committee at its next meeting in London.

Relations with UNESCO and ISSC

Harry Alpert (UNESCO), present as an observer, joined Klineberg in a discussion of the relations with UNESCO and ISSC. They indicated that many important changes were being planned in the structure of ISSC. Among the recommendations for change in ISSC were that it should become a federation of International Unions in a relationship with UNESCO (similar to that of ICSU), that subventions to the international non-governmental organizations (NGOs) be given by UNESCO to ISSC in a lump sum for distribution among the NGOs, and that the ISSC Council include representatives from National and Regional Social Science Research Councils, along with representatives from the NGOs. After an extended discussion, a resolution was adopted whereby the IUPS indicated its preference for the present system of separate subventions, but noted that it would accept the new arrangement if adopted. The second part of the resolution stated that the IUPS was strongly opposed to the idea of the National Social Science Councils having the same status as the international disciplinary associations.

Publications

One of the major functions of IUPS being to establish and maintain effective international communications among psychologists, a whole day of the Executive Committee meeting was devoted to the report of the Standing Committee on Communication and Publications, chaired by Nuttin.

Plans were reviewed for a third edition of the *International Directory of Psychologists*, which would involve a number of alternative methods of preparation (e.g. computer processing) and support. The role of the national societies in support of the *Directory* would have to be increased and a revised financial structure should be adopted. Taking into consideration the many suggestions made, the Standing Committee, in collaboration with the Secretary-General, was asked to develop a revised plan.

The second item considered was the *International Journal of Psychology*, then in its second year of publication under the editorship of Germaine de Montmollin and with Deputy Secretary-General Gerhard Nielsen as associate editor responsible for the International Platform Section. Fraisse reported that the *Journal* had published 14 articles on perception-cognition, 6 on psycholinguistics, 13 on child-intellectual development, 42 on aspects of social and cross-cultural psychology, and 7 on methodological and theoretical issues in cross-cultural research. Half the authors were from the United States. There were 400 subscriptions to the *Journal*. A number of questions were raised about the advisability of devoting so much space to cross-cultural research and it was proposed that the *Journal* should mainly be concerned with fundamental, theoretical issues in psychology. There was a general commendation of the editor for the quality of the *Journal* in its initial 2 years, and a number of suggestions were made to help the *Journal* better serve the purposes of psychology internationally.

A third publication of the IUPS, the *Trilingual Lexicon of Psychological Terms*, which had been in preparation for a number of years, was in its final stage of editing and revision. To be most useful, the first edition had to be published soon, with any additional changes being deferred to subsequent editions. The possibility of adding the Spanish language was considered and rejected as impractical at this time.

Leontiev and Luria reported on the 1966 International Congress of Psychology and the publication of its proceedings. They announced that the three volumes of proceedings would be published by the end of 1968. Selected papers from the 1966 congress were also to be published. All royalties from these publications were to be assigned to the IUPS.

Summerfield and Simon Biesheuvel, who chaired the Working Party on Performance Measurement of the International Biological Program, announced that a *Handbook on Approved Methods for Performance Measurement* had been submitted for publication as a result of their work.

Finally, the Secretary-General informed the committee that he was preparing a brochure on the IUPS and that he would circulate a draft for comments and suggestions.

Membership issues

Four membership issues were presented for discussion. First, the then current member society representing the Netherlands agreed to relinquish its membership in favor of the Nederlands Instituut van Psychologen, clearing the way for this request to be sent to members of the Assembly for approval by mail ballot. Second, the Executive Committee approved the membership of the New Zealand Society as successor to the previous New Zealand Branch of the British Psychological Society. Third, the applications for membership received from Hong Kong and Panama were deemed to need more information before recommendation to the Assembly. The Iranian application was judged to be acceptable and would be recommended for Assembly approval at the London meeting. Fourth, it was noted that recent efforts to re-establish mail communications with Egypt and Venezuela thus far had failed, but would be continued.

Statutory amendments

A proposed amendment sent out to national members in July 1967 regarding a statutory change allowing the retiring President of the Union to remain as an ex-officio member for 4 years was strongly endorsed. The necessary clarification of the Statutes regarding the membership in both the Executive Committee and the Assembly led to the suggestion (to be approved at the next Assembly meeting) that the Statutes should stipulate that "All members of the Executive Committee shall be members of the Assembly," and that "In the event that a representative of a member society becomes a member of the Executive Committee, the member society be entitled to an additional Assembly representative."

International exchange of students and scholars

As Chair of the Standing Committee on the International Exchange of Scholars and Students, Summerfield presented a review of current activities in international exchanges, and listed the current needs for increasing the opportunities for effective movement of younger scientists. It was decided that the Platform Section of the *Journal* should be used for this purpose. The Executive Committee approved the recommendation made by Summerfield that an International Young Psychologist's Travel Fund be established under the auspices of the IUPS and asked him to prepare plans for implementation in order that this program could be operational for the London congress.

Financial matters

Following the usual presentation by the Treasurer of the financial statement for the preceding year, there was a discussion on financial matters, where, inter alia, it was decided to discuss, at the next Assembly meeting, the possibility of national societies increasing their contributions to the IUPS in consideration of the increased costs of operation.

International relations

A report from the round-table on Psychology in International Relations recommended the preparation of a book on the relationship between psychology and international affairs.

In view of the creation by the United Nations of a new award for individual contribution to progress in human rights, the Executive Committee unanimously recommended that the name of Professor Otto Klineberg be submitted by the Union.

The 19th International Congress of Psychology, London 1969

Organization of the congress

The 19th International Congress of Psychology, the fourth to be held in Great Britain was held at University College London, from July 27 to August 2, 1969, under the auspices of the British Psychological Society (BPS) and the IUPS, with George C. Drew presiding. Table 9.2 presents the structure and composition of the Organizing Committee.

Total registration to the congress was 1921 members and 464 associates (Proceedings of the XIXth International Congress of Psychology, 1971). Forty-nine countries were represented. The entire cost of the congress was

---

TABLE 9.2

Organizing Committee:
19th International Congress of Psychology (London, 1969)

G.C. Drew, University College London, *Chair*
A. Summerfield, Birkbeck College, London, *Deputy Chair*
P.H. Venables, Birkbeck College, London, *Honorary Secretary*
D.M. Nelson, London School of Economics, *Honorary Assistant Secretary*
  (until August 1968)
D. Legge, University College London, *Honorary Assistant Secretary*
  (from November 1968)
R.J. Audley, University College London, *Co-Chair, Program Committee*
D.E. Broadbent, Medical Research Council Applied Psychology Unit,
  Cambridge, *Co-Chair, Program Committee*
Sheila Crown, Bedford College, London
C.B. Frisby, lately National Institute of Industrial Psychology, London,
  Chair, Finance Committee
M. Hamilton, University of Leeds
Marie Jahoda, University of Sussex
R.P. Kelvin, University College London, *Chair, Social Events Committee*
Grace Rawlings, University College Hospital, London
A. Rodger, Birkbeck College, London
R.W. Russell, University of California, Irvine
O.L. Zangwill, University of Cambridge
I.A. Drew, *Chair, Ladies Committee*
R.M. Farr, *Honorary Secretary, Program Committee*

---

met from registration fees. The British Council, the Commonwealth Foundation, and the Wates Foundation generously helped a limited number of psychologists with travel costs.

The Organizing Committee first met in November 1966. Throughout the different stages of preparation, it received help in particular from the staff of University College London and the BPS.

The congress was officially opened at the Royal Festival Hall, by the Rt Hon Richard Crossman, Secretary of State for Health and Social Security, on behalf of Her Majesty's Government. The presidential address, entitled "British psychology," was given by Drew. Other addresses were given by R.J. Audley as President of the BPS and Fraisse as President of the IUPS. The latter's talk was entitled "De la fonction des congrès internationaux de psychologie" (Proceedings of the XIXth International Conference of Psychology, 1971). Summerfield closed the formal opening ceremony with a vote of thanks to Secretary of State Crossman. The formal session was followed by a reception.

George C. Drew: President of the 19th International Congress of Psychology, London, 1969.

Scientific program

The scientific program consisted of five parallel sessions each day and contained 23 long symposia, 19 short symposia, 10 review papers, 5 specially invited papers, and 105 submitted papers. Table 9.3 presents the major themes of the scientific program. Film sessions were arranged as part of the program on three afternoons. Evening lectures were delivered by Broadbent ("Relation between theory and application in psychology") and Luria ("The origin and cerebral organization of man's conscious action"). Two book exhibitions were also available.

The film sessions and review papers, which were an innovation at this congress, were particularly well attended. Appreciation was also expressed for the numerous opportunities provided by informal meetings and discussions between participants.

The closing session, held at the Royal Festival Hall on August 2, consisted of a most successful symposium entitled "Psychology in the future," chaired by George A. Miller (Rockefeller University, USA). Participants were Karl Pribram (Stanford University, USA): "Psychology tomorrow: The immediate future," Harry Kay (University of Sheffield, UK): "Psychology: AD 2000: Facts, forecasting, fantasies and fallacies," and Masanao Toda (Hokkaido University, Japan): "Possible roles of psychology in the very distant future." The congress was officially closed by Summerfield and followed by a farewell luncheon. Many receptions were given during the week of the congress, offered by the Secretary of State for Education and Science, by the Vice-Chancellor of the University of London, and by the Provost of University College London.

TABLE 9.3

Main themes of the scientific program:
19th International Congress of Psychology (London, 1969)

Specially invited papers
- Autonomic learning: Clinical and physiological implications (N.E. Miller)
- The perception of syntactic structure (W.J.M. Levelt)
- Forgetting: Another look at an old problem (E. Tulving)
- Boolean analysis of cognitive structures and communications (C. Flament)
- The sharing of interrelated motor tasks among human operators (A.Leontiev)

Review papers
- Discrimination learning in children (H.H. Kendler and T.S. Kendler)
- The present status and future promise of computer simulation (E. Hunt)
- The social development of monkeys and apes (R.A. Hinde)
- Repeated measures designs and their analysis (A. Lubin)
- Social behaviour in infancy (H.L. Rheingold)
- Behavior-genetic analysis and its biosocial consequences (J. Hirsch)
- Experimental studies in abnormal psychology (R.W. Russell)
- Color vision (W.A.H. Rushton)
- Perceptual coding (H.-L. Teuber)
- Mathematical analysis of stochastic learning models (F. Norman)

Symposia
- Social factors in childhood and adolescence
- Behavior therapy
- Models for memory
- On-line computing in psychology
- Deductive thought
- Learning process of human infants
- Tracking skills
- The effects of intra-uterine stimulation
- Human aggression and social conflict
- Developmental and specific handicaps
- Strategies in learning and cognitive processing
- Temporal aspects of information processing
- The communication of psychological information
- Psychological research in developing countries and its application to social planning
- Cognitive development: The years 5 to 8
- Current trends in computer-assisted instruction
- Approaches to psychological stress and emotions
- Biological, social and linguistic factors in psycholinguistics
- Evolution of behavior
- Decision-making
- Cross-modal integration
- Learning and personality: I . Motor learning
- Learning and personality: II. Memory and interference in verbal learning
- Consistency and social influence
- The dimensions of arousal
- Temporal-lobe functions and behavior
- Models in personality theory

continued →

TABLE 9.3 *continued*
• Physiological and biochemical mechanisms of learning and habituation
• Stimulus generalization
• Nonverbal communication
• Pharmacological and biochemical aspects of mental illness
• Human curiosity and exploratory behavior
• Visual masking and meta-contrast
• Cognitive consistency: Contributions to restatement of theories
• Recent research in sleep and dreams
• Attention: Some growing points in recent research
• Some current issues in animal discrimination learning
• Imprinting
• The psychology of addiction
• The social context of language behavior
• Recent advances in the experimental psychology of aging
• Split-brain function
• Theory and practice of measurement
Film sessions
• Animal behavior
• Child behavior and abnormal behavior
• Miscellaneous

General Assembly, London 1969

This first (July 27) and second (July 31) sessions of the General Assembly were chaired by President Fraisse, in the presence of representatives from 25 member societies.

Reports of the Officers

After approval of the minutes of the 1996 Moscow meeting, Fraisse reported briefly on the activities of the IUPS, emphasizing the importance of communications among member societies and the strategic value of international congresses. Secretary-General Jacobson commented on his annual report of the IUPS to UNESCO. The Treasurer's report was then adopted and the Assembly considered the recommendation to raise the annual dues of the member societies, which had remained unchanged since 1951. It was unanimously agreed that the contribution should be doubled (from US$10 to $20 per unit), effective January 1, 1970. A suggestion that the maximum number of units should be raised from 40 to 80 was tabled until the second session of the Assembly meeting.

Publications

Concerning publications, Nuttin reported that work was continuing on the *Trilingual Lexicon*, while Summerfield indicated that the Standing Committee on International Exchange of Scholars and Students was considering a revised edition of the volume on *International Opportunities for Advanced Training and Research in Psychology*. Montmollin and Nielsen reported on the *International Journal of Psychology*, providing circulation figures (N=662) and the wide geographical distribution of its subscribers. The countries of origin of the authors and the topics of the papers published were outlined. A suggestion was made that members should advertise the *Journal* in their national publications.

Leontiev reported that the proceedings of the 18th congress (Moscow) were being mailed to the congress participants and that five other volumes, edited by Luria and Russell, based on special material and colloquia, would be published by Academic Press on behalf of the IUPS.

Future congresses

Preliminary plans and the state of preparation of the 20th congress to be held in Tokyo, Japan, in 1972, were presented to the Assembly. On behalf of the Société française de psychologie, Fraisse invited the Assembly and it unanimously accepted an invitation to convene the 21st congress in Paris, in 1976.

Following a discussion on the procedures towards the improvement of the scientific usefulness of international congresses and program development, the Assembly agreed that the host society should have the ultimate responsibility in these matters, but that final decisions should be made only after extensive consultations with the national societies and the Union. For this purpose, Fraisse proposed, and the Assembly approved, the creation of an International Advisory Program Committee.

Membership issues

The change in the representation of the Netherlands was unanimously approved. The situation of the Egyptian Society for Psychological Studies was still unclear; it had failed to respond to numerous calls for payment of dues. On the other hand, the Venezuelan College of Psychologists had re-established contact with the Union and was readmitted to active status. The reorganization of the Indian Psychological Association was under way, and hope was expressed that its status would soon return to normal. The applications of the Psychological Association of Iran and the Colombian Federation of Psychology for membership were approved. The applications of Pakistan and Bulgaria, however, were deemed to be incomplete, while the application of Hong Kong did not obtain the support of a majority vote. Additional information from Hong Kong would be requested before its application could be reconsidered.

Statutory amendments

The Secretary-General reported that the mail ballot on the proposed statutory changes related to the representation on the Executive Committee had received strong approval.

Executive Committee (1969–1972) at the 19th International Congress of Psychology, London, 1969—Back row (left to right): O'Neil, Westerlund, Summerfield, Pfaffmann, Russell, Nielsen, Bruner, and Mailloux. Front row (left to right): Leontiev, Fraisse, Tomaszewski, Tanaka, Nuttin, and Jacobson.

Unanimous approval was given to change Article 8 to increase from 40 to 80 the maximum number of dues units to be assessed to any national society.

Election of the Executive Committee

For the presidency, the nominations of Nuttin, Russell, and Summerfield were put to a vote; Russell was elected. For the vice-presidency, Luria, Mailloux, Nuttin, O'Neil, Summerfield, and Tomaszewski had accepted nominations; Luria and Nuttin were elected. Bruner, Duijker, Fraisse, Leontiev, O'Neil, Pfaffmann, Summerfield, Tanaka, Tomaszewski, and Westerlund were elected to the Executive Committee.

Relations with other organizations

Harry Alpert, Director of Social Sciences at UNESCO, led an extended discussion of UNESCO programs in the social sciences and the nature of the relationship between international NGOs, such as the IUPS, and UNESCO. It was noted that research support was available from UNESCO National Commissions in various countries for activities related to UNESCO programs.

Information regarding the present status of the relations with ISSC and ICSU (through the Section on Experimental Psychology and Animal Behavior of the IUBS) was given to the Assembly.

Executive Committee meeting, London 1969

Chaired by Fraisse, the first session held on July 26 was attended by all members of the Executive Committee, with the exception of Piaget.

Reports of the Officers

The President reviewed previous discussions related to the responsibilities of the Executive Committee concerning international congresses and explored the possibilities of assuming a more active role in the development of programs.

The Secretary-General discussed the relationships of IUPS with the United Nations, UNESCO, and ICSU in connection with the interests of those organizations in the problems of "Man and his Environment." He also distributed a report on the activities of the IUPS. The relationship with ICSU, through the section on Experimental Psychology and Animal Behavior of the International Union of Biological Sciences, was examined once again. It was deemed appropriate to maintain active contact and cooperation with this section.

The Treasurer presented the financial statements for 1968 and for the first half of 1969. Increasing costs, particularly those connected with the Executive Committee meetings each year, required additional funds. At the upcoming Assembly meeting, a proposition would be made to increase the annual dues from US$10 to $20 per assessment unit of 100 members.

Membership issues

Many issues related to membership were discussed by the Executive Committee. Arrears in dues payment of India and Venezuela were noted. The applications for membership of Colombia, Hong Kong, and Iran were approved for presentation to the Assembly. A mail ballot was approved for Pakistan and Bulgaria pending receipt of complete documentation. Further information was needed from Panama before any action could be taken.

Appointment of Officers

The second session (August 2 and 3) of the Executive Committee was called to order by the new President, Roger Russell. With the exception of Duijker, Leontiev, and Luria, all members were present.

The first task was the appointment of the officers. Jacobson was appointed as Secretary-General, Nielsen as Deputy Secretary-General, and Mailloux as Treasurer.

Relations with UNESCO

Alpert, of UNESCO, was present and reviewed with the Executive Committee five current UNESCO programs of particular interest to the IUPS. These were: (1) Man and his Environment, (2) Social Science and Development, (3) Peace Research, (4) Aggressiveness, and (5) Problems of

Youth. It was agreed to inform the national societies of the possibilities of obtaining UNESCO support in these areas.

The Executive Committee approved the contract with UNESCO for the publication of a survey of psychology and international relations to be directed by Klineberg. An Ad Hoc Committee was appointed to act as an editorial board for the publication.

Future congresses

Specific suggestions were made by Fraisse and approved by the Executive Committee regarding the organization of future congresses. For instance, it was agreed that the Japanese Psychological Association, host of the 20th congress, should draw up a provisional list of possible topics and send it to all members of the Executive Committee and member societies for their opinions and comments. Names of psychologists potentially capable of making original contributions to the program or suggestion of topics could be returned. Second, any psychologist would be encouraged to submit for consideration abstracts of papers on any recognized topic for the congress. Among the papers accepted some would be selected for oral presentation, whereas others would only be summarized by a designated speaker. Third, to assure international diversity, no more than two psychologists from a single country could be invited to participate in a given symposium. Finally, it was suggested that the scientific program include (a) reviews of important problems intended for the non-specialists, (b) round-table discussions of current problems, (c) invited addresses from well-known psychologists, and (d) some conferences intended for audiences made up not exclusively of psychologists. Pfaffmann spoke on the desirability of organizing satellite symposia with specially invited participants in order to encourage additional exchanges with colleagues from other disciplines. These meetings could be held before, during, and after the congress. It was also deemed desirable to have additional uncommitted room space so that seminars could be organized spontaneously during the congress.

Committee reports

Nuttin was reappointed Chair of the Standing Committee on Communication and Publications. The works in progress were reviewed. A manuscript on a UNESCO-sponsored survey on the teaching of psychology had been completed by Francès. Additional competitive bids for the publication of the third edition of the *International Directory of Psychologists* would be sought.

Summerfield remained as Chair of the Standing Committee on Exchange of Scholars and Students. It was agreed that he should prepare suggestions for a new structure of the committee, to be discussed in Tokyo. Regarding the support of young psychologists, the Secretary-General is to contact the national societies asking them for donations towards a travel fund.

Other issues

Westerlund reported that the next International Congress of Applied Psychology would be held in Liège, Belgium, in 1971, to be followed by one in Montréal, Canada, in 1974.

The idea of organizing a group of young psychologists called the "IUPS Forum on New Developments in Psychology" was approved, under the leadership of the Deputy Secretary-General.

Information was provided on the publication of the proceedings of the 19th London congress. With a format and content similar to previous proceedings, it would be published in 1970. Liaison officers to the different organizations related to the IUPS were appointed: Summerfield for UNESCO and International Biological Program, Montmollin for ISSC, and Nuttin for ICSSD.

Executive Committee meeting, Washington 1970

The meeting was held at APA headquarters on October 14–17, 1970. With the exception of Duijker and Luria, all members of the Executive Committee were present. In his customary report, President Russell referred to the need for considering long-term developments in the social sciences and future directions for psychology. The report of the Secretary-General contained a detailed review of the relationships between the IUPS and other international bodies. The Treasurer led the discussion on a membership issue, the status of the Indian Psychological Association. Although the association had paid its 1970 dues, due to special circumstances it had not been able to make the payments of the four previous years. The Executive Committee agreed to write off this non-payment and to continue the membership of the Indian Association. If future difficulties of this nature should again arise, the membership status of this association should be critically reviewed.

Relations with ICSU

After review by Russell and Pfaffmann of the history of the IUPS-ICSU relationship, it was decided that ICSU programs having psychological implications should be identified and attempts made to establish collaboration. The idea of full participation by IUPS in ICSU was once again discussed, noting that membership issues would be considered by ICSU only at its next Assembly meeting in 1972.

Publications

Fraisse reported on the *International Journal of Psychology*. He observed that the policy of the *Journal* had changed to make it more general in scope and that the number of subscriptions was slowly growing. Suggestions for changes in the *Journal* included: (1) the preparation of issues on special themes with invited papers; (2) the clarification of scientific controversy, with authors chosen to represent conflicting scientific positions; and (3) the screening of submitted papers in order to prepare issues with substantive focus. Nielsen spoke of the limitations placed upon the Platform Section by infrequency of journal publication, which made it difficult to have a truly current representation of issues dealing with international psychology. Summerfield suggested that the Platform Section be used to update international opportunities and information on the exchange of scholars and students.

Nuttin, reporting as Chair of the Communication and Publications Committee, noted that during the present year every effort would be made to complete the Lexicon project, which had been in preparation since the 1957 Brussels congress.

Function and purposes of international congresses

On the second day of the meeting, a long discussion took place on the function and purposes of international congresses. An introductory paper, analyzing the information exchange role of international congresses, was presented by Russell. Another paper based in part on research on international congresses conducted by the American Psychological Association, prepared by Harold Van Cott, was also distributed. Fraisse commented that congresses should serve to sharpen scientific questions, promote advances in the discipline, and report on the most recent developments. For his part, Nuttin drew attention to the characteristics of the communication processes during congresses, including audience readiness to understand and the factors that influence the effectiveness of scientific communication. He proposed increased use of discussion groups rather than paper-reading sessions, and noted that making use of opportunities for members of symposia to confront each other with opposing views could provide valuable contributions to a congress.

Nielsen remarked that the purposes of a large international congress are to provide opportunities for considering the objectives of psychology as a science, for obtaining information about subject matters outside one's field of competence, for initiating and facilitating exchanges between psychology and other groups in the international scientific, professional, and political communities, and for increasing dissemination of scientific materials. Mailloux observed that congresses provide models of scientific work for younger colleagues and syntheses of past research. For Bruner, the importance of congresses could be summarized in four functions: (1) mythological (developing the image of psychology through debate, confrontation and exposure), (2) educational (synopses, dissemination, interfaces, forms of presentation), (3) informational (new material, analytic and synthetic exercises), and (4) coalitional and affiliative (contacts, collaboration, exchanges, project development). Bruner added that opportunities for satellite meetings with representatives of other disciplines should be enhanced. Westerlund suggested that language problems were a major factor and that every effort should be made to increase the effectiveness of simultaneous translation. Finally, it was agreed by everyone that the excellent and innovative recommendations made should be translated into action and implemented at the earliest possible opportunity.

Membership issues

The Secretary-General reported on correspondence with the Hong Kong and the Panamanian societies. More information had been received concerning these two petitions and, after extensive discussion, it was decided to submit their applications to a mail ballot by Assembly members.

On the last day of the meeting, October 17, the candidacy of the Scandinavian Research Society was reviewed. Although not eligible for membership in the IUPS, it could be considered as an affiliate. More information was needed from this society before a recommendation could be made. It was reported that further attempts to establish contact with Egypt had not been successful.

The following year's meeting of the Executive Committee would be held at the end of July in Liège, Belgium, in conjunction with the International Congress of Applied Psychology. Westerlund, acting President of the IAAP, extended an invitation to the IUPS to be represented at both the opening and closing ceremonies of the congress.

Just before closing the session, the Executive Committee recommended that a third Standing Committee on Cross-Cultural Research be established following suggestions that had been made at the previous meeting in London.

Executive Committee meeting, Liège 1971

Reports of the Officers

Russell presented his presidential report outlining several important issues that were to be considered during the current meeting. He reviewed the UNESCO survey of International NGOs with member societies in South Africa asking them about membership practices relating to apartheid policies. The Secretary-General had been asked to conduct an inquiry on this issue and had reported that the policy of the South African Society was that professional qualifications were the only standards for admission to membership. The Executive Committee requested, however, that a further inquiry should be made of the South African Society about current participation of "non-whites" in the work of the society.

Secretary-General Jacobson reported on two positive financial aspects of the IUPS program. First, after many years of negotiation, the US National Science Foundation had agreed to support some of the costs of the third edition of the *International Directory of Psychologists*; it was now necessary to find a European co-editor for the project. Second, UNESCO had provided a small increase in the amount of its biennial subvention to IUPS.

Publications

The report of the Standing Committee on Communication and Publications began with a report on the *Lexicon*. Final drafts had been received and final arrangements were being made with the publisher, Huber Verlag. Concerning the *Journal*, the search for a new editor to replace Montmollin had begun. A policy of Special Issues for the *Journal* was suggested; it was thought that one issue per year could be "special." It could focus on current problems, the development of psychology in various parts of the world, or developments and reviews in various branches of psychology. All agreed that there was a need for making the *Journal* more attractive to a larger number of psychologists by making it multi-faceted. The problems of combining in one journal the functions of archival responsibilities, of encouraging communication among psychologists, of addressing current problems, and of supporting basic scientific developments were discussed.

Congratulations were addressed to Montmollin, present at the meeting, for her pioneering efforts in starting the *Journal* with very limited support. To summarize the extensive discussion on the *Journal* that went on during the afternoon session on July 22 and the morning session on July 23, it can be said that there was general agreement that: (1) the launching of the *Journal* had been a success and that it should be continued and improved, (2) that there should be Special Issues with guest editors , and (3) that the Platform Section serves an important function, but that it should perhaps be published separately. In addition to the Platform, the possibility of also circulating a newsletter should be considered.

Future congresses

Tanaka reported that plans for the Tokyo congress were nearing completion. He also observed that the organizers were planning a number of special events for the young psychologists who attend the congress. It was agreed that the Open Meeting, sponsored by the IUPS in London, had been useful and that a similar meeting should also be held in Tokyo.

Relations with ISSC and UNESCO

The fourth session of the meeting was held on the afternoon of July 23. Invited participants to this session were Eugene Lyons, current head of the Department of Social Sciences at UNESCO, and Samy Friedman, Secretary-General of ISSC. Lyons reviewed the current program of UNESCO in the social sciences. He expressed UNESCO's concern with the social sciences in the developing countries. He noted the interest of UNESCO in human problems related to the control of the environment and the quality of life. He reviewed programs on population issues and human rights and peace that have social science implications. In response to Pfaffmann's comments on the relevance of studies of man and the biosphere, Lyons informed the committee that UNESCO was convening a Working Group on Human

Factors in Environmental Change. All agreed that a fundamental task was the improvement of social science resources in the developing countries.

Friedman commented on the proposed new constitution of the ISSC and the new ISSC rules of procedure. He noted that these would allow the social sciences to present themselves in a more unified way and, potentially, make better use of their resources. There was an extended discussion of problems of financing new social sciences activities within the new ISSC, the role of UNESCO and the ISSC in the developing countries, and the administrative problems associated with effective ISSC operations.

Other issues

On July 24, the last session of the 1971 meeting started with a discussion on possible candidates for editor of the *Journal*. Responsibility for this selection was delegated to the Secretary-General and the Chair of the Communication and Publications Committee. Regarding membership issues, correspondence with the Scandinavian Federation of Research Psychologists, whose membership had been discussed at the previous meeting, indicated that the federation was now eligible for affiliate membership in the Union. Correspondence with African psychological societies seeking membership information was deemed encouraging.

As for research projects supported by IUPS, it was reported that the political situation in Pakistan made it impossible to continue with plans for the literacy studies in this country. Mailloux was happy to report that the Rwanda project had been successfully completed and that it needed only limited support to enable publication. Nuttin remarked on plans that he and colleagues were developing for research on time perspective and development in the Congo. It was agreed to consider this new research as part of the IUPS research program after more information became available.

Jacobson reported that the establishment of a Standing Committee on Cross-Cultural Research depended for its success on a reasonable prospect of finding funds, since funds for this kind of research were not as readily available as they had been. No committee had yet been established.

References

González Solaz, M.J. (1998). *Los congresos internacionales de psicología (1963–1984)*. Unpublished doctoral dissertation, Valencia, Spain.

Montoro, L., Tortosa, F.M., & Carpintero, H. (1992). Brief history of the International Congresses of Psychology. In M. Richelle & H. Carpintero (Eds.), *Contributions to the history of the International Congresses of Psychology: A posthumous homage to J.R. Nuttin* (pp. 75–89). Valencia, Spain: Revista de Historia de la psicología, and Leuven: Studia Psychologica.

Proceedings of the XIXth International Congress of Psychology, London, UK. (1971). London: British Psychological Society.

Solso, R.L. (1991). Institute of Psychology, USSR: 20-year retrospective. *Psychological Science, 2*, 312–320.

Psychology in Asia (1972): A first major step in the globalization of psychological science

10

Until 1972, all of the international congresses had been held in major cities of Europe, the United States, and Canada. In both the IUPS Assembly and its Executive Committee, discussion for several decades had frequently taken place of the need to reach out more effectively to psychologists in other parts of the world, but no major decision to hold the international congress elsewhere was made until the Moscow congress in 1966. Moving the 18th congress as far east as Moscow had been a bold but highly successful venture, and the 1966 Assembly unanimously accepted the offer of the Japanese delegation, led by Koji Sato, to hold the 20th congress in Tokyo.

Although the Japanese Psychological Association was a charter member of IUPS, it wasn't until 1960 that a Japanese psychologist, Professor Sato, was elected to the Executive Committee. Immediately thereafter, Sato began planning for a congress. At the Washington Congress in 1963, he broached the idea to the Executive Committee of holding the 20th International Congress of Psychology in Tokyo. They encouraged him to proceed with preliminary planning and a formal invitation. After a feasibility study, the Assembly of Representatives of the Japanese Psychological Association decided to issue a formal invitation, provided that a substantial number of Japanese psychologists personally pledged to contribute money and services. An enthusiastic response by many psychologists provided the necessary support to launch a major planning effort and to issue a formal invitation that was approved by the Assembly at the Moscow congress.

Sponsorship of the Tokyo congress by the Japanese government was granted in 1970, and the Science Council of Japan officially established the Organizing Committee. Moriji Sagara, the President of the Japanese Psychological Association, was elected Chairman of the Committee, and Hiroshi Azuma was appointed Executive Secretary. Major financial support for the Congress came from the Government of Japan, from funds raised from industries by the Japan Society for the Promotion of Science, and from the earlier pledges of individual psychologists. Contributions by individuals were particularly noteworthy; 400 Japanese psychologists each gave the equivalent of US$80 for a total of US$32,000 as underwriters of the congress.

The 20th International Congress of Psychology, Tokyo, Japan, 1972

The 20th International Congress of Psychology was held in Tokyo on August 13–19, 1972. As President of the Japanese Psychological Association, Moriji Sagara served as the President of the congress. The scientific program was organized primarily around 32 long symposia, 9 short symposia, and 8 review sessions devoted to topics of current interest ranging from physiological to social psychology. Fifty-six sessions consisted of submitted papers, 4 film sessions showed films on research, and 25 free discussion sessions were held. In addition to the general opening session that included welcoming addresses by Roger Russell, IUPS President, and Yukiyoshi Koga, senior member of the Japanese Psychological Association, two evening addresses and seven lectures were given by distinguished leaders of psychological science.

These major speeches and a symposium on implications of Asian psychology in world perspective at the closing session were printed in the congress proceedings, together with abstracts of all the other presentations (Science Council of Japan, 1974). The proceedings also contains an appendix listing all the participants and their addresses. A major innovative feature of the program was the free discussion session linked to each long symposium. A long symposium consisted of a main session followed by a 2-hour discussion period, providing plenty of time for extensive interaction.

The congress continued the tradition, started in 1963 for the Washington congress, of subsidizing the travel of young psychologists. The American Psychological Association supported 10 young psychologists from the United States and Canada, and the Japanese Organizing Committee arranged to have young Japanese psychologists with related scientific interests serve as their hosts.

A total of 2164 psychologists with 398 accompanying persons registered for the Tokyo congress. One half of the registered psychologists came from over 50 different countries, the remainder being from Japan. The largest number of foreign psychologists was 633 from the United States. Other countries with 10 or more psychologists present were Australia, Brazil, Canada, Denmark, France, Federal Republic of Germany, India, Israel, Korea, Mexico, Netherlands, Spain, Sweden, United Kingdom, and Union of Soviet Socialist Republics. Clearly, the Tokyo International Congress established a new standard of global participation of psychological scientists by drawing in large numbers of psychologists from Asia and the Pacific and introducing many European and American psychologists to Asian psychology.

Moriji Sagara (1903–1986): President of the Japanese Psychological Association and President of the 20th International Congress of Psychology, Tokyo, 1972.

As was now customary, the outgoing Executive Committee of the IUPS met before the congress on August 12 and the newly elected incoming Committee met immediately following on August 19. The Assembly held its meetings on August 13 and 16 during the congress. By the time of the Tokyo congress, the Assembly consisted of 51 representatives from 38 national member societies, most of whom were present for both sessions.

In the first meeting of the Executive Committee, President Russell led a discussion of opportunities for more concerted action by psychologists to deal with pressing human problems. Areas that were noted ranged from man in a changing environment to the impact of rapidly emerging new technologies. Russell's opening address at the congress expanded considerably on this theme. Secretary-General Jacobson reported that M. Jules Leroux, from the University of Louvain, had been appointed as the new editor of the *International Journal of Psychology*.

New Officers of the Union

The Assembly elected Joseph Nuttin, University of Louvain, Belgium, as President to succeed Russell. Arthur Summerfield of Birkbeck College, London, and Yoshihisa Tanaka, University of Tokyo, were elected Vice-Presidents. The 10 members elected to the Executive Committee consisted of 7 who were re-elected—Bruner, Fraisse, Jacobson, Leontiev, Russell, Tomaszewski, and Westerlund—and 3 new ones—Friedhart Klix, Humboldt University, Berlin, Boris Lomov, USSR Academy of Sciences, and Mark Rosenzweig, University of California, Berkeley. The appointment by the incoming Executive Committee of Noël Mailloux from Canada as Treasurer, Wayne Holtzman from the United States as Secretary-General, and Germaine Montmollin as Deputy Secretary-General completed the roster for the new Executive Committee that would hold office for 4 years rather than 3 as in the past, in keeping with the new 4-year cycle between international congresses. Rosenzweig was appointed Chairman of the Standing Committee on Communication and Publications, and Summerfield continued as Chairman of the Standing Committee on International Exchange of Scholars and Students. Montmollin was appointed liaison with UNESCO and Rosenzweig liaison for the Committee on Social Science Information and Documentation.

Joseph R. Nuttin (1909–1986): President of the IUPsyS (1972–1976).

Trilingual dictionary

In his report as retiring Secretary-General, Jacobson noted that the *Tri-Lingual Dictionary*, in English, French, and German, edited by Hubert C. J. Duijker, with support from UNESCO and IUPS, would be published in 1973 by Hans Huber. The *Dictionary* grew out of the early work of Dr W. Luthe, who started a compilation of psychological terms in the three languages.

The Union initially approved the project in 1954. As the first Chairman of the Committee on Communication and Publications established at the Bonn Congress in 1960, Duijker took a keen interest in finishing the task. Even though only three languages were represented, most psychologists would be familiar enough with one of the three to profit greatly from such a lexicon.

Executive Committee meeting, Rosny 1973

The first major meeting of the newly formed Executive Committee at Chateau de Rosny near Paris, September 3–6, 1973, took note of the highly successful Tokyo congress and discussed other ways in which further globalization of psychology could be advanced. President Nuttin raised the general question of how areas of the world such as Africa, which have no official voice in the Union, could be represented. He suggested that new rules be adopted for election of Executive Committee members so that no country would have more than one elected representative. Perhaps the election could be held in stages; in the second stage, one or two Executive Committee members could be elected at large from anywhere in the world. Both of Nuttin's ideas were adopted later in a major reform of the IUPS Statutes and Rules and Procedures.

As President of the International Association of Applied Psychology, Westerlund invited the IUPS to participate, officially, in the opening session of the 18th International Congress of Applied Psychology in Montréal, July 1974. Thus began a new era of close cooperation between the two major international associations that were now holding one or the other congress every 2 years. As President of IUPS, Nuttin was nominated to represent the Union by serving as an official speaker at the opening session of the 1974 Applied Congress in Montréal.

Relations with other international organizations

Of continuing concern to the Executive Committee were the relationships between the Union and such international bodies as UNESCO, ISSC, and the International Council of Scientific Unions (ICSU). The Union had been formally rebuffed in its previous attempts to gain membership in ICSU some years earlier. Obtaining full membership in ICSU would remain a long-standing piece of unfinished business until finally the question was favorably resolved in September 1982. UNESCO had always provided a small subvention directly to IUPS, but now there was some preliminary discussion of routing such subventions through ISSC. ISSC was undergoing a major reformation, the final outcome of which was not at all clear.

Samy Friedman, formerly with UNESCO's Department of Social Sciences and now Secretary-General of ISSC, joined the Executive Committee for a luncheon discussion of these several issues. Friedman explained that the new organization of ISSC would be more of a confederation of independent associations, each of which would maintain its full autonomy and its status as a Category B affiliate of UNESCO. He pointed out that through ISSC, IUPS and other member organizations could increase their influence in the various departments of UNESCO, particularly in the Department of Social Sciences. While some projects might be shared by IUPS and ISSC, others could be independently proposed by IUPS for funding as in the past. He cautioned, however, that the General Conference of UNESCO, where the underdeveloped countries were highly influential, was growing impatient with the non-governmental organizations such as IUPS for not working more vigorously on the problems of the developing countries.

Subsequently, the Executive Committee concluded, as urged by Montmollin, that IUPS should (a) propose research projects to ISSC on topics of interest to psychologists as well as other disciplines; (b) develop and maintain strong relations with other departments of UNESCO, including Education, Communication, and Natural Sciences; and (c) propose research ideas now through Friedman that could be implemented in the UNESCO program for 1975–76 and then carried out by IUPS with UNESCO funding. Montmollin and Holtzman were confirmed as delegates to ISSC, with Summerfield and Rogelio Diaz-Guerrero from Mexico as alternates.

In the next meeting of the ISSC General Assembly later in 1973, psychology proved to be well represented as part of the newly formed structure serving an expanded membership of 11 international societies. Montmollin was elected to the Executive Committee, Summerfield was appointed a member of the Research Committee, Tomaszewski was elected as a new Member-at-Large, and Holtzman served as a regular representative of IUPS.

Reaching out to Latin America and Africa

The small amount of remaining funds, US$5250, in the 1973 IUPS budget were assigned to Holtzman for support of training and research development in Latin America. These funds were subsequently used in support of travel and local costs for psychologists from throughout Latin America who participated in the First Latin American Conference on Training in Psychology, organized by Rubén Ardila of Colombia. The conference was held on December 17–18, 1974, in Bogota in conjunction with the 15th Interamerican Congress of Psychology. Five commissions were established and programs in many Latin American countries used the proposed models for improvement of their university programs (Ardila, 1975). The major papers presented at this highly successful conference were subsequently published (Ardila, 1978).

New contacts were also developed with psychologists in Africa that later led to a greater involvement of African psychologists in IUPS activities. Highest priority for research funds in the 1974 budget was given to expenditure in the English- and French-speaking countries of equatorial

Africa, as strongly advocated by Nuttin and others. Mailloux recalled a successful Union project years ago in Rwanda on cognitive development in children. By 1975, the major outline of another project dealing with child development in Africa had emerged.

Preliminary plans for the 1976 and 1980 congresses

A major portion of the meetings in Rosny was devoted to preliminary plans for the 1976 congress to be held in Paris and the 1980 congress in Leipzig. As requested by Fraisse, a limited subvention was provided from IUPS to the French Society of Psychology to prepare for the forthcoming congress. Klix announced that a series of international symposia, one per year, would be presented in East Germany as a prelude to the Leipzig congress. The first of these symposia took place in September 1973 and was devoted to organismic information processing, pattern recognition, and problem solving. It was anticipated that additional conferences in this pre-congress series would be held on such topics as biochemical, neurological, and physiological bases of memory; on language production and language understanding; and on emotions, motivation, and cognitive efficiency.

Encouraged by the successful participation of Korean psychologists in the Tokyo congress, a petition for membership in the Union was filed by the Korean Psychological Association (South) and approved by mail ballot in 1973. The Psychological Society of Ireland was admitted to the Union in early 1974 and then withdrew in 1988, remaining outside the Union until it was readmitted in 1996.

Executive Committee meeting, Montréal 1974

At its 1974 meeting, July 25–28, at Mount Gabriel near Montréal, the Executive Committee continued with a more detailed review of plans for the 1976 Congress in Paris. Jean-François Le Ny, Chairman of the Program Committee, joined Fraisse in presenting a plan for 40 symposia, each lasting over a period of two half-days, as well as special lectures, sessions of individual papers, and workshops. Themes and organizers for the 40 symposia would be selected from a larger number of suggested topics and leaders after extensive consultation with psychologists throughout the Union.

Sponsorship of young psychologists

Of special interest for the 1976 congress was the growing number of students and sponsored young psychologists, many of whom would need low-cost dormitories and travel subsidies from their national associations. The registration fee for the congress would be kept under 250 French francs. Harley Preston from the American Psychological Association Central Office described their special subsidy program for young psychologists from Canada and the United States. For the previous congress in Tokyo, 10 travel awards to the most deserving applicants were made consisting of free tickets provided by domestic air carriers and several private donors. Low-cost housing was made available by the host society. All recipients of grants had to be less than 30 years old. Similar plans for the Paris congress were successfully developed by the host committee and the IUPS Committee on Exchange of Scholars and Students under Summerfield.

Misuse of psychology

A growing concern of many psychologists in the early 1970s was the severe political oppression, disappearance of dissenters, and widespread tales of rape, torture, and murder evident in several countries of South America, most notably Brazil, Argentina, and Chile. Rumors that psychologists working for the military governments in these countries were aiding and abetting the mental breakdown of dissenters in order to force confessions were particularly disturbing. Public concerns regarding alleged abuses of political prisoners by psychiatrists who misused psychodiagnosis as a tool of oppression in the Soviet Union had already sensitized many Western psychologists to the problem. The American Psychological Association, among several IUPS members who voiced official concern, asked the Union to address these issues. Compounding the difficulty for the Union was the fact that only Brazil of the offending South American countries had a psychological society that was a member of IUPS, and the Brazilian Psychological Association claimed that none of its members were engaged in such activities, making it impossible to impose sanctions on the societies unless they expelled the offenders, if indeed, any member psychologists were engaged in such highly unethical behavior. But clearly something had to be done.

The Executive Committee strongly deplored the oppression of dissenters but realized it was ill-equipped to undertake deep investigation of the widespread rumors concerning the complicity of psychologists. (Later it turned out that several military officers who were implicated in forced confession-torture activities in Brazil had received some elementary training in psychology but were not recognized, professionally trained psychologists.)

After considerable discussion led by Russell, the Executive Committee asserted its leadership in promoting international communications regarding ethical standards for psychologists. A formal resolution was approved and widely disseminated promoting the following actions: (1) all national societies should establish formal codes of scientific and professional ethics and conduct; (2) a survey would be conducted immediately of all IUPS national member societies to determine which ones have already adopted such codes; (3) information about existing codes would be collated and made available to societies which had not adopted a code; (4) all societies would be urged to accept responsibility for monitoring the compliance of their individual members and for applying appropriate sanctions where their code had been violated; (5) ethical codes would be a primary subject for discussion and action at the next Assembly meeting in Paris; and (6) Holtzman as Secretary-General would be responsible for organizing a special symposium for the Paris congress on the subject of scientific and professional ethics and conduct, with particular reference to the issues of oppression and torture.

Executive Committee meeting, Austin 1975

An African project

At its 1975 meeting in Austin, Texas, October 6–8, the Executive Committee devoted considerable attention to special projects that materialized following the earlier commitment to work closely with UNESCO on ideas of mutual interest: (1) an African conference on child rearing; and (2) an international project on educational television and child development. The African conference was organized by Marcel Ebode in July 1975 at Yaounde, the Republic of Cameroon, with mainly French-speaking psychologists present. Support was provided by a UNESCO grant of US$3000 through the Population Council and matching funds from the IUPS budget. A grant of US$3000 from the Aquinas Fund augmented the conference funds and made it possible for key psychologists in the conference, both English- and French-speaking, to travel to Paris the following year for a planned symposium on child rearing at the Paris congress. Two of these African psychologists were also invited to attend the 1976 IUPS General Assembly meeting as official observers. The English-speaking psychologist, Michael Durojaiye, originally of Uganda and later of Nigeria, was then elected by the 1976 Assembly to the Executive Committee under the newly adopted Statutes.

Educational television of children throughout the World

The second project supported by UNESCO was directed by Isabel Reyes of Mexico and involved psychologists from Israel, India, Japan, the Federal Republic of Germany, Brazil, Mexico, and the United States. The Education Department of UNESCO provided US$12,000 in direct support and two grants of US$10,000 each from the UNESCO Participation Program made at the request of two national governments—Mexico and India. Two major conferences were held, one in Mexico City and a second in Tokyo. UNESCO's Education Department subsequently published a monograph, *Impact of Educational Television on Children*, containing major research articles by 11 of the participants (Holtzman & Reyes-Lagunes, 1983).

References

Ardila, R. (1975). The first Latin American conference on training in psychology. *International Journal of Psychology, 10,* 149–158.

Ardila, R. (Ed.) (1978). *La profesion del Psicologo.* Mexico: Trillas.

Holtzman, W. H., & Reyes-Lagunes, I. (Eds.) (1983). *Impact of educational television on young children.* Paris: United Nations Educational, Scientific, and Cultural Organization.

Science Council of Japan. (1974). *XXth International Congress of Psychology.* Tokyo: University of Tokyo Press.

The congresses return to Europe (1976–1982)

The 21st International Congress of Psychology, Paris, France, 1976

The Paris congress was held on July 18–25, 1976, and was attended by nearly 3000 psychologists and over 500 accompanying persons from 64 different countries. As President of the congress, Paul Fraisse joined IUPS President Joseph Nuttin, Vincent Bloch, President of the French Society of Psychology, and Robert Mallet, Chancellor of the University of Paris, in addressing the opening session of the 21st International Congress of Psychology, recalling the historic occasion of the 1st congress held in Paris in 1889 and pointing out the great progress made in psychology as a science in less than 100 years. A comparison of the scientific content and issues presented at international congresses prior to World War II with those of the 21st congress illustrates both the significant progress of scientific psychology in the past century and the changing nature of psychology. The maturity of basic psychological science together with the rapid emergence of professional and applied issues and topics of concern to developing countries throughout the world are clearly evident in the proceedings of the Paris congress of 1976 (French Society of Psychology, 1978).

In his opening address, following up on Russell's theme at the Tokyo congress that psychology can and must contribute to the understanding and resolution of big issues facing the world, Nuttin emphasized the importance of psychologists actively participating at the highest levels of international and interdisciplinary planning and policy-making as well as scientific research.

The Organizing Committee for the Paris congress, led by Fraisse, covered everything from finances and public affairs to publications. The scientific program was developed by a committee of 19 French psychologists under J.F. Le Ny as chairman. As analyzed more recently by González Solaz (1998) in her doctoral dissertation on the International Congresses of Psychology from 1963 to 1984, the program consisted of 6 invited major lectures, 40 symposia on contemporary topics ranging from the physiological basis of learning and memory to artificial intelligence and behavioral pharmacology, 35 thematic sessions of individual papers, a series of films on child development, psychopathology, social psychology, and animal behavior, and a special session honoring Jean Piaget, the internationally distinguished Swiss psychologist, on his 80th birthday.

The six invited speakers and their topics present some of the thematic interests of the times as viewed by the French committee: T.G.R. Bower (University of Edinburgh): "Concepts of development"; Barbel Inhelder (University of Geneva): "From the structural approach to the procedural approach: Introduction to the study of strategies"; Hans-Lukas Teuber (Massachusetts Institute of Technology): "The brain and human behavior"; Donald A. Norman (University of California, San Diego): "The role of active memory processes in perception and cognition"; Georges Noizet (University of Provence): "Strategies in the treatment of phrases"; and René Zazzo (Psychobiological Laboratory of the Child, Ecole Pratique des Hautes Etudes, Paris): "Brain and behavior". A more complete picture of psychology can be obtained from the symposia presentations and hundreds of individual papers that comprise the bulk of the scientific program. The invited lectures were published in full, together with the titles and authors of other presentations, in the proceedings (French Society of Psychology, 1978).

Ethical standards in psychology

During the 2 years preceding the 1976 congress, the Secretary-General corresponded regularly with the Union's national members concerning ethical standards and codes of conduct. The survey revealed that, while most societies were moving forward with discussion of appropriate codes of ethical standards, only a small number had actually adopted codes and were enforcing them. A special symposium was held at the Paris congress with a large, standing-room-only audience. Many in the audience were refugees from South American military oppression who demanded that psychology take a firm stand. Organized by Holtzman, the symposium was chaired by Otto Klineberg and had 14 speakers on a variety of ethical topics, including one by a Chilean refugee posing challenges to psychologists concerning techniques of torture used in Chile. Newspaper reports and television cameras were present, and some of the speeches were widely publicized, putting additional pressure on the IUPS Assembly to take some positive action.

The next day the Assembly debated the issues and finally passed a resolution proposed by Nuttin concerning professional ethics in psychology, taking into account the substance of a comprehensive Dutch proposal as well as an American proposal dealing with the misuse of psychiatric diagnosis to suppress political dissent. The final text of the resolution made reference to the United Nations Charter and to the 1975 UN Declaration on protection of all persons from being subjected to inhuman treatment (see Figure 11.1).

FIGURE 11.1

Resolutions approved by the IUPS Assembly, July 27, 1976, Paris

Keeping in view:

1. That the International Union of Psychological Science is an association of national associations;
2. That today its membership consists of 42 national associations from both developed and developing countries;
3. That its annual operation expenses amount to approximately US$20,000, partially because of its continuing responsibilities to UNESCO and its affiliated organizations; the Assembly of IUPS hereby resolves that:

> *it is essential to maintain the UNESCO funding of ISSC from which funds are derived for support of ongoing activities within IUPS; and requests that the member national societies of IUPS approach their national governments through appropriate organizations such as the National Commission to UNESCO, urging them to support fully the program and budget of UNESCO at the forthcoming General Conference of UNESCO in Nairobi.*

The International Union of Psychological Science, which includes national psychological societies of 42 nations from all over the world; which thus speaks in the name of over 70,000 professional psychologists which, because the subject of their science is behavior, are particularly concerned with any acts by which individuals in a systematic and deliberate way infringe upon the inviolable rights of human beings, regardless of race, religion, or ideology, these rights being guaranteed by the Charter of the United Nations; and which is concerned with strict observance of professional standards of ethics in the practice of psychology, therefore makes the following declarations:

> *It proclaims that no psychologist, in the exercise of his or her professional functions, should accept instructions or motivations that are inspired by considerations that are foreign to the profession;*

> *It protests solemnly against any use of scientific data or of professional methods of psychology that impair the above-mentioned rights;*

> *It formally condemns any collaboration by psychologists—whether actively or passively, directly or indirectly—with the above-mentioned abuses, and it urges its members to oppose any abuses of this sort;*

> *It requests each member-society to make certain that it has enacted a code of ethics and to take those actions required by its code against any member guilty of such abuses against human rights;*

> *It declares that the Executive Committee of IUPS is ready to support, with all means at its disposal, any action undertaken by a member-society in order to carry out the terms of the present resolution;*

It recalls the following statement made by its Executive Committee on July 27, 1974:

> *The Executive Committee wishes to make clear that the International Union of Psychological Science denounces vigorously all practices that are contrary to the high level of morality that must regulate the scientific and professional roles assumed by psychologists in modern society.*

It welcomes the United Nation's Resolution, adopted by the General Assembly (Third Committee: A/10408; 2423rd plenary meeting, 9 December 1975) on the Protection of All Persons from being subjected to Inhuman Treatment.

This Resolution was approved by a unanimous vote of the IUPS Assembly, Paris, July 22, 1976.

New officers of the Union

Meetings of both the outgoing and incoming Executive Committees and two sessions of the Assembly for the Union were held during the Paris congress. A total of 69 voting delegates representing 36 countries attended one or both of the Assembly meetings, a record attendance. Summerfield was elected President, and Lomov and Rogelio Diaz-Guerrero, National University of Mexico, were elected Vice-Presidents. Following the newly approved Statutes and Rules of Procedure, new procedures were used for electing the first eight Executive Committee members from delegates of current national member societies and then electing two more at large from anywhere. This two-step method increases the likelihood that a qualified psychologist or two from countries not currently represented might be elected. And, indeed, that is how the elections worked out.

Arthur Summerfield: President of the IUPsyS (1976–1980).

Michael O.I. Durojaiye, University of Lagos, Nigeria, joined Juan J. Guevara, University of Havana, Marianne Frankenhaeuser, University of Stockholm, and seven returning Executive Committee members—Fraisse, Klix, Nuttin, Rosenzweig, Russell, Tanaka, and Tomaszewski—to run the affairs of the Union. At their first meeting, Holtzman, Montmollin, and Mailloux were re-appointed as Secretary-General, Deputy Secretary-General, and Treasurer, respectively. With the announcement by Mailloux that he would retire after only one more year, the Executive Committee appointed his colleague at the University of Montréal, David Bélanger, as his replacement after retirement, thereby completing the committee for the next 4 years. Rosenzweig was reappointed chairman of the Committee on Communication and Publications, Diaz-Guerrero was appointed chairman of the Committee on International Exchange of Scholars and Students, and Nuttin was appointed chairman of a special committee to draft a plan for a new Committee for Research and Special Projects.

David Bélanger: Treasurer, IUPsyS, 1977–1992. Also, President of the 26th International Congress of Psychology, Montréal, 1996.

A necessary increase in dues

The Assembly also approved an increase in dues from US$20.00 to US$30.00 per membership unit, larger societies having a formula-based larger number of units in accordance with the revised Statutes and By-Laws. The Panamanian Association of Psychologists was approved as a new member, bringing the total number of member national societies to 42. Initially introduced to the Assembly in 1972 at its meeting in Tokyo, the formal invitation from the Society for Psychology in the German

Democratic Republic to hold the 22nd International Congress in Leipzig in 1980 was enthusiastically approved, as was the invitation from the Mexican Society of Psychology to hold the 23rd International Congress in Mexico in 1984.

Executive Committee meeting, Windsor 1977

A financial windfall from the Paris congress

The new Executive Committee met again in Windsor, England, October 11–13, 1977, to discuss unfinished business from the Paris congress and to plan for the future. In his final report before retiring, Mailloux announced, to everyone's relief, that the annual subsidy for IUPS from UNESCO through ISSC was US$15,310, only a small drop from the previous year. The support would remain the same for at least the next year. Moreover, the reserve fund from small surpluses in past budgets and congresses had now grown to US$31,922. This good news was further reinforced by Fraisse, who reported that a grant from the French Government of US$80,000 to support the Paris congress had arrived too late to be used for the congress. After much discussion, the Treasurer proposed a resolution which was unanimously adopted stating the following: (1) the French money should be used first to defray all remaining expenses incurred by the French Psychological Society in sponsoring the congress; (2) in accordance with the Union's Statutes, US$10,000 would be immediately available for work of the Executive Committee; (3) preference would be given two French projects: (a) a scientific colloquium on child development in memory of Henri Wallon to be held in Paris in 1979 as part of UNESCO's Year of the Child, and (b) a new abstracting journal to improve knowledge about French-language publications in psychology; and (4) these funds should be kept in a special, French-franc account in Paris where they would be considered part of the Union's Reserve Fund.

The finances of the Union were in good shape, thanks to the long and careful management of them by Noël Mailloux as well as to the success of the French congress and to the subsidy of the Secretary-General's office by the Hogg Foundation for Mental Health at the University of Texas. A great deal of work was accomplished with a very modest, if not meager, budget, largely because of the voluntary efforts of the Executive Committee and many others. The increase in member dues approved in 1976 would help stave off a financial crisis, provided that subsidies from UNESCO continued and there was no need to employ paid central office staff.

The new Committee on Research and Special Projects, consisting primarily of the active project directors with Bélanger as chairman, set out an ambitious agenda to respond to invitations for joint projects with other organizations, to serve as a broker of ideas from IUPS members, to take the initiative in generating new projects appropriate to the IUPS mission, and to review new program opportunities at UNESCO, recognizing that general subsidy of IUPS by UNESCO would probably be phased out. Renewed efforts to secure membership in the International Council of Scientific Unions were recognized as essential if the Union was to achieve its goals of promoting expanded international research activity in the basic psychological sciences other than those sponsored by ISSC. Such membership had been sought on several previous occasions without success during the past 25 years, and it would require a united effort on several fronts to persuade scientists in other disciplines that psychology had much to offer in such interdisciplinary endeavors.

A change in the secretariat

Bélanger moved quickly into his new role as Treasurer. Montmollin decided to retire, leaving open the position of Deputy Secretary-General. Within months, Kurt Pawlik, University of Hamburg, Federal Republic of Germany, was persuaded to accept appointment as Montmollin's replacement.

Executive Committee meeting, Leipzig 1978, and General Assembly, Munich 1978

In anticipation of the 1980 congress, the meeting of the Executive Committee, July 26–29, 1978, was held in Leipzig, a city rich in the history of psychology. A meeting of the Assembly for exchange of information was also held on July 30, 1978, in Munich, in accordance with the new custom of holding IUPS Assembly meetings in conjunction with the quadrennial meetings of the International Congress of Applied Psychology. This interim meeting of the Assembly was called on a trial basis for informational exchange only. A report of deliberations of the Executive Committee over the past 2 years was given, providing an excellent opportunity for a full discussion of future plans and possible new projects. It was clear to all who attended that such interim meetings for information exchange were an excellent means of furthering good communication between the Executive Committee and member national societies, and it was enthusiastically agreed that they should be continued.

As a follow-up to the 1976 International Congress of Psychology in Paris, a special symposium was organized at the Munich congress by the Union's project on ethical standards and conduct. The nine papers given at the symposium dealt primarily with ethical standards of scientific research in different cultures and were subsequently published (Holtzman, 1979).

New *Journal* editor and changes in publication policies

Growing dissatisfaction with the current arrangement involving Dunod as publisher of the *International Journal of Psychology* convinced the Committee on Communication and Publications that it was time for a major change. Moreover, Jules Leroux wished to retire as editor. North-Holland (Elsevier) offered the Union a favorable contract, including 6000 Dutch florins of subsidy annually for the editor. Beginning with Volume 14 in 1979, Géry d'Ydewalle, University of Louvain, was selected as the new editor, with US$5000 to be provided annually for support of editorial assistants. A new focus for the *Journal* would be international aspects of psychology other than cross-cultural issues, with special attention to some of the problems in the developing countries.

A new policy was approved for certain psychology journals such as the *German Journal of Psychology* and the anticipated new *French-Language Psychology*. When a reputable, scholarly publication that translates abstracts or articles into a language such as English to promote international scientific psychology asks for support from the Union, the guiding principle of providing non-financial, moral support would be considered. If approved, a brief statement for the journal title page would be authorized along the following lines: "Published under the auspices of the International Union of Psychological Science."

Preliminary plans for the 1980 congress

Considerable time was spent at the 1977 meeting of the Executive Committee discussing detailed plans for the 1980 International Congress of Psychology under the leadership of Klix, Professors Manfred Vorwerg (Leipzig), chairman of the Organizing Committee, and Jurgen Ruckert (Berlin), Secretary-General of the congress. Chairman of the Program Committee would be Hubert Sydow, and Adolph Kossakowski would be President of the Society for Psychology of the GDR. The German Democratic Republic would provide a subsidy of 300,000 marks. A historical exhibit on Wilhelm Wundt and other pioneers of psychology would be featured, together with a display of early psychological instruments, and major receptions and cultural events were being planned. A loan of up to US$4000 from IUPS in support of pre-Congress activities was approved, with the understanding that the loan would be paid back to IUPS from revenues received in registration of participants for the congress.

Members of the Committee for Research and Special Projects reported on several major projects, as well as two small ones supported in part by IUPS funds: an international study of the role and status of women (Montmollin); another international survey of ethical standards and conduct (Holtzman); research on child rearing and socialization in Africa (Durojaiye); the impact of educational television upon young children (Holtzman); and the results of two small IUPS grants of US$1600 to Jean Morval for an environmental psychology project headquartered in Canada and of US$1000 to Otto Klineberg for completing an international project on college student attitudes.

The first Executive Committee meeting in Latin America, Mexico City 1979

A meeting of the Executive Committee on July 15–18, 1979, in Mexico City was the first of many to follow in which the time and place of the meeting were chosen to take advantage of travel subsidies for Executive Committee members offered by a national society in exchange for lectures at a local university or at a national meeting of the society. Such support proved to be an important way of conserving the very modest funds within IUPS for such travel, while also developing stronger ties between the Executive Committee and national member societies. The second Mexican Congress of Psychology was being held during this period, and the sponsoring Mexican Society had issued an invitation earlier for the Union to hold its 23rd International Congress of Psychology in Mexico. The National University of Mexico provided generous travel support for most of the Executive Committee members in return for their active participation on the program of the Mexican Congress of Psychology. The congress was attended by over 3000 psychologists and students. It was important for members of the Executive Committee to see at first hand the resources and capabilities of the Mexican psychologists to hold a major world congress. The meetings in Mexico City clearly demonstrated such capabilities although the 1984 International Congress of Psychology was actually held in Acapulco, a resort city well equipped for large meetings.

Contributions to the International Year of the Child

The Union made several important contributions to UNESCO's International Year of the Child in 1979. First, UNESCO's Education Division agreed to publish and distribute the results of the 3-year study by IUPS on the impact of educational television upon children. Then the French conference on the Psychology of the Child was held, sponsored jointly by IUPS and the French Society of Psychology, using reserve funds from the 1976 Paris congress. And finally, a second conference was held in September 1979 at the University of Texas in Austin, sponsored by UNESCO and the Hogg Foundation for Mental Health under the auspices of IUPS. Entitled "Trends in Social Science Research on Children," this conference was initiated by the Division for the Study of Development within UNESCO and involved psychologists from throughout the world, including Diaz-Guerrero, Tomaszewski, Durojaiye, and Holtzman from the Union's Executive Committee. The conference's recommendations were well received by UNESCO and resulted in collaborative program activities for some years to come between IUPS and the Division for the Study of Development.

Women's role and status

A 2-year grant of US$34,000 was also received from UNESCO through ISSC for the IUPS project on Women's Role and Status initiated by Montmollin.

An initial research conference was held in Austin in the spring of 1979 at which a four-country cross-cultural study was developed involving principal investigators from France (Germaine Montmollin), Tunisia (Taoufik Rabah), Mexico (Graciela Rodriguez), and the United States (Georgia Babladelis). Eduardo Almeida from the National University of Mexico agreed to serve as the overall project coordinator. A report of findings on several thousand women surveyed in the four countries was presented at a special symposium at the 1980 International Congress of Psychology and was published as a Special Issue of the *International Journal of Psychology* (Montmollin, 1983).

Final plans for the 22nd International Congress of Psychology to be held in Leipzig on July 6–12, 1980, were also presented and approved at the 1979 Executive Committee meeting. By mail ballot, the Dominican Association of Psychology was admitted as a new member and the International Association for Cross-Cultural Psychology was welcomed as a new affiliate of the Union.

Revised procedures for admission of new members

Taking note of a resolution by the French Society of Psychology to discontinue mail ballot procedures for admission of new members, the Executive Committee proposed revised procedures that were later unanimously approved by the Assembly in 1980. Henceforth, the Secretary-General would send out the petition for membership and accompanying information to all members of the IUPS for informal review and comment prior to review by the Executive Committee at its next annual meeting. The voting representatives of all member societies would be urged to communicate with their societies concerning the petition, so that comments could be collated by the Secretary-General in preparation for Executive Committee discussion. As in the past, only after review and approval by the Executive Committee would formal mail ballots be sent to the voting representatives of member societies.

A change in publisher

The *International Journal of Psychology* underwent major changes in 1979. In addition to the successful transfer of publisher from Dunod to North-Holland and the appointment of d'Ydewalle as the new editor, steps were taken to facilitate subscriptions from socialist countries, plans were made for widely publicizing the *Journal* under a new format by North-Holland, and the Executive Committee approved a new set of principles proposed by Rosenzweig for subsidizing free subscriptions. Member societies with less than 500 members would receive 1 free subscription, societies with less than 1000 but more than 500 would have 2 subscriptions, societies with more than 1000 would receive 3 subscriptions, and each member society would be asked to name the recipients who should receive the allotted journals.

International Directory of Psychologists, third edition

Continuing delays in completion of the third edition of the *International Directory of Psychologists* were discouraging to the Executive Committee in 1979. After 12 years of planning and delays, there were rumors that Gunther Reinert, the European co-editor, was ill and that no publisher had yet been contracted. North-Holland offered to publish the *Directory* in time for the Leipzig Congress, provided the manuscript was completed in short order. Eugene Jacobson, the American co-editor of the *Directory*, was under pressure from the US National Science Foundation, a financial sponsor, to complete the *Directory*. With the help of Reinert's assistant, Detlef Herrig at the University of Trier, Jacobson quickly finished the manuscript, North-Holland published the third edition of the *International Directory of Psychologists*, and it was finally presented at the Leipzig International Congress in 1980. Unfortunately Reinert failed to live long enough to see the final product of his many years of effort. The third edition contained information on approximately 17,000 psychologists from 100 countries, exclusive of the United States. (It was considered unnecessary to include the United States because the American Psychological Association's annual directory provided a listing of most American psychologists.)

Psychology returns to its origins by sponsoring the 22nd International Congress of Psychology, Leipzig, German Democratic Republic, 1980

The 22nd International Congress of Psychology was held in Leipzig, on July 6–12, 1980, with 4015 individuals registered from 58 countries. The congress attracted a large number of psychologists from the socialist countries of Eastern Europe. Opening addresses were given by Friedhart Klix, President of the congress, Hans-Joachim Bohme, Minister for Higher and Technical Education of the GDR, and Arthur Summerfield, President of the IUPS. Klix spoke on the evolution of cognitive processes from animal to contemporary human problem solving, and Summerfield commented on the special historical significance of meeting in Leipzig 100 years after the founding by Wilhelm Wundt of the first psychological laboratory at the University of Leipzig.

The main body of the congress consisted of 37 invited lectures by distinguished psychologists from throughout the world; 57 symposia on a wide range of topics; 62 thematic sessions comprised of individual papers; 10 psychological films; and 36 free sessions—nearly 1300 contributions. A total of 42 young psychologists were welcomed from 13 countries; 72 exhibitors displayed their materials and instruments; and 13,000 tickets were sold for cultural events associated with the congress. Income was approximately 500,000 marks, and the Government of the

GDR paid the difference between income received and expenses for the congress.

The opening addresses and invited lectures were bound and distributed at the congress in a preliminary version of the congress proceedings. All of the symposia and papers presented in the thematic sessions were also listed in this early version by title and author, together with an alphabetical listing of most registrants and their mailing addresses. The authors of presentations came from 40 different countries, the largest number being from the host country, the GDR. Large delegations of at least 100 psychologists also attended from neighboring Czechoslovakia, Hungary, Poland, and the Federal Republic of Germany, as well as from the United States and Japan, testifying once again to the importance of holding international congresses in different parts of the world as a way of involving a greater diversity of psychologists in global activities.

Selected papers presented at the Congress were edited and published in 1982 by North-Holland in a series of ten volumes as follows:

- Richter-Heinrich, E., & Miller, N.E. (Eds.), *Biofeedback—Basic Problems and Clinical Applications*
- Schmidt, H.D., & Tembrock, G. (Eds.), *Evolution and Determination of Animal and Human Behavior*
- Kossakowski, A., & Obuchowski, K. (Eds.), *Progress in Psychology of Personality*
- Hacker, W., Volpert, W., & von Cranach, M. (Eds.), *Cognitive and Motivational Aspects of Action*
- Bachmann, W., & Udris, I. (Eds.), *Mental Load and Stress in Activity*
- Klix, F., Hoffmann, J., & Van der Meer, E. (Eds.), *Cognitive Research in Psychology*
- Glaser, R., & Lompscher, J. (Eds.), *Cognitive and Motivational Aspects of Instruction*
- Hiebsch, H., Brandstatter, H., & Kelley, H.H. (Eds.), *Social Psychology*
- Geissler, H.-G., & Petzold, P. (Eds.), *Psychophysical Judgement and the Process of Perception*
- Groner, R., & Fraisse, P. (Eds.), *Cognition and Eye Movements*
- Sinz, R., & Rosenzweig, M.R. (Eds.), *Psychophysiology: Memory, Motivation and Event-Related Potentials in Mental Operations.*

The IUPS Assembly met twice during the congress, once on July 9, when they heard various reports and drew up nomination slates for election of the President and the two Vice-Presidents, and again on July 11 when officers were elected and other items of business were conducted. A total of 63 voting representatives were present from 33 different countries at one session or the other. Representatives of the five international associations affiliated with the Union were also present and gave brief reports of their activities. The Assembly accepted the invitation of the Australian Psychological Society to hold the 1988 International Congress in Sydney.

New officers elected

Friedhart Klix was elected President of the Union for the next 4 years, and Rosenzweig and Tomaszewski were elected Vice-Presidents. Hiroshi Azuma (University of Tokyo), Géry d'Ydewalle (University of Louvain, Belgium), Germaine Montmollin (University of Paris), Ronald Taft (Monash University, Australia), Martti Takala (Jyvaskyla University, Finland), and Durganand Sinha (Allahabad University, India) were newly elected members of the Executive Committee, joining Diaz-Guerrero, Durojaiye, Lomov, and Summerfield, who were re-elected.

The Assembly also elected the Chinese Psychological Society as the 44th member of the Union and heard brief reports from the Secretary-General, the Treasurer, and each of the committee chairmen. As proposed by the International Social Science Council, a Resolution on Free Circulation of Scientists was reviewed and unanimously adopted by the Assembly (see Figure 11.2). Diaz-Guerrero and Mario Cicero, President of the Mexican Society of Psychology, gave a brief report on preliminary planning for the 23rd International Congress of Psychology to be held in Mexico early in September 1984.

Friedhart Klix: President of the 22nd International Congress of Psychology, Leipzig, 1980, and later President of IUPsyS 1980–1984.

The Wilhelm Wundt Special Fund

Upon the invitation of Manfred Vorwerg, Chairman of the Organizing Committee for the Leipzig Congress, the Assembly approved the establishment of the Wilhelm Wundt Special Fund under the auspices of the Union to support research in the field of psychological history and to provide for scientific exchange with the aim of preserving the Wundt legacy. Support from the Government of the GDR for this international project was assured. Execution of the plan was left in the hands of psychologists within the GDR, with external advice to be provided by an international committee formed for the purpose.

Organization of the new Executive Committee

At the closing session of the 1980 Executive Committee meetings, Holtzman, Pawlik, and Bélanger were reappointed as Secretary-General, Deputy Secretary-General, and Treasurer, respectively. Continuing as Chairman of Communication and Publications, Rosenzweig reported that North-Holland had agreed to increase the number of pages per volume of the *International Journal of Psychology* by at least one third. The actual number of pages increased from 308 in 1980 to 420 in 1981, and to 504 in 1982, an increase of 64% in only 2 years. Plans were also launched for the compilation and publication by North-Holland of a new edition for the *International Directory of Psychologists*. Pawlik was named chairman of a committee consisting of Montmollin, Rosenzweig, d'Ydewalle, and Holtzman to

FIGURE 11.2

Free circulation of scientists

Considering that IUPS is a non-political organization strongly adhering to the principle that scientists from all parts of the world have the right to participate in its activities and in those of its Member Associations with regard to race, religion, political philosophy, ethnic origin, citizenship, language, or sex;

Considering that IUPS exists in order to promote active cooperation in scientific matters among scientists from all parts of the world, regardless of the political structure of their governments and that it is a well-established principle that scientific meetings shall not be disturbed by political statements or by any activities of a political nature;

Noting that invaluable work carried out by the International Council of Scientific Unions (ICSU) to improve scientific communication and cooperation, also reflected in the Resolution on Political Non-Discrimination adopted by ICSU in 1958, in the Resolutions on the Free Circulation of Scientists adopted by ICSU in 1963, 1972, 1974, and 1976, and in the Resolution on the Free Circulation of Scientists adopted by the International Social Science Council in 1979,

The General Assembly of IUPS has unanimously adopted at Leipzig, GDR, the following Resolution:

> The IUPS affirms the right of the scientists of any country or territory to adhere to, or to associate with, international scientific activity without regard to race, religion, political philosophy, ethnicity, or sex and confirms its basic policy of political non-discrimination.

Such adherence or association has no implication with respect to recognition of the government of the country or its policies.

The IUPS is prepared to recognize the academy, research council, national committee, or other bona fide scientific group representing scientific activity of any country or territory acting under a government de facto or de jure that controls it, subject only to payment of subscription and submission of required reports.

Meetings or assemblies of IUPS or of its dependent organisms such as special committees and commissions shall be held in countries which permit participation of every national member of IUPS or of the dependent organisms of IUPS concerned, and allow free discussion and prompt dissemination of information related to such meetings.

In holding IUPS meetings and meetings of IUPS scientific and special committees, the Union shall take all measures within its powers to ensure the fundamental right of participation, without any discrimination, of the representatives of every member of IUPS concerned and of invited observers.

develop a proposal for support of the fourth edition by the Regional Participation Fund of UNESCO. The proposal was subsequently submitted through the Federal Republic of Germany's National Commission to UNESCO as part of the 1981-83 Participation Program, but only US$2000 was approved. Although the American Psychological Association donated US$500 for the new directory, the available amount fell short of what was needed. Pawlik later agreed to work out a new plan involving the publication services of North-Holland and close cooperation by IUPS member societies, who would have to submit camera-ready copy that he could then edit.

Executive Committee meeting, Caracas 1981

Erik Becker Becker, a member of the Assembly from Venezuela, invited the Executive Committee to hold its 1981 meeting in Caracas on September 8–11. Travel support was generously provided by the Venezuelan Federation of Psychologists in return for lectures at the National University by Executive Committee members.

Major new projects

Several new projects as well as ongoing activities were reviewed by the Executive Committee under the leadership of President Klix, who emphasized the importance of involving more psychologists from member societies in the Union's projects. Five major project areas were outlined, together with the naming of individuals responsible for each: (1) Child and human development (Holtzman); (2) Man-machine systems (Klix); (3) Psychology and the Third World (Sinha); (4) Man and the biosphere (Rosenzweig and Klix); and (5) Professional and legal issues in psychology (Montmollin). Reports from a 2-day meeting in January 1981 of Klix, Holtzman, Pawlik, and Montmollin with officials of ISSC, UNESCO, and ICSU concerning these and other possible new IUPS programs were sufficiently encouraging to stimulate extensive discussion by the Executive Committee.

Among the major projects under way, a second international conference on human development with substantial involvement of IUPS, supported financially by UNESCO's Division for the Study of Human Development, was held in Doha, State of Qatar, May 9-12, 1981. Papers dealing with childhood inequalities and development presented by Diaz-Guerrero, Durojaiye, Holtzman, and Tomaszewski, together with contributions by 16 other social scientists, were published for UNESCO by the University of Qatar in both English and Arabic editions (UNESCO, 1982). Plans were also announced for a third UNESCO-sponsored conference concerned with the impact of psychology on Third World development to be held in conjunction with the 20th International Congress of Applied Psychology in July 1982. Organized by Sinha and Holtzman, this 2-day symposium was subsequently published in a special issue of the *International Journal of Psychology* (Sinha & Holtzman, 1984).

The Secretary-General announced that the Foundation for Child Development in New York had granted IUPS US$4900 to support the planning of a new international network of child research centers, an idea that grew out of the Austin UNESCO conference in September 1979. Originally under the leadership of Nicholas Hobbs of Vanderbilt University, the project had been taken over by Holtzman and IUPS with assistance from Wolfgang Schwendler of UNESCO. A 2-day meeting earlier in 1981 in Ottawa, Canada, under the auspices of the Canadian National Commission to UNESCO, resulted in a list of nearly 70 centers across the world, most of which subsequently joined the network. Through the Secretary-General's office, a periodic newsletter was issued to reinforce the network. At its meeting in July 1983, the International Society for the Study of Behavioural Development formally adopted the network. A world-wide *International Directory of Human Development Research Centers* was compiled under the direction of Harold Stevenson, University of Michigan, and was widely distributed in 1985.

The success of the *German Journal of Psychology* as an English-language journal containing abstracts and reviews of psychological publications in German spawned not only a review journal for original articles in French as an outgrowth of the 1976 Paris congress but also a third journal for Spanish language articles. Under the auspices of IUPS, all three English-language review journals aimed at a world-wide distribution of psychological theory and research originally published in a language other than English. Unfortunately, only the *German Journal of Psychology* survived beyond the first few years, the other two succumbing to the pressure of financial deficits. The Federation of German Psychological Associations provided the *German Journal of Psychology* with an annual subvention, assuring its financial stability.

Admission to the International Council of Scientific Unions

A major achievement for IUPS shortly after the 1980 congress in Leipzig was admission to the International Council of Scientific Unions (ICSU) as an Associate Member. For many years the Union had been trying to gain admission to ICSU, but for one reason or another it had never succeeded. Associate membership was viewed as a first step in gaining recognition as a full member, the status enjoyed by other primary scientific disciplines. Recognition by ICSU of psychology as a scientific discipline was important, not only to extend the range of projects and cooperation to other scientific disciplines, but also to accelerate the acceptance of psychology as a science in those countries where it was still classified among social, philosophical, and humanistic disciplines.

Considerable time was spent at the 1981 Executive Committee meeting in developing a multi-faceted plan to ensure successful admission as a full member by the ICSU General Assembly meeting in Cambridge, September 13–17, 1982. Rosenzweig prepared a brief working paper on past relations of IUPS to ICSU. A special committee was appointed by Klix consisting of Rosenzweig, Lomov, and Klix to strengthen the current relations with ICSU, to seek full membership in ICSU, and to develop relevant scientific projects to be undertaken by IUPS in cooperation with ICSU. Together with Summerfield, they agreed to contact influential scientists from other disciplines who were active in ICSU affairs.

Klix, Rosenzweig, and Bélanger met in Paris with the Executive Secretary of ICSU in March 1982, where they learned that assurance of formal support for IUPS admission as a full member must be obtained in advance of the General Assembly meeting. Rosenzweig wrote on behalf of the IUPS to several international unions and national members of ICSU to secure their support. By July, three international unions and six influential national councils or academies had agreed to support the Union's petition. In the drive to become a full member of ICSU, a minor problem arose concerning the use of IUPS as the acronym for the International Union of Psychological Science, since this particular acronym has been used by the International Union of Physiological Science from 1955 when it was admitted to ICSU. It was proposed that IUPS be changed to IUPsyS to avoid conflict, once the Union has been recognized as a full member of ICSU. All of these efforts proved fruitful, and the Union was formally admitted to full membership at ICSU's General Assembly meeting in Cambridge on September 13, 1982.

Executive Committee and Assembly meetings, Edinburgh 1982

Strengthening relations with other international organizations

The Union's Executive Committee meeting in 1982 was held on July 22–24 in Edinburgh immediately prior to the 20th International Congress of Applied Psychology. Relations with international organizations, especially ICSU and ISSC, were reviewed. The International Social Science Council was still going through major changes as a result of negotiations with the International Federation of Social Science Organizations (IFSSO), a loosely knit group of largely governmental agencies and analogous bodies that wanted to have a major role in deliberations by the non-governmental, discipline-oriented organizations that comprised the ISSC. As immediate past-President of ISSC, Summerfield reported that IFSSO was now an integral member of ISSC with voting power but with a status different from the traditional members such as IUPsyS. The addition of IFSSO broadened the base of support for ISSC activities since the social sciences in many countries, especially the socialist and Third World nations, were largely represented by government agencies rather than by private associations. Although IUPsyS would continue to get a small UNESCO

Participants at an international research conference organized by the IUPsyS and held at the 20th International Congress of Applied Psychology in Edinburgh, in July 1982—Front row (left to right): José M. Salazar (Venezuela), Jai B. Sinha (India), *C.C. Jing (China), unidentified woman, *Michael O.A. Durojaiye (Nigeria), Cigdem Kagitcibasi (Turkey), Albert Charns (UK), *Durganand Sinha (India), *Hiroshi Azuma (Japan), *Alfredo V. Lagmay (Philippines). Back row (left to right): Ida Fisher (Assistant to Wayne Holtzman), Wolfgang Schwendler (UNESCO), *Rogelio Díaz-Guerrero (Mexico), Levon Melikian (Qatar), Robert Serpell (Zambia), Harry Triandis (USA), *Wayne Holtzman (USA). *Members of the Union's Assembly in 1982.

subsidy through ISSC, direct research contracts with UNESCO or with ISSC, especially where an interdisciplinary, international project was undertaken, would be the area of greatest potential future growth for IUPsyS as far as the social sciences were concerned. Summerfield gave as an example a new ISSC project on which his network of environmental psychology was working, the outcome of which would be published in an ISSC monograph.

With respect to other international organizations, Pawlik represented the Union at meetings of the International Test Commission, and d'Ydewalle was the Union's representative at meetings of the International Committee for Social Science Information and Documentation. Several members of the Finnish Psychological Society under the leadership of Kirsti Lagerspetz, had proposed that IUPsyS initiate a discussion among members concerning the establishment of an international group of psychologists interested in promoting peace and resisting nuclear arms. Although the Union was unable to provide any financial support for this effort, the topic was judged to be an important one. The 1984 International Congress of Psychology in Mexico presented an ideal venue for launching the special interest group called Psychologists for Peace and Against Nuclear War.

Review of the Statutes

Once again it was deemed necessary to propose revisions in the Union's Statutes and Rules of Procedure to take account of a proposed change in the structure and amount of dues and to include committee chairmen as ex-officio members of the Executive Committee. A major unresolved problem was how to deal with delinquent dues payments, especially in view of the world economic recession and serious distortions of currency exchange that were severely impairing the ability of some members to make timely payments. The Treasurer was instructed to prepare for approval by the 1984 Assembly a new scale of payments that would allow a member to continue in a non-voting status while paying no dues.

International Directory of Psychologists, fourth edition

Considerable progress under the leadership of Pawlik was made on the fourth edition of the *International Directory of Psychologists*. The Australian Psychological Society voluntarily contributed US$500 in support of the preparation of the *Directory*, thereby matching the earlier amount donated by the American Psychological Association. Shortly thereafter, the Federation of German Psychological Societies and the Japanese Psychological Association also made substantial contributions. All but 1 of 16 member societies responding to Pawlik's earlier survey were strongly in favor of submitting camera-ready copy of individual entries, which could then be compiled by the editor and published by North-Holland.

Given the very small available budget and the press of time, each society would have to take full responsibility for the precise typing of each entry on blue-line paper that could then be photocopied directly into the printing process. By the time of the 1983 Executive Committee meeting in Sydney, Australia, 85% of IUPsyS members had responded favorably. Several non-member societies from Third World countries were also included, thanks to the cooperation of the Union's affiliate, the International Association of Cross-Cultural Psychology. A deadline of September 1984 was established for receipt of final copy, and the fourth edition of the *International Directory of Psychologists* was published on schedule (Pawlik, 1985), a major accomplishment requiring skillful management and the excellent cooperation of many individuals.

The attractiveness of the *International Journal of Psychology* had improved considerably under d'Ydewalle's editorship and North-Holland's management. In 1982, 26 articles out of 139 submissions had been published. By 1984, of 164 manuscripts received, 47 were published representing first contributors from 39 different countries. Special Issues were proving particularly attractive and the number of pages per volume had grown to almost 600 by 1982. However, paid subscriptions tended to hover around 800. The contract with North-Holland was up for renewal in December 1983, and renegotiation was undertaken by d'Ydewalle as editor and Rosenzweig as Chairman of the Committee on Communication and Publications.

New projects with ICSU

New projects within IUPsyS continued to grow as a result of ICSU membership. A first international workshop on man-machine systems was organized by Klix and was held on July 29, 1982, in conjunction with the Edinburgh Applied Congress. This area later proved to be particularly relevant to the interests of other scientific disciplines within ICSU, as evidenced by a grant to the Union from ICSU of US$4000 in 1983 and US$8500 in 1984 to support international conferences. The Man-Machine Interactive Network (MACINTER) that developed from these activities under the Union held its first international seminar on October 15–19, 1984, at Humboldt University, Berlin, attended by 94 scientists from 16 different countries (Klix, 1985). These initial efforts were sufficiently encouraging that ICSU invited IUPsyS participation in its Science Education Project, in particular, conferences on science education to be held in Bangalore, India, and Ottawa, Canada in 1985. It was generally agreed that the Union could make significant contributions in learning, cognition, and instructional psychology. IUPsyS invited Robert Glaser, an expert from the University of Pittsburgh on instructional psychology and its contribution to science education, to represent the Union at both conferences, but he could only attend the Ottawa conference.

References

French Society of Psychology. (1978). *Proceedings of the XXIst International Congress of Psychology*. Paris: Presses Universitaires de France.

González Solaz, M.J. (1998). *Los congresos internacionales de psicologia (1963–1984)*. Unpublished doctoral dissertation, Valencia, Spain.

Holtzman, W.H. (Ed.) (1979). The IUPS project on professional ethics and conduct. *International Journal of Psychology, 14*, 107–149.

Klix, F. (1985). Report on the first network seminar of the International Union of Psychological Sciences on man-computer interaction research (MACINTER). *International Journal of Psychology, 20*, 373–378.

Montmollin, G. de, (Ed.) (1983). Roles and status of women: A psychological perspective. Special issue of *International Journal of Psychology, 18*, 1–142.

Pawlik, K. (Ed.) (1985). *International Directory of Psychologists (Exclusive of the USA)*. Amsterdam: North-Holland.

Sinha, D., & Holtzman, W.H. (Eds.) (1984). The impact of psychology on Third World development. Special issue of *International Journal of Psychology, 19*, 1–192.

UNESCO (1982). *Childhood inequality and development*. Doha: University of Qatar.

Continued initiatives in the globalization of psychology (1984–1988)

12

Final plans for the 23rd International Congress of Psychology to be held in Acapulco, Mexico, in early September 1984 were presented by Diaz-Guerrero to the rest of the Executive Committee for discussion at their meetings in 1982 and 1983. Preliminary plans for the 1988 congress to be held in Sydney, Australia, were outlined by Taft, who stated that the Australians would have to raise $300,000 by 1986 in order to hold 3,000 hotel rooms for the congress. A meeting of the Executive Committee in Sydney, Australia, on August 28–September 1, 1983, at the same time that the Australian Psychological Society was holding its annual meeting, was made possible by a generous travel subsidy from the Australians. In return for the travel grant of US$11,383, the members of the Executive Committee gave major presentations, participated in social receptions, and held conversation hours with Australian psychologists as a featured part of the society's meeting.

A special joint session of the Executive Committee and the Australian Congress Planning Committee, as well as a tour of the congress facilities under construction, proved very advantageous to both groups. Many questions arose that could easily be settled in conference. Australia would be celebrating its national bicentennial throughout 1988, and many international conferences were being planned for the new facilities that had not yet been constructed.

The 23rd International Congress of Psychology, Acapulco, Mexico 1984

The 23rd International Congress of Psychology was held in Acapulco, Mexico, September 2-7, 1984, the first time that a psychological congress of this magnitude had ever been held in Latin America. The occasion was a challenging one for the members of the Mexican Society of Psychology, but they carried it off well in spite of a number of crises arising from financial difficulties. The Mexicans had counted on substantial government support, only a small part of which was forthcoming due to a severe economic depression and currency collapse that hit Mexico in the early 1980s. The organizers had to rely almost entirely on registration fees to support the

Rogelio Diaz-Guerrero: President of the 23rd International Congress of Psychology, Acapulco, 1984.

congress. Difficulties in communications and delays in advance registration created considerable anxiety among the congress organizers, who revised their budget downward to the low level of US$156,000, requiring fewer than 2300 registrants to break even financially. Rogelio Diaz-Guerrero was President of the congress, Graciela Rodriguez served as Chairman of the Organizing Committee, Isabel Reyes was Secretary-General, and Juan José Sanchez-Sosa was Chairman of the Program Committee—all senior professors at the National University of Mexico who were dependent largely upon hundreds of volunteers to organize and host the congress. Fortunately, nearly 3200 individuals participated in the congress.

The scientific program consisted of 17 invited lectures, 77 symposia (several with additional discussion sessions), 98 thematic sessions with an average of 10 papers each, 10 thematic sessions of the young psychologists program with an average of 8 papers in each, 18 workshops, and 24 sessions of special interest meetings. Although previous congresses had encouraged other international groups to hold special interest meetings at the congress, the number of such satellite meetings at the 1984 congress was impressive. Among the groups holding such meetings at the congress were the International Society of Comparative Psychology, the International Test Commission, the International Network for Child Development, the Experimental and Animal Behavior Section of the International Union of Biological Sciences, the Division of Environmental Psychology of the International Association of Applied Psychology, and the Cheiron Society for the History of the Social and Behavioral Sciences. Most of the sessions

Presidium of the opening ceremony at the 1984 Congress in Acapulco, Mexico. From left to right: Friedhart Klix, Union President; Cervantes-Delgado representing the Governor of the Mexican State of Guerrero; Guillermo Soberon, Mexican Minister of Health representing the President of Mexico; Darvelio Castano, Dean of the School of Psychology at the National University of Mexico; Wayne Holtzman, Secretary General of the Union; and Salvador Malo, Director for Scientific Research at the Ministry of Education.

were held in the Acapulco Convention Center while others were held in nearby hotels.

The presentations covered almost every field of scientific and applied psychology as well as the theory and history of psychology. Within the area of experimental psychology there was special emphasis on neuropsychology of cognition and information processing, sensation and perception, ocular movements in learning, motivation, and psycholinguistics. A great many contributions of an applied nature were concerned with topics of health psychology, peace psychology, assessment, psychotherapy, and with advances in clinical, educational, and organizational psychology, as well as problems of labor and social psychology.

Publication of the congress proceedings followed a different plan from that used in the past. Major presentations, individual papers, and symposia were organized under the overall editorship of Diaz-Guerrero, Holtzman, and Rosenzweig in a series of nine books, each containing a relatively homogeneous set of contributions, published by North-Holland in 1985. Each book was organized and edited by one or two well-known psychologists who attended the congress. The areas covered by the nine books and their editors were as follows:

- James L. McGaugh (Ed.), *Biological Processes and Theory*
- Rogelio Diaz-Guerrero (Ed.), *Cross-Cultural/National Social Psychology*
- Géry d'Ydewalle (Ed.), *Cognition, Information, Motivation*
- Juan José Sanchez-Sosa (Ed.), *Health and Clinical Psychology*
- Janet T. Spence and Carroll E. Izard (Eds.), *Motivation, Emotion, and Personality*
- Charles J. Brainerd and V.F. Reyna (Eds.), *Developmental Psychology*
- Florence L. Denmark (Ed.), *Social/Ecological Psychology and Psychology of Women*
- E.E. Roskam (Ed.), *Measurement and Personality*
- R. Groner, G.W. McConkie, and C. Menz (Eds.), *Eye Movements and Human Information Processing*

New officers

The Union's Assembly met on two afternoons, September 4 and 6, to hold elections and conduct other business. A total of 72 voting representatives from 36 countries were present at one or both sessions. After 12 years as Secretary-General, Holtzman retired and was elected President. Diaz-Guerrero and Lomov were elected Vice-Presidents. Qicheng C. Jing (Institute of Psychology, Chinese National Academy of Science) was elected as a new member of the Executive Committee, joined by Azuma, Durojaiye, d'Ydewalle, Klix, Montmollin, Rosenzweig, Sinha, Taft, and Takala who were re-elected.

Wayne H. Holtzman: Secretary-General of the IUPsyS (1972–1984), and later President of the IUPsyS (1984–1988).

Revision of the Statutes to accommodate a different kind of national member

Revision of the Statutes and Rules of Procedure to change the dues structure and amount (Statutes II–8 and Rules II–1) and to permit a different kind of national member (Statutes II–6 and 7) proved to be important items of business for the Assembly. As a member of the US National Academy of Sciences, Rosenzweig had been sounding out his colleagues concerning the desirability of following the lead of all the other scientific organizations represented in the Academy: by having the national member of the Union from the United States be the US National Academy of Sciences, rather than the American Psychological Association (APA). The Academy then would appoint psychologists to a new US National Committee for IUPsyS who were drawn from slates of distinguished psychologists nominated by the several leading psychological associations in the United States. Funded in part by the Academy, the National Committee would designate two of its members to represent American psychological science as delegates to the Union's Assembly. Since because of its large size the APA would have the right to nominate a majority of the committee's founding members, it graciously consented in advance to relinquish its role as the national member of the Union. Moreover, under the proposed new dues structure for IUPsyS, APA would have had to pay a substantially larger amount of dues each year, a prospect that would be eliminated by the new plan since the National Academy of Sciences would be responsible for the dues.

The stage had been carefully set in advance so that no opposition was encountered when the Assembly was asked to approve Statutes 6 and 7. Shortly thereafter, the US National Academy of Sciences became the official national member as the APA stepped down (Rosenzweig & Flattau, 1988). Getting the Academy to become a national member of the Union required successive actions that were carefully coordinated. The Union had to change its Statutes, the APA had to agree to the exchange, and the Academy had to agree to become the Union's national member with its National Committee serving as its active representative in the Union. Fortunately, Rosenzweig was in a key position to aid in these steps as a member of the Union's Executive Committee, of the APA Council, and of the US National Academy of Sciences. At about the same time, a Canadian National Committee for Psychology was formed by the Canadian National Research Council and accepted as Canada's national member by the Union.

Only very few countries have thus far taken advantage of this new idea. Nevertheless, the plan has proved to be highly valuable in those countries where the change has taken place. Not only has it been a useful mechanism for involving more than one national psychological organization in IUPsyS affairs, but it has also resulted in substantially increased support for international initiatives in psychology by assuring the support of prestigious national science academies for special projects. A variation of the US plan with some of the same advantages has been adopted by Belgium

(Nuttin, 1986) and Sweden (Nilsson, 1988). In each case, a National Committee of Psychology has been formed under the Royal Academy of Sciences. The committee appoints delegates to the IUPsyS Assembly from the national society of psychology that still retains its official membership in the Union. This plan works well where there is only one recognized major national society of psychology.

At the 1984 Assembly meetings, the Nicaraguan Association of Psychology was admitted to the Union as its 45th member, and the International Society for Comparative Psychology was approved as a new affiliate of the Union. Of several attractive invitations received, the Assembly voted to hold the 1992 congress in Brussels, Belgium.

The Union's Executive Committee met on two occasions in Acapulco, the outgoing one on September 1–2 when most of the Union's business was discussed just prior to the congress, and the newly elected one late on September 7 for organizational purposes only. Klix invited all members to participate in the Ebbinghaus Symposium, July 1–6, 1985, at Humboldt University, Berlin, a symposium that he had organized with IUPsyS encouragement following the Leipzig Congress (Klix & Hagendorf, 1985). One of a series of special international conferences held in the German Democratic Republic, this symposium reviewed current trends in the psychophysics of cognitive processes, organizational principles of human memory, mechanisms underlying intelligence, and related topics in honor of the pioneering experimental work of Hermann Ebbinghaus on memory in Berlin 100 years earlier.

Relations established with the World Health Organization

A new project was announced by Holtzman involving collaboration between IUPsyS and the Division of Mental Health, World Health Organization (WHO), in Geneva. Stimulated initially by an invitation received from Norman Sartorius, a psychologist/psychiatrist serving as Director of Mental Health for WHO, the project involved a comprehensive review of roles and functions of psychologists in the provision of health care, in teaching in health care settings, and in health-related research in different countries throughout the world. With minor financial support and good cooperation from many psychologists, a report on this project was first published by WHO (Holtzman, Evans, Kennedy, & Iscoe, 1987) and then reprinted and translated elsewhere to insure wide international circulation among public health officers as well as psychologists. The publication spawned a new IUPsyS Network on Health Psychology that still continues to operate.

Continued relations with UNESCO, ISSC, and ICSU

Interest in the support of IUPsyS projects by the other three primary international agencies, UNESCO, ISSC, and ICSU, continued to grow. The International Network of Child Research Centers was gradually being taken over by the International Society for the Study of Behavioral Development, the MACINTER program on cognition and computers received financial support from ICSU, and three new interdisciplinary initiatives were getting underway, two with ISSC and one with ICSU. The small group of psychologists under Finnish and German leadership who were concerned with promoting psychological research on international peace joined forces with like-minded social scientists under a broader ISSC mandate. A related development occurred at ICSU, when Arthur Summerfield was invited to represent IUPsyS as a member of the ICSU Committee on the Environmental Consequences of Nuclear War. And finally, still another opportunity for psychology opened up with ISSC support of a new interdisciplinary study of Youth, Employment, and Technological Change. The mid-1980s proved to be a time of vigorous expansion of research and special projects under the leadership of the IUPsyS Executive Committee, leading to a new era of international collaboration among psychologists.

Executive Committee meeting, Austin 1985

The 1985 meetings of the Executive Committee were held in Austin, Texas, on August 29–31, at the Hogg Foundation for Mental Health, The University of Texas, with partial subsidy of meeting expenses by the Foundation. Robert Farr, London School of Economics and Political Science, was appointed Deputy Secretary-General, completing the roster of psychologists on the Executive Committee. As Deputy Secretary-General, he also served as co-editor, together with Pawlik, of the Platform Section for the *International Journal of Psychology*. Rosenzweig was reappointed Chairman of the Committee on Communication and Publications, with the three *Journal* editors—d'Ydewalle, Pawlik, and Farr—as members.

Guidelines for new projects

As Chairman of the Committee on Research and Special Projects, Klix proposed, and the Executive Committee adopted, guidelines for the promotion of new projects based on three goals: (1) To develop the exchange of ideas and scientific information among psychologists in different countries; (2) to aid scholars or graduate students in different countries to go abroad to work at universities and laboratories; and (3) to cooperate with other international and national organizations, especially within interdisciplinary research projects of WHO. ISSC, and ICSU. Based upon these guidelines, five international network projects and their coordinators were approved for modest funding from IUPsyS funds for one year: Child Research Centers (Holtzman); Man-Computer Interaction (Klix); Behavioral Ecology/Environmental Psychology (Pawlik); Psychology in the Third World (Sinha); and Cognitive Science, Artificial Intelligence, and Neuroscience (d'Ydewalle).

Relations between IUPsyS and both ICSU and ISSC had settled down somewhat in the past year with greater involvement of the Union in the two international organizations. Klaus Helkama of Finland represented the Union on the ISSC peace project and Taft served as liaison to the ISSC project, Youth, Employment, and Technological Change. Pawlik and d'Ydewalle agreed to serve as official representatives to the ISSC General Assembly. In addition, d'Ydewalle was elected Chairman of the International Committee on Social Sciences Information and Documentation. With respect to ICSU, Klix participated in the Ottawa Symposium on Global Change as well as the Ringberg Conference in Europe dealing with ICSU policies, Pawlik was a participant in the SCOPE project, and Roger Russell served on the steering committee for the International Biosciences Network.

Subvention funds from ISSC and ICSU continued as in the past in spite of serious budget cuts at UNESCO. This strengthened relationship between IUPsyS and both ICSU and ISSC was due largely to closer attention to global concerns in project planning. A better understanding between the Union and all three Paris-based international organizations was achieved by a series of informal meetings between officers of the Union and leaders of UNESCO, ISSC, and ICSU that were held in Paris on March 13–16, 1985.

A final report on the 1984 Acapulco congress revealed that the Mexican Organizing Committee produced a net profit of approximately $10,500 in spite of initial fears of a deficit. In view of the heavy responsibilities and stringent cost-saving efforts of the understaffed Organizing Committee, the Executive Committee approved a request by the Mexican Society of Psychology to allocate these funds for the purpose of obtaining permanent offices in Mexico City for the society's headquarters. Detailed plans for the 1988 congress in Australia and advance planning for the 1992 congress in Belgium were approved as presented by Taft and d'Ydewalle, respectively.

Assembly and Executive Meetings, Jerusalem and Zurich 1986

Jerusalem

A meeting of the Union's Assembly for the purpose of information exchange took place on July 15, 1986, in Jerusalem, Israel, in conjunction with the International Congress of Applied Psychology. Reports of Union activities since the 1984 Assembly meetings and plans for forthcoming project activities and international congresses formed the basis for discussion by the 26 Assembly members present.

Zurich

Immediately following the International Congress of Applied Psychology, the Executive Committee met in Zurich, Switzerland on July 19–23. The committee's meeting was joined by Ronald King and Barry Fallon, Chairman of the Organizing Committee and Treasurer, respectively, for the 1988 congress to be held in Sydney, Australia. Norman Sartorius, Director of the WHO Division of Mental Health, was also present part of the time to discuss ways in which the relationship between WHO and the Union could be strengthened.

Preparations for the Sydney congress

An extensive written report on the organizational and current state of preparations for the 1988 congress, augmented by the commentary of King and Fallon, led to a detailed discussion that comprised a major part of the meetings. A Congress Management Committee was formed consisting of the eight primary executives ranging from President and Secretary-General to Marketing Director. The policy-setting International Congress Committee was comprised of the Management Committee plus nine additional psychologists, including Taft as a member of the Union's Executive Committee and Roger Russell as IUPsyS liaison. Fallon presented a detailed budget based upon the assumption that at least 2000 participants would be needed to break even financially, given a registration fee of US$170–200. It was assumed that registration fees would comprise 85% of the needed income, the remainder coming from a variety of other sources. In addition to invited speakers and a wide range of symposia, three kinds of individual presentations would be noted on the printed program—individual papers presented in thematic sessions, interactive poster sessions, and announcements of prepared papers to be handed out.

It was anticipated that travel expenses for most participants would be unusually high due to the great distance to Australia from Europe, America, and much of Asia. Special efforts were made to organize satellite scientific meetings of a topical nature for which travel might be at least partially covered by national sponsors. Of particular note was the special effort by Roger Russell, Holtzman, and the US National Committee for IUPsyS under the chairmanship of Rosenzweig to organize a major international conference on behavioral toxicology that was held just prior to the Sydney congress at the Australian National University in Canberra. This conference enabled a number of psychologists to obtain travel support to Australia from funds provided to the US National Commission by its parent organization, the National Academy of Sciences/National Research Council in the United States. The behavioral toxicology conference required nearly 3 years of advance planning to be successful. Papers presented at the Canberra conference were subsequently published by the US National Academy of Sciences (Russell, Flattau, & Pope, 1990).

Non-payment of dues, a persistent problem

The collection of dues from members continued to be a difficult problem in spite of the change in Statutes approved in 1984. The Psychological

Society of Ireland was threatening to drop its membership due its inability to pay the required dues, and seven other national members were in danger of being dropped for non-payment of dues over the previous 2 years. Moreover, several national societies had apparently reduced their dues payment by claiming fewer individual members than they actually possessed. Clearly, it was again time for more changes in the Statutes and in the Rules and Procedures for governing such matters, and a special ad hoc committee was formed under the chairmanship of Bélanger to investigate the issue and recommend additional refinements to the 1988 Assembly.

Most scientific unions in ICSU had adopted a category system of members for the purpose of paying dues. Thus was born the idea for IUPsyS of a category system of national members based on the number of individual psychologists represented, carrying with it a designation of the number of authorized voting delegates, from zero to two, permitted within the Assembly. A non-paying national member would only be allowed a non-voting observer in Assembly meetings but would still retain its official membership in the Union. Based upon a dues unit value of $100 for 100 individual psychologists, the 8 categories ranged from Category 0 with no voting delegate; through Categories A (1 unit), B (3 units), C (5 units), and D (10 units) with one delegate; to Categories E (30 units), F (50 units), and G (80 units) with two delegates. The plan was circulated to all Assembly members and approved by the Assembly at its next meeting in Sydney during the 1988 Australian congress. The complete Statutes and Rules of Procedure as adopted by the 1988 Assembly were then published in the *International Journal of Psychology* (1989).

Expansion of Union publications

With financial assistance from the American Psychological Association, a new brochure was produced by Rosenzweig in 1986 describing IUPsyS, the main activities of the Union, publications, affiliate organizations, Union membership, and officers. The brochure was widely distributed. National societies were encouraged to reproduce, translate, and re-publish the brochure on their own in the hope that many more psychologists throughout the world would thereby have a better appreciation of the Union and its activities on behalf of psychology.

Other publications under the Committee on Communication and Publications were also reviewed. Arrangements were made with North-Holland Publishers for shortening the delay in publishing news items in the Platform Section of the *International Journal of Psychology*. National members were encouraged to appoint special correspondents charged with providing the associate editor with timely news items for the Platform Section, but with only limited success.

For the main body of the *Journal*, d'Ydewalle reported that from mid-1985 until mid-1986, 140 manuscripts had been submitted of which 36 were published, the average publication lag being reduced to 10 months. d'Ydewalle announced his intention to step down as editor in one more year. By the time he had finished his term as editor, d'Ydewalle had succeeded in reducing the publication lag to less than 6 months. In his last year as editor, 143 manuscripts from 30 different countries were reviewed, 46 were published, and 3 Special Issues were published, a notable improvement in less than 1 year. Michel Sabourin, University of Montréal, was nominated in 1987 as his replacement and served as the new editor of the *Journal* beginning with the first issue in 1988.

The Union's role in mental health

After reviewing the progress of research and special projects initiated under the auspices of the Union, the Executive Committee listened with considerable interest to an overview of WHO developments in mental health that was presented by Norman Sartorius. He emphasized three areas of special concern to psychologists: (1) the classical problems of mental health such as mental illness and drug abuse; (2) potential contributions of psychologists to health care; and (3) the psychological aspects of major social adjustments such as the resettlement of refugee families. Sartorius emphasized that WHO was now beginning to stress the application of the behavioral sciences to general health as well as mental health. Sartorius' encouragement, together with publication of the findings of the recent IUPsyS project on psychology and health in several journals including the *International Journal of Psychology* (Holtzman et al., 1987) led to the formation of a new Committee on Psychology and Health, with Holtzman as Chairman, to collaborate with the WHO Division of Mental Health in promoting an international network of health psychology.

A revised application for membership in the Union was received from the Egyptian Association for Psychological Studies and was approved by the Executive Committee for preliminary review and comment by all Union members. The application was then formally submitted in 1986 to the Assembly for mail ballot, resulting in official approval of the Egyptian Society as a reinstated member of IUPsyS. (Egypt had originally been admitted as a member in 1951 but became inactive shortly thereafter.) The same procedure was employed for the Pakistan Psychological Association, which was approved by mail ballot in 1987. Preliminary petitions from Greece and Costa Rica were judged not yet ready for formal review, and advice was given their psychologists concerning what must be done to meet the standards for membership in the Union.

A major new Asian initiative, the Executive Committee meeting in China 1987

The 1987 meetings of the Executive Committee were held in Beijing, China, on September 14–17, and in Hangzhou on September 20, thanks to a welcome invitation from the Chinese Psychological Society, one of the newest members of the Union. In return for partial subsidy of the meeting expenses, members of the Executive Committee gave lectures at meetings of the Chinese Psychological Society in Hangzhou. Farr expressed his wish to resign for personal reasons as Deputy Secretary-General, and d'Ydewalle agreed to accept an appointment as his successor. Guests for the meeting were Michel Sabourin, the new editor of the *Journal*, and Ronald King, Chairman of the Organizing Committee for the 1988 Australian Congress.

The number of project proposals from various sources under consideration for possible Union support had grown to such an extent that a set of guidelines concerning applications for international projects, as proposed by Klix, was reviewed and adopted. The guidelines consisted of eight principles to be followed in preparing proposals of projects to be initiated or supported by IUPsyS, how they should be established, their management, their termination and the necessary tendering of accounts. Even where little or no funds from IUPsyS were involved, official sponsorship by IUPsyS was a serious matter that should be granted sparingly. The eight principles adopted were as follows:

1. An application for a project should be presented in writing to the Secretary-General 3 months before the forthcoming session of the IUPsyS Executive Committee, and copies should be forwarded to the members of the Executive Committee who are invited to send their comments to both the Secretary-General and the Chairman of the Committee on Research and Special Projects.
2. The application should specify the project's aims and the basic procedures to be employed; it should also include details as to the institutions and/or research groups to be included.
3. The description of the project should, when relevant, include information concerning international bodies (e.g., UNESCO, WHO) or major projects of other scholarly associations (e.g., ISSC, ICSU, IFFSO) with which the project can be coordinated or related.
4. If interdisciplinary activities are suggested, relations with other scientific fields should be stated and justified. Existing agreements with other scientific associations concerning the project are welcome.
5. The applications should specify the time at which results will be reported and the forms of publication (e.g., research reports, books, symposia, or conferences). In general, a brief progress report should be given every 2 years to the members of the IUPsyS Executive Committee. In the intervening 2 years, a comprehensive report should be given to the Secretary-General.
6. The Union's own research funds should be used mainly as "seed money" to help initiate projects. This support should not be given for a period longer than 4 years. When the coordinator wishes to continue the project under sponsorship of the Union beyond the

4-year period without Union funding, the coordinator must apply every 2 years for approval. Continuation of sponsorship depends upon progress.

7. A statement of costs should be presented specifying the amount of funds expected to be given by IUPsyS as well the financial support anticipated from other scientific institutions, societies, and/or governmental bodies. It should also contain information concerning financial gains, if any, to be returned to IUPsyS. Evidence of support for the project by other institutions would be commendable.

8. A project must be relevant to the aims of the Union.

Application of these guidelines to existing, ongoing projects led to the following decisions by the Executive Committee: *Human Development and Child Research* (4th year, Holtzman)—continued for one more year as a collaborative effort with UNESCO and the International Society for Behavioral Development; *Man-Machine Interaction Research* (5th year, Klix)—continued IUPsyS sponsorship but no further funding; *Behavioral Ecology/Environmental Psychology* (2nd year, Pawlik)—funding approved with recommendation that it be implemented by establishing a task force for the ICSU International Geosphere-Biosphere Program; *Psychology in the Third World* (2nd year, Sinha)—funding approved; *Cognitive Science, Artificial Intelligence and Neuroscience* (2nd year, d'Ydewalle)—funding approved; *Communication Studies* (2nd year, Lomov)—funding approved; *Psychology and Health* (1st year, Holtzman)—funding approved; *Chinese-English Dictionary* (new, Jing)—funding approved.

In each of the approved projects, funding ranged from zero to US$2000 from the small IUPsyS budget, primarily subvention funds from ISSC and ICSU, most amounts being US$1000 or less for the 1987–88 year, barely enough to carry on network communications or plan for conferences where other funding is involved.

Several other activities were encouraged but considered unready for formal sponsorship or funding. The ad hoc group under Finnish leadership dealing with peace was urged to plan a specific international research project on peace and the avoidance of nuclear war, keeping in mind ISSC's continuing interest in the same topic. Azuma was asked to explore the possibility of a new standing committee on how the Union could contribute more effectively to the development of psychology as both a science and a profession in countries where there has been considerable lag in such developments. A special committee was formed for this purpose, consisting of Azuma as Chairman and Diaz-Guerrero, Pawlik, and Taft as members.

The Standing Committee on International Exchange of Scholars and Students had not been active since the 1984 congress. A small related study by Rosenzweig to determine the views of national societies in collaborating to produce an International Roster of Experts, an initiative that had been encouraged by ISSC and ICSU, revealed little interest and the project was dropped. A much larger project, the possible gathering of new information on tens of thousands of individual psychologists, exclusive of the United States, for a fifth edition of the *International Directory of Psychologists*, loomed as a more important issue that had to be decided no later than the 1988 Sydney congress. The current fourth edition had been highly acclaimed, but the explosive growth of psychology since it had been compiled made the task a formidable one, and financial support was uncertain.

The newly formed European Federation of Professional Psychologists Associations (EFPPA) was viewed by the Executive Committee with much interest and some concern since one of its mandates was to consider ways of improving, recognizing, and possibly standardizing professional training programs, codes of ethics, and professional services by psychologists throughout Europe. While generally viewed as positive, the long-range impact of EFPPA's initiatives upon training and research in psychological science was unclear. Secretary-General Pawlik met with officers of EFPPA and arranged for regular communication between the Union, EFPPA, and IAAP as well as with the associated organizers of the proposed 1st European Congress of Psychology to be held in 1988.

The 24th International Congress of Psychology, Sydney, Australia, 1988

The 24th International Congress of Psychology was held in Sydney, Australia, on August 28–September 2, 1988, with a total of 2600 individual and symposium contributions covering all areas of psychology, plus an additional 38 workshops and a series of satellite conferences. Peter W. Sheehan was President of the Congress. The Union had taken another major step in the progressive globalization of psychology by holding the International Congress of Psychology for the first time in the southern

Venue of the 24th International Congress of Psychology, Sydney, 1988.

hemisphere. Over 4000 individuals participated as delegates or accompanying persons from 50 different countries. The opening session was held in the beautiful new opera house on the harbor, with a full complement of national dignitaries present as well as most of the psychologists attending the congress. After a brief welcome by IUPsyS President Holtzman, several short addresses by Australians and musical entertainment, the congress adjourned to the opera house foyer for a reception.

In the final weeks before the Congress opened, the organizers were under considerable stress due to delays in construction of the highly anticipated, new convention center where nearly all of the scientific sessions were to be held. Australia was straining to accommodate all the international activities and conferences associated with its bicentennial celebrations in 1988, and the International Congress of Psychology was one of its most prestigious events. Drastic steps were taken and the congress barely opened on time, much to the relief of the overworked organizers!

Patterned after previously successful programs at earlier International Congresses, the Young Psychologists Program in Sydney was noteworthy, and parts of the program with keynote speakers were well mixed with the program involving the young psychologists. Although the congress was a complete success in most respects, a slight financial deficit of about US$5000 was incurred after paying back the loan from IUPsyS received by the Australian organizers for start-up purposes several years earlier.

A large number of papers presented at the congress that were judged to be of high quality were published and distributed in nine volumes similar to the plan adopted following the Mexican congress. Requiring camera-ready copy facilitated the work. Publication of the nine books by North-Holland within the year following the congress was a major accomplishment, given the large number of individual authors and the magnitude of the editorial task. An Executive Editorial Committee comprised of six Australians supervised the editorial work. An 11-man Publication Management Board consisting of both Australians and members of the Union's Executive Committee provided general oversight. Syd H. Lovibond served as general editor of the series. Editors of each of the individual books, together with the substantive areas covered, were as follows:

- Joseph P. Forgas and J. Michael Innes (Eds.), *Social Psychology*
- Douglas Vickers and Philip L. Smith (Eds.), *Human Information Processing*
- Adrienne F. Bennett and Kevin M. McConkey (Eds.), *Cognition*

- John A. Keats, Ronald Taft, Richard A. Heath, and Syd H. Lovibond (Eds.), *Mathematical and Theoretical Systems*
- Barry J. Fallon, H. Peter Pfister, and John Brebner (Eds.), *Industrial Organizational Psychology*
- Nigel W. Bond and David A.T. Siddle (Eds.), *Psychobiology*
- Mary A. Luszcz and Ted Nettelbeck (Eds.), *Psychological Development*
- Ronald C. King and John K. Collins (Eds.), *Social Applications and Issues*
- Peter F. Lovibond and Peter H. Wilson (Eds.), *Clinical and Abnormal Psychology*

The Union's Assembly met on two occasions, August 30 and September 1, with 63 voting members from 30 countries present at one or both of the sessions. Five affiliated organizations were also represented and nine observers attended. Delegates from two new national members, the Indonesian Psychologists Association and the Nigerian Psychological Association, were welcomed to join the Assembly once the petitions for membership received from their associations were approved as a first order of business, bringing the total number of national members in the Union to 50. The Royal Society, the UK Academy of Science, was approved as the successor to the British Psychological Society as the national member from the United Kingdom, following in the footsteps of the Americans and Canadians, with the British National Committee of Psychological Science serving as the UK Academy's representative in IUPsyS.

The Assembly approved the proposed revisions in the Statutes and Rules of Procedure, including the change to a category system of representation in the Assembly and of dues payment, and authorizing the immediate Past-President to be a voting member of the Executive Committee. The Assembly endorsed the continuation of the international network projects as well as the appointment of a new Committee for the Psychological Study of Peace. Based upon the recommendations of Azuma's special committee, a third standing committee was established, the Committee on Development of Psychology as a Science and Profession.

New officers

Mark Rosenzweig was elected President of the Union for the next 4 years. Hiroshi Azuma and Martti Takala were elected Vice-Presidents. Five former Executive Committee members were re-elected—Diaz-Guerrero, Jing, Klix, Lomov, and Sinha. The five new members elected to the Executive Committee were Rochel Gelman, University of Pennsylvania; Terrence P. Hogan, University of Manitoba, Canada; Cigdem Kagitcibasi, Bogazici University, Turkey; Lars-Göran Nilsson, University of Umea, Sweden; and Peter Sheehan, University of Queensland, Australia. Under the newly

Mark R. Rosenzweig: President of the IUPsyS (1988–1992).

approved Statutes, as immediate Past-President, Holtzman continued on the Executive Committee for one more term.

Before adjourning, the Assembly also heard from a Belgian task group headed by d'Ydewalle concerning preliminary plans for the next international congress to be held in Brussels, approved an invitation from Canada to hold the 1996 congress in Montréal, and received an invitation from Sweden to consider Stockholm for the international congress in 2000.

The outgoing Executive Committee met on August 26–28 just prior to the congress to hear reports from the standing committees and the project coordinators, to review matters for consideration by the Assembly, to consider new petitions for membership, and to seek ways of improving the financial condition of the Union. Reduced subventions from ICSU and ISSC, the continued failure of some national members to pay their annual dues, and the major travel expenses incurred as a result of holding the Executive Committee in Australia put an unusual strain on the budget, making it necessary to draw upon the Union's small Reserve Fund kept for emergencies or to reduce IUPsyS funding of research and special projects.

The new Executive Committee met primarily for organizational purposes on September 3, reappointing Pawlik, d'Ydewalle, and Bélanger as Secretary-General, Deputy Secretary-General, and Treasurer, respectively. After serving continuously since 1972 as Chairman of Communication and Publications, Rosenzweig took office as President of the Union and Holtzman was appointed in his place as Chairman of Communication and Publications. Klix continued as Chairman of the Committee on Research and Special Projects, and Azuma was appointed Chairman of the third standing committee, the newly authorized Committee on Development of Psychology as a Science and a Profession. Adolph Kossakowski, German Democratic Republic, was appointed Chairman of the new Committee for Psychological Study of Peace with the understanding that no funds would be provided at this time, most of the Committee's work being carried out by correspondence. Takala agreed to serve as Vice-Chairman and liaison between the Committee for the Psychological Study of Peace and the Executive Committee. Germaine de Montmollin was asked to be the Union's official liaison to the 25th International Congress of Psychology to be in held in Brussels in 1992.

A major unsettled question concerned the feasibility of compiling and publishing a fifth edition of the *International Directory of Psychologists*. Many national societies were already periodically publishing directories of their members. Restricting the new directory to research psychologists in keeping with the primary focus of the Union upon psychological science would be one alternative to consider. Nevertheless, not only would it still be an expensive undertaking, but the problem of defining who is a research

Executive Committee members and journal editor at meeting in 1989 with Belgian officials to plan the 1992 Congress—From left to right: (front row) Géry d'Ydewalle, Rochel Gelman, Friedhart Klix, C.C. Jing, Hiroshi Azuma, Terrence Hogan, Mark Rosenzweig, Cigdem Kagitcibasi, Leni Verhofstadt-Denève (President, Belgian Psychological Society), Kurt Pawlik, (and in back) Peter Sheehan, David Bélanger, Belgian official, Durganand Sinha, Michel Sabourin, Martii Takala, Belgian official, Wayne Holtzman (missing from the photo are Executive Committee members Rogelio Diaz-Guerrero, Boris Lomov, and Lars-Göran Nilsson).

psychologist rather than a practitioner or counselor would require a great deal of cooperation and understanding among the growing number and diversity of member societies and the Union's editorial board. A primary objective would be to produce a directory that could be sold for about US$25 by keeping it fairly simple and using modern computer technology.

After obtaining the views of leaders within the member societies in 1989 and being discouraged by the responses, the Executive Committee at its next

Key Union Officers (1988–1992)—From Left: Géry d'Ydewalle, Kurt Pawlik, David Bélanger, and Mark Rosenzweig.

meeting in 1989 decided to postpone further action while reconsidering the task significantly and to focus on compiling an international directory of recognized psychological research centers and institutes, including their key scientists, rather than pursuing the much more difficult task of publishing a new directory of individual psychologists.

References

Holtzman, W.H., Evans, R.I., Kennedy, S., & Iscoe, I. (1987). Psychology and health: Contributions of psychology to the improvement of health and health care. *International Journal of Psychology, 22,* 221–227.

International Union of Psychological Science. (1989). Statutes and Rules of Procedure. *International Journal of Psychology, 24,* 217–236.

Klix, F., & Hagendorf, H. (Eds.) (1985). *Human memory and cognitive capabilities: Symposium in memoriam Hermann Ebbinghaus, Vols. 1–2.* Amsterdam: Elsevier Science.

Nilsson, L.-G. (1988). The Swedish National Committee of Psychology. *International Journal of Psychology, 23,* 649–652.

Nuttin, J.R. (1986). The Belgian National Committee of Psychological Science. *International Journal of Psychology, 21,* 785–791.

Rosenzweig, M.R., & Flattau, P.E. (1988). The US National Committee for the International Union of Psychological Science. *International Journal of Psychological Science, 23,* 367–375.

Russell, R.W., Flattau, P.E., & Pope, A.M. (1990). *Behavioral measures of neurotoxicity: Report of a symposium.* Washington, DC: National Academy Press.

Strengthening linkages and international networks (1989–1992)

13

By the end of the 24th International Congress of Psychology in Australia, it was apparent that a genuine global expansion of international psychology had been achieved. Not only had there been highly successful world congresses of psychology in Asia, Latin America, and the far reaches of the South Pacific, but the subsequent years following each congress were characterized by the involvement of psychologists from new national member societies representing the nations of the developing world where modern scientifically based psychology had more recently taken root. These changes were also gradually evident not only in the Assembly but also in the composition of the elected Executive Committee members who were responsible for carrying out the programs and policies of the Union.

Most of the Executive Committee meetings and the next three world congresses of psychological science sponsored by the Union were held in familiar settings within Europe and North America where previous IUPS congresses had been held earlier in the century. This move permitted the Union to build upon existing strengths in psychology and to consolidate the major gains of the past several decades. At the same time, vigorous efforts were made to strengthen ties with psychologists from the less well-developed countries of the world and to encourage additional Union membership from Asia, Latin America, and Africa. By the early 1990s, with the end of the Cold War involving the Soviet Union and the United States as primary antagonists, major political, economic, and social changes occurred in Eastern Europe that resulted in the breakup of the Soviet Union and the creation of new nation-states, as well as the restoration of former ones. The decade of the 1990s would see new petitions for IUPsyS membership from states that were formerly part of the Soviet Union, in addition to an increase in membership petitions from countries of the Third World.

The next three congresses were held in Western Europe and Canada. An important goal for the first of these congresses, the 25th International Congress of Psychology in Belgium, was the cross-area communication of the latest scientific findings in emerging specialized areas of psychology. The rapid expansion and specialization of theory and research in psychology had led to a situation where few, if any, psychologists could keep up with the latest developments, especially across different languages and countries. The next three meetings of the Executive Committee were focused upon these important issues as well as new publications, the expansion of projects and special interest networks, and the development of advanced research training workshops to be held as satellite meetings immediately prior to the international congress.

Executive Committee meeting, Brussels 1989

The 1989 meeting of the Executive Committee was held in Brussels on July 16–21, under the generous auspices of the Belgian National Fund for Scientific Research, one of the sponsors of the forthcoming international congress. A major consideration was the review of plans for the 1992 congress. In addition to Géry d'Ydewalle, key members of the Belgian Task Group who attended the Executive Committee meeting were Paul Bertelson, Piet J. Janssen, and Leni Verhofstadt-Deneve. The different kinds of scientific activities being planned were described, together with a timetable for invitations and announcements, a tentative budget for the congress, and an overview of expected satellite conferences. Following a visit to the proposed site of the congress and an inspection of the facilities, the Executive Committee expressed its approval of the plans and thanked the Task Group for the advanced and well-organized state of their planning.

Advanced Research Training Seminars (ARTS)

Several suggestions were also made for organizing advanced training workshops in conjunction with the 1992 Belgian congress. Kagitcibasi and d'Ydewalle agreed to contact departments of psychology in neighboring countries as well as the affiliate members of the Union, such as the International Association of Cross-Cultural Psychology (IACCP), while Pawlik would submit workshop proposals to ICSU, especially to obtain travel funds for psychologists from developing countries. Their efforts elicited an enthusiastic response from psychologists at universities in four cities of Germany and The Netherlands, which offered to host workshops. Ype Poortinga, University of Tilburg and current President of IACCP, agreed to coordinate the planning of the seminars.

By 1991, US$12,000 was obtained from UNESCO for supporting the seminars, to which sum was added generous support from Finland, Japan, the United Kingdom, and the United States, making it possible to hold two ARTS. Held on July 25–August 1, 1992 in Berlin, one ARTS was led by Ute Schönpflug and Klaus Boehnke. The ARTS was devoted to Life Span Development from a Cross-Cultural Perspective and was attended by 33 psychologists, 15 of whom were from less affluent countries and received financial support. Held at the same time, the Tilburg seminar on Coping with Adverse Conditions was led by Guus van Heck and Fons van de Vijver and was comprised of 14 psychologists, all but 1 of whom were from economically poor countries. Primarily from disadvantaged nations, these participants could then go earlier to the International Congress in Brussels immediately before the ARTS. Both ARTS were declared highly successful, and the 1992 Assembly in Brussels voted to continue the ARTS as a featured satellite program at future international congresses.

Advance preparations were also announced for the 26th International Congress of Psychology to be held in Montréal, Canada. The Executive Committee approved the nomination by the Canadians of David Bélanger as President of the congress, as well as the proposed financial agreement involving support of the congress by the National Research Council of Canada. A contractual agreement was established with the National Research Council that involved a sharing of the surplus, if any, as well as an understanding that any deficit would be completely covered by the Council.

Executive Committee and Assembly meetings, Kyoto 1990

The 1990 meeting of the Executive Committee was held in Kyoto, Japan, on July 19–22, in conjunction with the 22nd International Congress of Applied Psychology. A meeting of the Union's Assembly was also held at the time of the congress for the purpose of exchanging information with members who could be present.

Change of publisher and improvements in the *International Journal of Psychology*

Negotiations by Holtzman, Pawlik, and d'Ydewalle with North-Holland/Elsevier Publishers at the time of contract renewal for the Journal proved unsatisfactory, and efforts were made to find a more attractive publisher. The best proposal was received from Lawrence Erlbaum Associates Ltd, UK, which contained several advantages for the Union: (1) a substantial increase in royalties, particularly on sales of Special Issues; (2) reimbursement of secretarial expenses for the editor; and (3) much lower subscription prices for individuals while providing a more attractive plan for subscriptions using non-convertible currency and from Third World countries, as well as for bulk purchase of 100 subscriptions by the Union.

Clause 18 of the former contract with North-Holland created a problem that required delicate negotiation before the transfer could be completed. In the same manner as the price paid by North-Holland to Dunod in 1979, this clause provided that reasonable compensation was due North-Holland for transfer of the subscription list and the stock of back volumes of the *Journal* to a new publisher. North-Holland's charge of US$44,000 in fulfillment of Clause 18 was negotiated down to US$25,000, all of which was paid by Erlbaum UK, including US$12,500 to be charged against future royalties due the Union. The Executive Committee formally approved the new contract once agreement was reached among the three parties, and henceforth Erlbaum UK, known after 1996 as Psychology Press, has been the publisher.

Under the editorship of Sabourin since 1988, publication lag of the main scientific section of the *Journal* was reduced to 5.5 months by 1992, the number of manuscripts submitted from 30 different countries had increased to 121 by 1992, several Special Issues had been published under guest editors, and the Consulting Editorial Board had been expanded. Started by d'Ydewalle in December 1981 while he was editor, Special Issues have been a successful way of focusing on timely topics of international interest by appointing a guest editor who solicits appropriate articles on the chosen topic. Special Issues have the added value of being marketable as single numbers of the *Journal*, the royalties of which flow back to the Union's treasury.

The Platform Section of the *Journal*, under the leadership of d'Ydewalle and Pawlik as associate editors, continued to publish reports, national activities, brief notes, and special articles of a timely international nature. The most successful of these regular features has been the calendar of international congresses and scientific meetings that first appeared in 1987 when the *American Psychologist* discontinued its international calendar.

Executive Committee meeting, Berkeley 1991

When the Executive Committee met in Berkeley, California, on August 19–23, the international networks of special interest groups, the relationships of the Union with ICSU, ISSC, WHO, and UNESCO, the communication and publication activities of the Union, and plans for the international congress in Belgium a year later were all developing very well. Moreover, the financial health of the Union had improved considerably after passage of the new dues structure and category system for members that was adopted in 1988 at the 24th International Congress of Psychology in Australia. By 1991, the total annual budget had grown to US$62,000, about one half of which was devoted to projects while the remainder helped cover administrative expenses of the Union. A reserve fund of approximately twice the annual budget had also been built up to cover unforeseen emergencies in the future.

Given the sound condition of the Union's finances and considering his long term of service to the Union, Bélanger announced that he was planning to retire after 15 years as Treasurer of the Union at the end of the 1992 congress. Similarly, Pawlik stated that he would be stepping down after 8 years as Secretary-General after the Brussels congress, and Sabourin said he would be resigning upon completion of a 4-year term as editor of the *Journal* the end of 1992. Both Past-Presidents of the Union, Klix and Holtzman, would also be leaving the Executive Committee in 1992. Clearly, 1992 would be a watershed year concerning the turnover of leadership within the IUPsyS.

Search for a new editor for the *International Journal of Psychology* began immediately. The editor must have a wide knowledge of current psychological science, previous editorial experience, a working knowledge of English and French, and an ability to deal effectively with a diversity of authors as well as the publisher. After numerous exchanges and several interviews, Jean Pailhous, CNRS, Marseilles, France, and editor of the *European Bulletin of Cognitive Psychology*, was selected as the person who appeared to possess all of the desirable qualities and was willing to devote himself to this demanding task. As agreed upon in the negotiations, pending manuscripts for the *Bulletin* were merged with those of the *Journal*, beginning with Volume 28 (1993) of the *Journal*, to the advantage of readers of both journals. Unfortunately, the merger proved unsuccessful, and, at its 1993 meeting, the Executive Committee had to dissolve the merger and appoint a new editor.

In addition to extensive discussion of continuing issues and future plans, in 1991 the Executive Committee adopted a new logo for its stationery and publications. It also agreed that the changing times and successful globalization of psychology compelled the Union reluctantly to drop its requirement that French be an official language, while retaining English, in all future congresses of IUPsyS. Although French would obviously be the second language of choice for the next two international congresses in Brussels and Montréal, where French was a native language, in Sweden and other countries where future congresses would be held, requiring French for all international congresses placed too heavy a burden for simultaneous translation upon the congress organizers. Henceforth, only two languages would be required, English and the host country's national language, although additional languages could certainly be adopted if the congress organizers chose to add them and provisions were made for the necessary simultaneous translation. This decision applied only to the quadrennial congresses and not to other activities of the Union, such as the *International Journal of Psychology*, which continued to encourage articles in either of two official languages, English or French.

Research, special projects, and networks

International projects initiated or supported by the Union usually involved networks of like-minded psychologists with a member of the Executive Committee serving as the organizer/chairman/coordinator or at least as a key member of the special interest group. Financial support from Union funds for such networks was always nominal, generally ranging from US$500 to US$1500. Occasionally a project director was successful in obtaining more substantial funding elsewhere once the network was established. By the time of the 1992 international congress, the following networks were actively under way:

Young Child and the Family Environment. Formerly the International Network of Human Development and Child Research Centers dating back to 1984 under Wayne Holtzman, the creation of the UNESCO Project on the Young Child and the Family Environment and its collaboration with IUPsyS led to a realignment of this interest group with Cigdem Kagitcibasi as the coordinator. The network continued to operate under the joint auspices of the Union and its affiliate, ISSBD.

Psychology-based Man-Computer Interaction research (MACINTER). Begun in 1981 by Friedhart Klix, this activity was taken over by Hans Wundtke of Germany when Klix retired from the Union in 1992. At that time the network comprised 280 members who periodically received MACINTER News and participated in annual conferences or workshops. Since then the News merged with the newsletter of the European Association of Cognitive Ergonomics, with which the network was associated.

Healthnet. A network of several hundred health psychologists had been formed and managed with a periodic newsletter by Holtzman after successful completion in 1987 of the World Health Organization project on Psychology and Health.

Psychology and the Third World. The origins of this network can be traced back to 1981, when a project was conceived by Durganand Sinha to stimulate research conferences and exchanges in Asia. A directory of psychologists interested in psychological studies of problems in developing countries, containing 427 entries from 46 countries (Sinha, 1992), was distributed at the 1992 congress.

Terminology and classification of concepts. Begun by Géry d'Ydewalle in 1985 as the International Network of Cognitive Science, Artificial Intelligence, and Neuroscience and taken over by Lars-Göran Nilsson in 1992, this network was closely aligned with the CODATA standing committee of ICSU. A first step of the realigned network was to establish a large database for concepts in cognitive psychology as used in current textbooks, handbooks, and journal articles.

Psychology of Global Environmental Change. Begun in 1985 by Kurt Pawlik, who had been the Union's liaison with the Human Dimensions of Global Environmental Change Program of ISSC and with the International Geosphere-Biosphere Program of ICSU, this network supported symposia at several international meetings, including the 1988 and 1992 International Congresses of Psychology. A Special Issue of the *International Journal of Psychology* was devoted to papers presented at a symposium on the psychological dimensions of global change, held at the 22nd International Congress of Applied Psychology in Kyoto (Pawlik, 1991). A first Regional Advanced Research Training Seminar was held in March 1992 in Malaysia dealing with the psychology of global change. Pawlik continued a coordinator of this network while heading up a related ISSC project on the Perception and Assessment of Environmental Change.

Communication research. Originated in 1985 by Boris Lomov as a project dealing with psychological issues of communication and then taken over by his co-worker in Moscow, Alexandra Belyaeva, after his sudden death, this network project survived for several years under the joint coordination of Belyaeva and Michael Cole, University of California, San Diego. Their efforts were devoted largely to investigating problems of communications in the context of new technological realities, especially as they arose among scientists in Russia and Eastern Europe. By 1992 the project had been transformed into a large-scale social research project involving 40 institutions, partly as a result of the social-political changes in the countries of the former USSR and Eastern Europe.

Two other projects under the auspices of the Union during the 4 years between the Australian and Belgian congresses deserve brief mention. The first was a study fostered by the Standing Committee on the Development of Psychology as a Science and as a Profession under the chairmanship of Hiroshi Azuma. A questionnaire survey was carried out by Mary Nixon of Monash University, Australia, to identify in universities of countries which were members of the Union the minimum requirements and course content for training psychologists. After much effort and some uncertainty regarding the meaning of responses received from 23 national members of IUPsyS, a preliminary manuscript was circulated and a symposium on the subject was organized for the Belgian congress.

The second project involved the Committee for the Psychological Study of Peace, which had its origins in a symposium organized by Adolph Kossakowski at the 1980 International Congress of Psychology in Leipzig. Kossakowski remained as Chairman of the committee until 1991, and in 1988 Martii Takala was appointed Vice-Chairman, thereby assuring a closer linkage to the Executive Committee. A reorganization of the committee in 1992 resulted in Michael G. Wessells of the United States being named as interim Chairman. Under Kossakowski and Takala, the committee prepared an international directory of scientists active in research on the psychological aspects of peace. Several symposia were sponsored at different international conferences, the latest of which at that time was the Second International Symposium on Contributions of Psychology to Peace that took place in Jena, Germany, on September 16–18, 1991 (Boehnke & Frindte, 1992).

New publications also appeared under the auspices of the Union just prior to the Belgian congress. Noteworthy is the *Concise Encyclopedia of Psychology* (published by Hunan Educational Publishers; Jing, 1991), partially funded by the Union, which was compiled by Qicheng Jing as general editor and an editorial board of 11 Chinese psychologists. Written in Chinese, the book has 2800 entries covering the main areas of psychology, descriptions of psychology in different countries, and brief biographies of important psychologists from across the world. At the end of the book are indexes of English, Chinese, and Japanese terms, as well as indexes of English, Chinese, and Russian biographical names.

A second book under the auspices of the Union during this period was *International Psychological Science: Progress, Problems, and Prospects*. Edited by Mark Rosenzweig (1992) and published by the American Psychological Association, the book contains nine chapters, two dealing with the nature of psychological science and resources for conducting it around the world and seven covering key scientific advances in psychology on topics ranging from the neural bases of learning and memory to psychotherapy.

A third IUPsyS book, completed in 1992, that appeared a year after the Belgian congress was the *IUPsyS Directory of Major Research Institutes and Departments of Psychology*, edited by Géry d'Ydewalle (1993). After several years of surveys, a large database was compiled concerning institutions throughout the world that were active in research and advanced training in psychological science, forming the basis for the *Directory*. Rather than try to compile and publish a fifth edition of an international directory containing entries for individual psychologists, a task that proved to be impractical due to the high mobility of psychologists and the great expansion of psychology throughout the world in the previous two decades, a directory dealing with institutions was deemed more appropriate. Even this new directory could hardly claim to be truly comprehensive, since the field was changing rapidly and some institutions were omitted due to lack of response to the surveys. It was expected that subsequent editions of the Directory would be more inclusive as the omissions became apparent.

The 25th International Congress of Psychology, Brussels, Belgium, 1992

The 25th International Congress of Psychology was held in Brussels, Belgium, on July 19–24, 1992. Géry d'Ydewalle and Paul Bertelson served as Co-presidents. Organization of the congress followed traditional lines established by previous congresses. The Scientific Program Committee consisted of nine Belgians with Marc Richelle as Chair. Géry d'Ydewalle was chairman of the 12-member Management Committee. Paul Bertelson was Chairman of the overall Executive Board, which consisted of the chairmen of all the committees plus the current and immediate Past-Presidents of the Belgian Psychological Society and the IUPsyS liaison, Germaine de Montmollin. A Scientific Advisory Board of nearly 80 additional Belgian psychologists completed the organizational plan.

Wide international participation in the congress was fostered in several ways. The Scientific Program Committee invited psychologists from many countries and made sure that symposia included members from several different countries. Funds were obtained from several sources so that those psychologists from the developing countries and from Eastern Europe who requested financial aid could receive exemption from the registration fee. Free or inexpensive accommodations were provided for a large number of psychologists who requested help. Over 4000 individuals from 70 countries attended the congress, a record number.

For the first time, abstracts of the keynote addresses, state-of-the-art lectures, and all the papers to be presented at the Congress were published just in advance of the Congress as a special issue of the *International Journal of Psychology*, Volume 27, Issues 3 and 4, June/August 1992. The book was made possible by the diligence and efficiency of the Belgian Scientific Program Committee, by the journal editors, and by excellent cooperation from the publisher, Erlbaum UK. In addition to 3785 abstracts, the book contained a brief report of the IUPsyS Committee on Communication and Publications, the Annual Report of IUPsyS, and a Directory of the Union's national members. A final section of the book was devoted to abstracts of special sessions organized under the IUPsyS—an open forum and round-table for journal editors and 8 thematic sessions totaling 50 individual presentations sponsored by the Union's research and special project networks. It was an impressive publication, running to 694 pages, that provided a ready reference for congress participants as well as a permanent archive summarizing the scientific content of the congress.

Géry d'Ydewalle: Co-president of the 25th International Congress of Psychology, Brussels, 1992. He became Secretary-General of the IUPsyS (1992–1996), and then President of the IUPsyS (1996–2000).

Altogether, the main scientific program consisted of 13 keynote addresses by distinguished scientists, 22 state-of-the-art lectures highlighting the latest research findings in selected areas, 129 symposia, 115 thematic sessions of individual papers, and 123 interactive poster sessions. Following the congress, 10 of the keynote addresses were published in Volume 1 (Bertelson, Eelen, & d'Ydewalle, 1994) of a two-volume series— five by Americans and one each from five other countries. Volume 2 contained 18 of the state-of-the-art lectures (d'Ydewalle, Eelen, & Bertelson, 1994)—8 by American authors, 2 each by British and German authors, and 1 each by psychologists from Colombia, Italy, Israel, Poland, Sweden, and France. These two volumes focused primarily on experimental, laboratory-based research, with a heavy emphasis on cognition. But when combined with the Special Issue of the *Journal* containing abstracts of all the presentations, a thorough account of international perspectives on psychological science in the early 1990s was given.

General Assembly, Brussels 1992

The Union's Assembly met during the congress on two occasions, July 21 and 23, to hear reports, act upon recommendations from the Executive Committee and national member delegates, to conduct the two-stage election process for new officers to lead the Union until the Montréal congress

Paul Bertelson: Co-president of the 25th International Congress of Psychology, Brussels.

in 1996, and to consider new business. Four new national members were admitted to the Union—the Union of Estonian Psychologists, the Hellenic Psychological Society, initially representing Greece with the proviso that the representation would be changed shortly to a new National Committee of Psychology, the Portuguese Society of Psychology, and the Singapore Psychological Society—bringing the total number of national members to 51. In addition, representation from Colombia was changed from the Colombian Federation of Psychology to the Colombian National Committee of Psychology. Both Greece and Colombia followed in the footsteps of several other countries by forming a National Committee representative of two or more psychological societies as the Union member. In addition, the European Association of Personality Psychology was welcomed as a new affiliate member, bringing the number of affiliates to nine.

The Assembly formally accepted the invitation by the Swedish Psychological Association to hold the 27th International Congress of Psychology in Stockholm in the year 2000. In other action, the Assembly approved the Executive Committee's recommendation that a permanent legal venue be established in Montréal, with the understanding that the "Société du centre de conférences internationales de Montréal," a non-profit organization founded by the federal and provincial governments of Canada and the city of Montréal, would provide the Union with office space and support staff for at least 2 years, in addition to conference facilities, general assistance, and advice.

Further revisions in the Statutes

Consistent with the above action, Article 4 of the Statutes was amended to read, "the Union has a legal venue in Montréal."

A second recommended change in the Statutes was also approved by the Assembly. Although the change to a category system at the 1988 Assembly meetings had produced a necessary increase in income, there were still some minor problems resulting from having only eight categories for dues payment. Several members had expressed a preference for a finer grading in the number of units offered and a higher top category. Article 8 of the Statutes was amended to contain 13 categories rather than only 8. The value of one unit was still maintained at US$100, and the top Category M was raised to 100 units, a sum of US$10,000 per year for the United States, the only country in the top category. Category 0 was still used to designate observer status only, with no annual dues. Category D (10 units) and above allowed two voting delegates in the Assembly, and Categories A, B, and C permitted only one delegate.

Election of new officers and reorganization of the Executive Committee

Pawlik was elected President of the Union for the next 4 years. Jing and Nilsson were elected Vice-Presidents. New members elected to the

Executive Committee were Michel Denis, University of Paris, France; Hiroshi Imada, Kwansei Gakuin University, Japan; D. E. Blackman, University of Cardiff, UK; Jan Strelau, University of Warsaw, Poland; Rubén Ardila, National University of Colombia, Bogota; and F. A.-L. H. Abou-Hatab, Ain-Shams University, Cairo, Egypt, joining Gelman, Hogan, Kagitcibasi, and Sinha who were re-elected for another four-year term.

At a subsequent organizational meeting immediately following the Brussels Congress, the new Executive Committee appointed d'Ydewalle and Sabourin as Secretary-General and Treasurer, respectively. Later in the year, Bruce Overmier, University of Minnesota, was appointed Deputy Secretary-General, completing the Executive Committee membership until the next international congress in 1996. The following were named as chairmen of the three standing committees: Rosenzweig, Communication and Publications; Nilsson, Research and Special Projects; and Imada, Development of Psychology as a Science and as a Profession. As established earlier, the Budget Committee was comprised of the President, the Treasurer, and the Secretary-General. Kagitcibasi agreed to coordinate planning for the next Advanced Research Training Seminars to be held in 1994 in conjunction with the International Congress of Applied Psychology in Madrid.

Other leading appointments by the new Executive Committee concerned the chairmen of the several working groups and special interest networks. The Communication Research Project was upgraded to a

Kurt Pawlik: Secretary-General of the IUPsyS (1984–1992) and later President of the IUPsyS (1992–1996).

Executive Committee (1992–1996) at the International Congress of Psychology, Brussels, 1992—From left to right: Derek Blackman, Michel Denis, Lars-Göran Nilsson, Cigdem Kagitcibasi, David Bélanger (1992), Mark Rosenzweig, Kurt Pawlik, Fouad Abou-Hatab, Michel Sabourin (1993–1996), Géry d'Ydewalle, Jan Strelau, Qicheng Jing, and Hiroshi Imada. Durganand Sinha is missing from the picture (being the photographer), as are Rubén Ardila, Rochel Gelman, Terrence Hogan, and Bruce Overmier.

Michel Sabourin:
Treasurer of the
IUPsyS (1993–)

Working Group with Nilsson as Chairman. The International Networks had the following persons appointed to head them: Kagitcibasi, Young Child and the Family Environment; Sinha, Psychology and the Third World; Pawlik, Psychological Dimensions of Global Change; Hogan, Healthnet; and Nilsson, Taxonomy and Classification. Denis agreed to develop a new initiative on cognitive science, and decisions concerning the psychological study of peace were deferred pending further consultation.

Pawlik was named as the Union's delegate to ICSU; Denis and Pawlik were chosen as official delegates to ISSC, joining d'Ydewalle who was already a member of the ISSC Executive Committee, and Hogan was named the Union's representative to WHO while d'Ydwalle agreed to be liaison to EFPPA.

The Executive Committee took note of national member recommendations that the Union help organize more regional scientific meetings, promote more discussion on the teaching of psychology, expand the international exchange of information, and provide better communication to the public at large. As a first step, Ardila proposed that a regional meeting be organized at the time of the 24th Interamerican Congress of Psychology in Santiago, Chile.

With the success of the 25th congress in Brussels, the expanding program activities as reported to the Assembly, and the strong support of the Assembly for actions that greatly strengthened both the global reach and the firm scientific base of the Union, it was apparent that the International Union of Psychological Science had become a mature organization with a permanent office and a bright future.

References

Bertelson, P., Eelen, P., & d'Ydewalle, G. (Eds.) (1994). *International perspectives on psychological science Vol. 1: Leading themes.* Hove, UK: Lawrence Erlbaum Associates Ltd.

Boehnke, K., & Frindte, W. (1992). Report of the second international symposium on contributions of psychology to peace. *International Journal of Psychology, 27,* 258–260.

d'Ydewalle, G. (Ed.) (1993). *IUPsyS directory of major research institutes and departments of psychology.* Hove, UK: Lawrence Erlbaum Associates Ltd.

d'Ydewalle, G., Eelen, P., & Bertelson, P. (Eds.) (1994). *International perspectives on psychological science, Vol. 2: The state of the art.* Hove, UK: Lawrence Erlbaum Associates Ltd.

Jing, Q. (Ed.) (1991). *Concise encyclopedia of psychology.* Hunan, China: Hunan Educational Publishers.

Pawlik, K. (Ed.) (1991). The psychological dimensions of global change. Special Issue of the *International Journal of Psychology, 26*, 545–673.

Rosenzweig, M.R. (Ed.) (1992). *International psychological science: Progress, problems, and prospects*. Washington, DC: American Psychological Association.

Sinha, D. (1992). IUPsyS international network of psychology and the developing world. *International Journal of Psychology, 27*, 508.

New initiatives and preparations for the Montréal congress (1993–1995)

14.

For the first time since the Union's formative years when it sponsored its first congress in Montréal in 1954, after the Union's founding in 1951 at the 13th international congress in Stockholm, preparations were underway for holding the 26th International Congress of Psychology once again in Montréal. Discussion of plans for the 1996 Montréal congress occurred at every meeting of the Executive Committee during the 4 years between Brussels and Montréal, as well as during the Assembly meeting in 1994 at the International Congress of Applied Psychology in Madrid. In addition, the newly reconstituted Executive Committee continued to move forward with new initiatives as well as execution of previous ones, using its expanded committee structure to carry them out.

Executive Committee meeting, Montréal 1993

The Executive Committee met at headquarters of the Société du Centre de Conférences Internationales in Montréal on August 24–28, 1993. In addition to the congress plans, major issues to be discussed at the meeting included (1) how to provide badly needed assistance to psychologists in Eastern Europe, where newly independent countries were still undergoing major transitions, (2) how to stimulate more regional meetings in between the quadrennial world congresses, and (3) how to implement effectively the expanding list of important international projects the Union had agreed to sponsor through its networks, committees, and organizational ties.

Sabourin, as Treasurer, reported that the annual budget was still severely limited, making it very difficult to undertake all the ambitious projects of interest unless additional external funding could be provided. Extra costs of the 1992 meetings in Brussels led to a reduction in total assets of the Union from US$190,520 to US$179,360. Based upon the Executive Committee's evaluative judgments, internal funds of US$10,000 were available to distribute as follows among the Union's continuing networks and projects: Psychological Dimensions of Global Change—US$2000; Human Development and Child Research Centers—US$2000; Psychology and Cognitive Science—US$1500; Researchers' Perceptions of Factors Facilitating and Impeding Research (as a part of Developing World Network)—US$500; Development of Psychology as a Science and as a

Profession—US$500; East-West Presidential Task Force—US$500; Advanced Research Training Seminars (ARTS)—US$2000; remaining reserve for later appropriation—US$1000.

Communication with some of the national member societies as well as their designated representatives continued to be a problem. Some had failed to pay their dues and had not requested a change to Category 0 status, which recognizes financial hardship cases among some of the smaller societies from developing countries. Overmier volunteered to develop an e-mail bulletin board on a trial basis for the Union in order to facilitate more rapid and effective communication, especially among members of the Executive Committee. The rapid expansion of electronic mail capability on a worldwide basis through the Internet during the 1990s vastly improved communication among members of the Executive Committee and between them and national member societies. And yet, some of the smaller societies in several underdeveloped countries still did not have e-mail capability by the end of the century, placing them at a disadvantage.

New developments in publications

In his report for the Committee on Communication and Publications, Rosenzweig introduced the new edition of the IUPsyS brochure published for the Union by the American Psychological Association (APA). Together with Oxford Press, APA had also launched a major new publication project to produce a comprehensive *Encyclopedia of Psychology* and had asked for nominations from IUPsyS of individuals who could serve on the International Advisory Board. A list drawn up by d'Ydewalle as Secretary-General was approved and sent forward to the Editor-in-Chief with the following names: Max Coltheart, Susan Pick De Weiss, Hiroshi Imada, Cigdem Kagitcibasi, Kurt Pawlik, Lea Pulkkinen, Maurice Reuchlin, Jai B. P. Sinha, Alexander Sokolov, Jan Strelau, and Zhou-Ming Wang.

Somewhat disturbing was the announcement that APA would no longer include abstracts of articles originally published in a language other than English in *Psychological Abstracts*. Such abstracts would still be included in *PsycLIT*, APA's electronic media CD-ROM product. APA had offered to publish a stand-alone SCAN print product of the such non-English abstracts if the Union would guarantee its financial viability or if overseas publishers would share in the cost, but such alternatives were not judged feasible at that time by the Executive Committee.

Also disappointing was the failure of the merger the year before of the *European Bulletin of Cognitive Psychology* and the *International Journal of Psychology* under the editorship of Jean Pailhous. Pailhous had asked for the merger as part of his agreement to become the new editor of the *International Journal of Psychology* since he wanted to continue editing the *European Bulletin* and thought the merger of the two journals might make the task more manageable. Unfortunately, the distortions in the content of the *International Journal of Psychology* created by this merger, as well as other problems associated with it, led Rosenzweig reluctantly to recommend that the merger be dissolved and that a new editor be named for the *Journal*, a recommendation that the Executive Committee unanimously approved.

Preliminary discussions held earlier with Francois Doré, University of Laval, Québec, Canada, indicated that he would be interested in serving as the new editor of the *Journal*. A review of his credentials by the Executive Committee led to his approval as the new editor, with the following general conditions stated in the editor's contract: (1) appointment for 4 years, renewable once and possibly with the suggestion of a 1-year probation; (2) continued service as a function of a yearly assessment by the Executive Committee of IUPsyS; (3) appointments of the consulting editors by the editor to be made in consultation with the Standing Committee on Communication and Publications; (4) attendance of the editor at portions of the Executive Committee meetings by invitation of the Union's President; and (5) IUPsyS payment of an annual stipend to the editor and the publisher's payment of the editor's office expenses. The editorial appointment became effective with the first issue of the *Journal* in 1994.

Research and special projects

As Chairman of this standing committee, Nilsson summarized the progress of seven networks and working groups, calling upon project directors for the details. The network on global change under Pawlik's leadership organized a regional research training seminar in Malaysia in February 1993 on the psychology of global change. This network was also particularly active in a project under the auspices of ISSC called Perception and Assessment of Global Environmental Change.

The Network on the Young Child and Family Environment under Kagitcibasi had reported plans for an Advanced Research Training Seminar on Human Development to be held in Istanbul in 1994, recognizing the International Year of the Family. It was also noted that a multidisciplinary, international symposium on child development and family in China had been sponsored by IUPsyS and UNICEF in Beijing, July 7–11, with over 300 participants.

As reported by Sinha, a regional conference, Psychology and the Developing World, was sponsored by the IUPsyS in Katmandu, Nepal. Healthnet was taken over from Holtzman by Hogan, who stated that he wanted to address issues of behavioral medicine in developing countries and would be continuing the newsletter. Gelman, the new Chair of the Committee on Teaching of Psychology as a Science, expressed a desire to focus both upon psychology's contribution to the teaching of science and the teaching of psychology as a scientific discipline. The project on Psychological Issues of Communication, initiated by Boris Lomov before his untimely death and carried on thereafter by Alexandra Belayeva of

Moscow and Michael Cole of the University of California, San Diego, was deemed sufficiently successful in demonstrating the feasibility of an electronic network for international communications to justify terminating the project without prejudice.

Several new proposed projects were discussed and tabled for lack of funds. During the course of the discussion, three minimal criteria were adopted as a basis for approved funding: (1) existing networks/projects must have been active in the past year and must have submitted a written progress report when solicited by the Secretary-General for inclusion in the Union's annual report; (2) for both new and old projects, a written plan for future action must have been submitted; and (3) there must be favorable review and a priority established by the appropriate committee as well as the Executive Committee. Henceforth, each standing committee would be expected to hold a meeting just prior to the annual Executive Committee meetings for the purpose of discussing plans and making recommendations for consideration by the Executive Committee.

As Chairman of the Committee on the Development of Psychology as a Science and a Profession, Imada presented a written proposal for compilation of a bibliography of selected materials on psychology in countries throughout the world and for conducting an analysis of the degree of coverage given to psychology in different countries. As a start, members of the Executive Committee were asked to send him relevant items from their own countries by November 30, 1993.

A proposal was also received from Michael Wessells (USA) to continue Union sponsorship of the Committee for the Psychological Study of Peace although, as in the past, no funding would be involved. Ardila reported on the Third International Symposium on the Contributions of Psychology to Peace that was held on August 15–19, 1993, at Randolph-Macon College, Virginia, USA. He also agreed to serve as liaison to the committee in place of Takala because of his interest in peace research. The Executive Committee agreed to support Wessell's request for one more year, provided the committee broadened its scope to include issues of conflict resolution and prevention in its manifest national, social, cultural, racial, and religious forms. In subsequent months, the committee broadened its mandate but made no change in its name.

Relations with the International Social Sciences Council

A new structure was adopted for ISSC at its last Assembly meeting, allowing three kinds of members: (1) Member Associations—non-governmental international social and behavioral science associations such as IUPsyS; (2) Member Organizations—national social science councils and corresponding sections of national academies; and (3) Associate Members—international and national non-governmental social science professional organizations, such as the International Association of Applied Psychology. d'Ydewalle announced that he had been re-elected to the Executive Committee of the

ISSC, where he could represent psychology as a major influence on future policy and program decisions of ISSC.

Nilsson reported that a related, though independent, group, the International Committee on Social Science Information and Documentation (ICSSID), had thus far neglected to include psychology as a central part of its programs on bibliographic directories.

Relations with the International Council of Scientific Unions

Both Pawlik and d'Ydewalle were the Union's representatives to the ICSU General Assembly that met every 3 years, and Pawlik served on the General Committee of ICSU that met annually. As a member of the Bioscience Group, and with the expected admission later in 1993 of the International Brain Research Organization and the International Union of Anthropological and Ethnological Sciences as new ICSU members with close ties to psychology, IUPsyS could be expected to play a larger future role in major ICSU projects. One of ICSU's projects, the Committee on Data for Science and Technology (CODATA), involved psychology. Nilsson, the Union's representative to CODATA, reported on their last meeting and stated that IUPsyS could become more active in two areas—management of large databases and environmental and global change.

Relations with UNESCO

A new UNESCO program entitled "Management of Social Transformation" (MOST) presented the Union with an opportunity to draft several new proposals. Kagitcibasi and Sinha agreed to prepare a proposal for funding on the management of change in multi-ethnic and multi-cultural society contexts. Imada, Ardila, Abou-Hatab, and Gelman agreed to prepare a proposal on city contexts, and a proposal dealing with the problems of coping locally with economic and technological transformation was chosen by Pawlik as his responsibility. d'Ydewalle incorporated the several texts into a more comprehensive one entitled *Psychological Perspective on the Management of Social Transformations* which was sent to UNESCO and circulated widely. Denis agreed to serve as the Union's official representative to UNESCO.

Other international collaborations and regional development

After considerable discussion of how the Union could help psychology in newly independent Eastern European nations, a special Presidential Task Force to Promote East-West Relationships was formed comprised of Strelau, Blackman, d'Ydewalle, and Pawlik. The main objective of the task force was to provide guidance to emerging national psychology associations of Eastern Europe concerning how they should organize and the kind of petition they must submit if they wish to become members of the Union.

Regional congresses

Regional congresses to be held under Union auspices were also discussed as a means of encouraging different regions to strengthen scientific psychology. Such congresses were expected to be primarily limited to a defined geographic region and to deal with topics of special regional significance. The Executive Committee approved a new regional congress dealing with psychology and social development in the Asian and Pacific region to be held in Guangzhou, China, in 1995. At meetings of the Executive Committee in 1995, following conferences between officers of the Union and of the International Association of Applied Psychology (IAAP), an agreement was reached that primary sponsorship of regional congresses should be alternated between the IUPsyS and the IAAP, with the other organization cooperating where appropriate. The Asian-Pacific Regional Congress of Psychology, under IUPsyS sponsorship with the full cooperation of IAAP and IACCP, would be the first of many officially sponsored, regional congresses to come in the future.

Advanced Research Training Seminars

Kagitcibasi announced that three seminars were being organized to take place in July 1994 close to the time of the International Congress of Applied Congress in Madrid, provided that funding could be obtained. Two of the three were actually held, with the majority of participants from developing countries. One was held on July 28–August 3 under the leadership of Lutz Eckensberger in Saarbrücken, Germany, on Eco-Thinking from a Cross-Cultural Perspective, funded by the Volkswagen Foundation, the Ministry of Science and Culture of the Saarland, and the University of the Saarland. Thirty-two participants were present, most of whom went on to the Applied Congress in Madrid. The second ARTS, led by Kagitcibasi with the help of Sevda Bekman and Banu Oney, was held on July 29–August 3 in Istanbul, Turkey, on Human Development and Assessment, funded by the Bernard van Leer Foundation, the Mother-Child Education Foundation, the Turkish Ministry of Culture, and Bogazici University. Twenty-nine participants from 12 different countries participated (Kagitcibasi, 1995).

Planning for the 1996 congress

A primary reason for convening the Executive Committee meetings in Montréal was the opportunity to meet with the congress organizers to discuss preliminary plans. In addition to Bélanger, who had been appointed President of the forthcoming congress and Sabourin who agreed to head the congress Organizing Committee, other officers present from Canada were Pierre Ritchie, Secretary-General; John Adair, Chairman of the Scientific Program and Scientific Publications Committee, and Laurier Forget, Director of Congres Services for the Canadian National Research Council.

Planning followed closely the pattern of pre-congress activity that had proved successful in the past. The first formal announcement was to be mailed in fall 1993. A Scientific Advisory Council and seven subcommittees had been appointed to manage various sections of the scientific program. Over 250 suggestions for symposia and a similar number of suggestions for invited speakers had already been received. Scheduled for August 16–22, the 1996 congress could handle 42 to 56 presentations per hour of paper sessions, organized topically, permitting an appropriate number of coordinated social hours to be held as well. A common problem yet to be worked out was the timing of submissions and subsequent notifications of acceptance sufficiently early to permit participants to obtain travel funds from local sources.

A practice established for the planning of the International Congresses has been to include a recent or current member of the IUPsyS Executive Committee, knowledgeable about the congresses, as a member of the congress organizing committee. Mark Rosenzweig served this liaison function on the Montréal Congress Council, participating in its meetings and corresponding with its officers.

As always, costs for participants would be an important factor determining the number of psychologists who could attend, particularly from developing countries very distant from Canada. The Canadian National Research Council proposed a novel approach to this problem in the future. Any deficit from the congress would be covered completely by the Canadian NRC. Any surplus would be shared by the NRC and the Union as follows: the first US$10,000 would go to the Union to repay seed money advanced by the Union. The next US$20,000 would be shared equally by the NRC and the Union. Two-thirds of any additional surplus would go the the Union, leaving one third for NRC. Half of the Union's share of the surplus would be placed under the control of the Canadian Psychological Association and dedicated to Canadian projects related to international psychology.

Executive Committee and Assembly meetings, Madrid 1994

The Executive Committee held its 1994 meetings in Madrid, July 14-17, in conjunction with the International Congress of Applied Psychology, a previous custom that had become a tradition with the added advantage that a non-voting meeting of the IUPsyS Assembly could also be held at the same time. All members were present. Others attending various parts of the meeting included François Doré, the new editor of the *International Journal of Psychology*; Bélanger, Ritchie, and Adair, representing the organizers of the Montréal congress; Marina Manthouli and James Georgas, Presidents of the Fourth European Congress of Psychology; and two representatives of the Union's publisher, Rohays Perry and Paul Dukes of Lawrence Erlbaum UK.

Expansion of the Union and further globalization of its reach continued at the same time as strengthening and consolidation of gains in Europe and North America were occurring. Two new national members representing Chile and Malta had been approved by mail ballot of the Assembly and were expected to attend the Madrid meeting of the Assembly. The Presidential Task Force on Eastern Europe was actively assisting psychologists in newly independent nations of Eastern Europe to organize and to petition for Union membership. The European Congresses initiated by the European Federation of Professional Psychologists Associations (EFPPA) were beginning to attract academically based scientists, and plans were being developed to transform the organization into a European association to which all qualified psychologists in Europe would be welcome. The determination of the Union to foster the development of regionally based, international meetings continued to yield promising results. For example, the Fourth European Congress, to be held in Athens in 1995 under the joint auspices of IUPsyS, IAAP, and EFPPA, would be the first to involve representatives of the Union's European National Members as active participants. Overmier's electronic communication system, known as IUPsySX, was also making communication among the Executive Committee members far easier than in the past.

Other good news conveyed by the Treasurer at the meeting concerned the achievement of a healthy budget surplus for 1993 of US$24,855, substantially more than originally anticipated. The Executive Committee approved distribution of the surplus as follows: (1) an advance loan of US$10,000 to the Montréal congress Organizing Committee; (2) a grant of US$5000 to help support the regional conference in China in 1995; (3) US$1000 for the bibliographic project under Imada's leadership on psychology throughout the world; and US$5000 to the Union's Reserve Fund, leaving the remainder as a current, small contingency fund. As in the past, US$12,000 in funds from the 1994 budget were allocated on a modest basis to the existing, ongoing projects, leaving a small remainder for additional expenditures that would have to be approved in advance by the Finance Committee. Clearly, the Union was in better financial shape than ever before, but it still had to be careful to limit expenditures. If the Union were to maintain this good financial state in the future, it was believed that the dues of national members would have to be increased by at least 25% by the Assembly at the Montréal congress or the expanding program and responsibilities of the Union would have to be sharply curtailed.

As agreed upon in 1993, each of the major committees met the day before the formal Executive Committee meetings to discuss their progress and plans and to formulate any recommendations for consideration by the entire group.

Communication and publications

Doré, the new editor of the *Journal*, reported that psychologists from 25 countries submitted 97 manuscripts in 1993. In 1994 the number dropped to 79 manuscripts from 21 countries, but was expected to pick up again in 1995. The excessive publication lag in 1993, due in part to many Special Issues in 1992, had dropped in 1994 to a normal 8–10 months. The Executive Committee approved a policy change to incorporate formally at least one Special Issue per year, noting that such issues often attract large sales when properly advertized. Following the successful model employed for the Brussels congress, the Executive Committee agreed that a double issue of the *Journal* containing abstracts of papers to be presented at the Montréal congress should be published just prior to the congress in 1996. It was recognized that a larger format for the *Journal* to accommodate the large number of abstracts would be highly desirable. Lawrence Erlbaum UK agreed as publisher to print 6 issues of approximately 100 pages each in large format, beginning with Volume 31 in 1996.

The *IUPsyS Directory of Major Research Institutes and Departments* had attracted sufficient interest since its publication in 1993 to justify consideration of a second edition. Overmier agreed to be editor of the revised *Directory*, and the publisher approved the plan to set a target date of mid-1996 for its publication—perhaps in time for distribution at the Montréal congress. By dropping individual names from the Directory and concentrating on institutes and departments, the project was made more manageable.

One of the problems concerning international journals brought out in the discussion was the fact that English-language journals published in the United States dominate psychological science. And yet, only rarely do they include articles or have editorial board members from other countries, especially those where other languages are employed. Pawlik proposed, and others agreed, that special efforts should be made to "internationalize" what are essentially national journals since psychological science knows no geographic boundaries. Gelman pointed out that the Committee on International Relations in Psychology of APA has already endorsed such an internationalization proposal, and Overmier added that the APA Publications and Communications Board acted to endorse this idea at its June 1994 meeting. But in the last analysis, such decisions still require the full cooperation of journal editors, who have the final say on the appointment of board members and the acceptance or rejection of submitted articles.

Research and special projects

Nilsson reported that at the committee's meeting the previous day, each of the six projects or networks was judged to be continuing in a highly active and successful mode in spite of minimal funding. The International Network on Terminology and Classification of Concepts in Cognitive

Science that he chaired, for example, had completed a first analysis of terms used for indexing articles on cognitive processes in the 1987-92 CD-ROM version of *Psychological Abstracts*. Pairs of concepts were then used as input to a clustering routine that links each term by its strongest pair. A map representing the resulting cluster structure of index terms was constructed using a MDS program that takes a matrix of co-occurrences as inputs and then yields the coordinates for a two-dimensional, best-fitting solution to the input matrix. Most of the international networks had developed plans to present symposia on their activities at the Montréal congress (d'Ydewalle, 1995).

As Gelman reported, the US National Committee for IUPsyS had been developing plans for a conference it would sponsor just prior to the Montréal congress. This international conference would address the life-span development of careers in science and technology and would involve major contributions by well-known psychologists, many of whom would then participate in the Montréal congress. The plan was enthusiastically endorsed by the Executive Committee, recognizing that the development of scientific and technical competencies and careers was an issue of concern to both ICSU and ISSC. Rosenzweig mentioned that a second workshop by the US National Committee was being planned devoted to the ethical and social consequences of future drugs that affect memory and intelligence. This plan was also strongly endorsed by the Executive Committee.

Relations with ICSU

Relations with ICSU had grown at a steady pace over the previous year. A new priority had been established within ICSU focusing upon brain research and issues of animal research, two areas of special interest to psychology, arousing interest in the possibility of new initiatives in partnership with other disciplines within the Biosciences Group of ICSU. Jing was nominated to the Committee on Science and Technology in Developing Countries, Strelau agreed to represent the Union at an ICSU Symposium on Ethics in Science, d'Ydewalle agreed to represent the Union at the forthcoming General Assembly of CODATA, and Peter Johnson of the UK planned to participate in a CODATA symposium on mental models and representations.

Before adjourning, the Executive Committee reviewed and approved once again plans for the Montréal congress, preliminary organization and plans for the Stockholm congress in 2000, and plans for the Asian-Pacific Regional Congress to be held in Guangzhou, China, August 28-30, 1995. The importance of this first IUPsyS-sponsored regional congress and the invitation of the Chinese Psychological Society to host the 28th International Congress of Psychology in 2004 convinced the Executive Committee that their 1995 meeting should be held in Guangzhou at the time of the regional congress.

Assembly meeting

Following the Executive Committee meetings, an informal session of the Union's Assembly met with 48 representatives of 29 countries present to exchange information about the latest activities of the Union and its national members.

Executive Committee and the Asian-Pacific Congress, Guangzhou 1995

The Executive Committee held its 1995 meeting with all members but Rosenzweig present in Guangzhou, China, on August 23–27, 1995, in conjunction with the IUPsyS-sponsored Regional Asian-Pacific Congress. The budget for 1995 was similar to that for 1994, although the funding policies of ISSC and ICSU had changed from small direct subsidies of a general nature to the awarding of grants for specific projects submitted by member organizations. The Executive Committee distributed internal funds totaling US$12,500 in small amounts among 10 projects and networks, including three new ones—the Cognitive Bases of Education, the final reporting of the Ethical Codes, and the organizing of an IUPsyS Homepage on the World Wide Web. The largest amounts were given for the International Network Project on Psychological Dimensions of Global Change (US$3000) and the 1996 ARTS (US$2600). Earmarked grants of

Photograph taken at the Asian-Pacific Regional Conference of Psychology, Guangzhou, China, August, 1995—From left to right: Dr Houcan Zhang* (China), Dr Bruce Overmier* (USA), Dr Joan Bazar (USA), Dr Qicheng Jing (China; former members of the IUPsysS Executive Committee and designated as President of the 2004 International Congress of Psychology), Setsuko Imada (Japan), Dr. Hiroshi Imada* (Japan), Dr. Michel Denis* (France), and Maryvonne Carfantan (France). *Members of the IUPsyS Executive Committtee.

UNESCO money funneled through ISSC and ICSU accounted for approximately one third of the budget.

Concerns about delinquent members

Considerable discussion was held regarding the relatively large number of national members who had failed to pay their annual dues or who were going through major transformations. Among the members in arrears for 2 or more years were Brazil, the Dominican Republic, India, Indonesia, Pakistan, Panama, the Philippines, and Italy. Serious questions were raised as to whether the associations presumably representing psychologists in India, Brazil, and Italy were either moribund or no longer representative of the most active psychologists. Special efforts would have to be made to determine the nature of these difficulties, to resolve them if possible, and to recommend appropriate action to the Assembly at its 1996 meeting.

New members

Three new members were approved by mail ballot of the Assembly—the Croatian Psychological Association, the Slovenian Psychological Association, and the Vietnam Association of Psycho-Pedagogical Sciences. In a similar manner, the European Association of Psychological Assessment was approved as a new affiliated organization. After reviewing new petitions, the Executive Committee recommended for mail ballot that four additional societies—the Bangladesh Psychological Association, the Russian Psychological Society, the Moroccan Association of Psychological Studies, and the Irish Psychological Society—be admitted as new national members of the Union.

Communication and publications

Pawlik presented a new proposal to compile and publish an international reference work, tentatively titled *International Handbook of Psychological Science*, to be edited by Pawlik and Rosenzweig. Sage Publishing Company had already informally agreed to publish and distribute the handbook, leaving open the rights for foreign language editions. Since Sage had offered 10% royalty payments to the Union as well as an advance of £12,500, the Executive Committee enthusiastically endorsed the project and urged the editors to move forward with the plan.

Efforts to strengthen communication with national members as well the general public led to the creation by d'Ydewalle of an electronic homepage for the Union on the World Wide Web. Related was the notable success of the electronic network established by Overmier called IUPsySX for communication among members of the Executive Committee.

Research and special projects

Written reports by project directors stimulated extensive discussion on how projects could be made more relevant to the Union's members and how more such members might be attracted to join Union-sponsored activities. Unfortunately, readily available funds have always been severely limited for starting up new projects, requiring special voluntary efforts by the initiator. Most projects thrive only because of strong individual initiative and external funding. Nevertheless, one new project proposed by Gelman for studying the Cognitive Bases of Education was approved. She proposed that a casebook be developed to advance the role of psychology as a basis of science education, perhaps with the involvement of Ardila and Abou-Hatab from the Executive Committee and of Giyoo Hatano and Houcan Zhang from Japan and China, respectively. The tiny sum of US$300 was approved to help her get started.

Three other projects aside from those presented by the Committee on Research and Special Projects were also reviewed. Imada reported on progress of the projected Bibliography of Psychology Around the World with a series of recommendations as to how to proceed. Overmier reported on his survey of national member codes of ethics. And it was announced that a manuscript by Wessells on the work of the Committee for the Psychological Study of Peace was completed.

Relations with ISSC

The relations of the Union with ISSC had begun to improve once again. At the last ISSC Assembly meeting d'Ydewalle was elected Vice-President and a new Secretary-General, Leszek Kosinski, was appointed. Kosinski was familiar with IUPsyS and had already improved the financial circumstances at ISSC by major reductions in staff. The announcement of new funding priorities at UNESCO provided an opportunity for the Union to propose new projects to ISSC for support. Proposals submitted by the Union covered such topics as social integration in southern Africa; urban problems and the status of psychology in the developing world, particularly Asia; dealing with poverty and social integration by focusing upon child rearing practices of women with low socioeconomic status; the perception and assessment of global environmental change; and exchange and communication among national scientific organizations of psychology.

Other cooperative activities

After brief reports of ongoing relations with ICSU, WHO, and UNESCO, a Pan-Arab Regional Conference of Psychology was proposed by Abou-Hatab, to be held in 1999. The Executive Committee approved the plan. The highly successful Fourth European Congress of Psychology held in Athens in July 1995 encouraged the Executive Committee to initiate joint efforts with the European Federation of Professional Psychologists Associations and IAAP to develop a forum of European organizations. A first step would be for the officers of the three organizations to plan a workshop of European behavioral scientists for the purpose of promoting European psychological science and research, especially in Eastern Europe.

Asian-Pacific Regional Conference, Guangzhou 1995

The first of what was hoped to be the forerunner of a series of regional congresses was held the week following the Executive Committee meetings. Co-sponsors included IAAP, the International Association for Cross-Cultural Psychology, and nine national psychological associations. Focusing on psychology and social development in the region, 173 papers were presented, 9 keynote speeches were given by distinguished psychologists from different countries, and 4 special symposia were organized by the 3 international co-sponsors.

Forthcoming International Congresses of Psychology

With only a year to go, final preparations for the 26th International Congress of Psychology were presented by Hogan and Sabourin, who reviewed the scientific program, special events for young psychologists, ceremonial events, housing, exhibits, and advance publication of abstracts, pointing out that travel grants and congress assistance program totaled US$80,000 of much-needed support. Considerable progress was reported by Nilsson on plans for the 2000 congress in Stockholm. The budget of 4,000,000 Skr was based on a registration fee of only 2600 Skr, assuming over 6000 participants. Nearly half of the necessary funds had already been acquired and marketing was underway. In addition to an invitation to hold the 28th congress in China in 2004, Ardila, Abou-Hatab, and Kagitcibasi announced that invitations would probably be forthcoming from Colombia, Egypt, and Turkey as well. Formal invitations would be welcomed at the Assembly meetings in 1996, where a final decision would be made.

References

d'Ydewalle, G. (1995). Annual report for 1994 of the International Union of Psychological Science (IUPsyS). *International Journal of Psychology, 30,* 762–768.

Kagitcibasi, C. (1995). Final report on ARTS, 1994. *International Journal of Psychology, 30,* 507–509.

Renewing historic strengths, initiating new ventures (1996–2000)

15

The Union began the final quadrennium of its first half-century at the Montréal congress. By all accounts, the 26th International Congress of Psychology was a resounding success. It was characterized by the scope and vigor of its scientific program, offered in an ambience that blended old-world charm with new-world features. It was in this context that the 1996 Assembly undertook its deliberations and in which the outgoing and incoming Executive Committees met. This chapter reviews the issues which the Union addressed in the period from the Montréal congress to the Executive Committee meetings in Durban, 1999. The final events of this quadrennium will coincide with publication of this volume.

The dramatic growth in Union membership was sustained. Including actions taken at the 1996 Assembly, there were now 61 national members; 8 new members were approved in 1996: Albania, Austria, Bangladesh, Czech Republic, Ireland, Morocco, Russia, and Uganda. The membership of Brazil was terminated resulting from the defunct status of the adhering organization. On petition from the respective countries, South Africa was re-admitted with a new adhering body, and the adhering body for Spain was also changed.

The 26th International Congress of Psychology, Montréal, Canada, 1996

The 26th International Congress of Psychology was held in Montréal, Canada, August 18–23, 1996, under the auspices of the IUPsyS and the joint sponsorship of the National Research Council of Canada and the Canadian Psychological Association. Montréal is the second largest French-speaking city in the world and one of North America's most cosmopolitan venues. This was the first time that the congress was entirely under Canadian responsibility, since the 1954 congress had been under the joint responsibility of the Canadian and American Psychological Associations.

While David Bélanger, a past Treasurer of the Union (from 1977 to 1992), assumed the presidency of the congress, the two essential Scientific Program and Organizing Committees were chaired respectively by John Adair and Michel Sabourin. Terrence P. Hogan acted as Chair of the Finance Committee and Pierre Ritchie as Secretary-Treasurer to complete the main

TABLE 15.1

Organizational structure and composition of the committees:
26th International Congress of Psychology

Congress Council
David Bélanger, Université de Montréal, *President*
John G. Adair, University of Manitoba, *Chair, Scientific Program Committee*
Michel Sabourin, Université de Montréal, *Chair, Organizing Committee*
Laurier Forget, National Research Council Canada, *Director of Congress Services*
Terrence P. Hogan, University of Manitoba, *Chair, Finance Committee*
Pierre L.-J. Ritchie, University of Ottawa, *Secretary-Treasurer*
Mark R. Rosenzweig, University of California, *IUPsyS Liaison*
John Service, *CPA Liaison*

Scientific Program Committee
John G. Adair, University of Manitoba, *Chair*
John W. Berry, Queen's University
Fergus I.M. Craik, University of Toronto
Kenneth L. Dion, University of Toronto
Michèle Robert, Université de Montréal
Gordon Winocur, Rotman Research Institute, Toronto

Organizing Committee
Michel Sabourin, Université de Montréal, *Chair*
Hélène Cauffopé, Université Laval
Marcelle Cossette-Ricard, Université de Montréal
François Doré, Université Laval
Jacques Forget, UQAM
Andrée Fortin, Université de Montréal
Robert Haccoun, Université de Montréal
Jacques Lajoie, UQAM
Luc Lamarche, Université de Montréal
Jean-Roch Laurence, Concordia University
Jean-Claude Lauzon, SOBECO Inc, Montréal
Paul Maurice, UQAM
Stéphane Sabourin, Université Laval
Donald Taylor, McGill University

core of the Congress Council. Table 15.1 presents the complete picture of the congress organizational structure and committee resources.

A total of 5018 participants (including 4200 delegates and students) from over 80 countries attended this meeting. Participants came from all regions of the world including some that had seldom been represented at the congress (Sabourin, Craik, & Robert, 1998). A special financial assistance program, designed for colleagues from developing countries with limited financial support, allowed 114 participants to be awarded travel bursaries and complimentary registration to the congress. Many foreign colleagues were also given either complimentary rooms in certain hotels or in the private homes of Montréal area psychologists.

A colorful opening ceremony, combining artistic expression (a display of circus arts in a musical context in the tradition of the Quebec-based and world-renowned "Cirque du Soleil") and official welcoming addresses, was held on the evening of August 16 at the Palais des congrès de Montréal. The Canadian Minister of International Cooperation, the Hon Pierre Pettigrew, and the Quebec Minister of State for the Métropole de Montréal, the Hon Serge Ménard, represented respectively the federal and provincial governments. Other speeches were given by the representative of the Mayor of Montréal, by David Bélanger as President of the Congress, by Kurt Pawlik as President of IUPsyS, and by Francine Fournier, Deputy Director for Human and Social Sciences, UNESCO.

The scientific program, composed of more than 400 items in 24 concurrent sessions during the 5 days of the congress, "provided participants with the latest research developments in psychology from around the world" (Sabourin et al., 1998). The highlights of the program (see Table 15.2) were the 15 keynote addresses, the 45 state-of-the-art lectures, and the IUPsyS presidential address. Covering a wide range of topics representing the whole discipline, 140 invited symposia and 49 submitted, integrated paper sessions constituted the core of the scientific program. To these can be added the 116 thematic oral sessions and the 1700 interactive posters.

TABLE 15.2

Highlights of the scientific program:
26th International Congress of Psychology (Montréal, Canada)

IUPsyS presidential address
Kurt Pawlik (Germany): The psychology of individual differences: The
  personality puzzle

Keynote addresses
Paul Bertelson (Belgium): Starting from the ventriloquist: The perception of
  multimodal events
Vincent Bloch (France): Mémoire et vigilance
John T. Cacioppo (USA): Somatic responses to psychological stress
Pierre R. Dasen (Switzerland): Cadres théoriques en psychologie (inter-)
  culturelle
Alice H. Eagly (USA): Attitudes and the processing of attitude-relevant
  information
Martha Farah (USA): The neural basis of face, object and visual world
  recognition
Giyoo Hatano (Japan): Comprehension activity in individuals and groups
Susan D. Iversen (UK): Schizophrenia: The dark side of the mind
Marc Jeannerod (France): Représentations motrices
David Magnusson (Sweden): The person in developmental research
Ronald Melzack (Canada): Pain and stress: Toward a theory of chronic pain
Odmar Neumann (Germany): Conscious perception and the sensory control of
  motor responses
Robert Rescorla (USA): Nature and persistence of associative structures
Evgeny N. Sokolov (Russia): Geometrical model of cognitive processes
Endel Tulving (Canada): Brain/mind correlates of human memory

State-of-the-art lectures
Renée Baillargeon (USA): Infant's understanding of the physical world
Paul B. Baltes (Germany): The psychology of aging: Facts and frontiers
Albert Bandura (USA): Personal and collective efficacy in human adaptation
  and change
Peter M. Bentler (USA): Causal modeling
Michael H. Bond (Hong Kong): Social psychology across cultures
Rupert Brown (UK): Intergroup relations
Patrick Cavanagh (USA): Research in visual perception: The 25th millennium
Michael Corballis (New Zealand): Evolution of the human mind
Paul T. Costa Jr (USA): Personality theory in the wake of the five-factor model of
  personality
Pieter J.D. Drenth (The Netherlands): The psychology of work: Scientific inquiry
  and professional care
Rocio Fernandez-Ballesteros (Spain): Quality of life: Concept and assessment
Bennett G. Galef (Canada): Animal social learning: A decade of progress in
  interdisciplinary behavioral research
Rochel Gelman (USA): Cognitive development, domain specificity, and cultural
  variation
Patricia Goldman-Rakic (USA): Working memory and pre-frontal cortex
Claes von Hofsten (Sweden): Early development of perception, action, and
  cognition

continued ➡

TABLE 15.2 *continued*

Qicheng Jing (China): China's reform and challenges for psychology
Cigdem Kagitcibasi (Turkey): Human development in cross-cultural perspective
Nancy Kanwisher (USA): The brain basis of visual object recognition
Bryan Kolb (Canada): Neural plasticity and behavioral development
Asher Koriat (Israel): Metamemory: The feeling of knowing and its vagaries
John R. Krebs and Nicky Clayton (UK): Adaptative specialisation in memory
    and the brain
Anna B. Leonova (Russia): Occupational stress, health, and personal adpatation
N.J. Mackintosh (UK): Perceptual learning in people and animals
Neil M. Malamuth (USA): The confluence model of sexual aggression
Jacques Mehler (France): Langage et cognition
Susan Mineka (USA): Experimental approaches to understanding the anxiety
    and mood disorders
Risto Näätänen (Finland): Memory trace of a sound in the human brain as
    reflected by event-related potentials
J. Bruce Overmier (USA): Learned helplessness for studying the effects of stress:
    State or stasis of the art ?
Susan Pick (Mexico): Sexual and reproductive health: What next ?
Kim Plunkett (UK): Connectionism and development
Ype H. Poortinga (The Netherlands): Methodological and theoretical dilemmas
    of cross-cultural psychology
Anik de Ribaupierre (Switzerland): Développement cognitif et différences
    individuelles
Giacomo Rizzolatti (Italy): Spatial attention: Mechanisms and theories
Robert Rosenthal (USA): Meta-analysis: Concepts, corollaries, and controversies
Mark R. Rosenzweig (USA): The growing role of neuroscience in psychology
Pierre L. Roubertoux (France): Behavior-genetic analysis
José Miguel Salazar (Venezuela): Permanence and modification in national
    identities
Peter W. Sheehan (Australia): Contemporary trends in hypnosis research
Shepard Siegel (Canada): Learning and homeostasis
Jai B.P. Sinha (India): Work culture in a developing country: The case of India
John E.R. Staddon (USA): Animal models of memory
Jan Strelau (Poland): Individual differences in temperament: An international
    perspective
Carolyn Zahn-Waxler (USA): Social-emotional development in children and
    adolescents
Mark Zanna (Canada): The effect of intoxication on behavioral intentions

Activities were also planned for young psychologists and students, including discussion sessions with prominent psychologists, with journal editors, and on the topic of alternative employment opportunities. A scientific exchange program was also offered to facilitate the creation of personal links and networks between local psychologists from universities or private research centers, and international colleagues attending the congress.

An international commercial exhibition with more than 50 exhibitors (mainly book and psychological test publishers, manufacturers of research instrumentation and computer software, new psychopharmacological products, etc.) was available to congress participants in an area adjacent to the interactive poster sessions.

Over 15 satellite meetings of psychological associations affiliated or in relation with the IUPsyS were organized independently and presented before or after the congress. Even the American Psychological Association had decided to hold its Annual Meeting in Toronto, Canada, during the week that preceded the congress, to facilitate the participation of American psychologists and exhibitors to the Montréal congress.

Following the tradition initiated at the 1992 Brussels congress, in order to give an archival value to the presentations made, the Congress Abstracts were published as a Special Issue of the *International Journal of Psychology* (Vol. *31*, Issues 3 and 4). The congress proceedings presented the contributions of the invited speakers arranged in two equal-size volumes. Volume 1 (Adair, Bélanger, & Dion, 1998) covered the contributions to the social, personal and cultural aspects of psychological science; it also featured the address of Kurt Pawlik, President of the IUPsyS. Volume 2 (Sabourin et al., 1998) covered the biological and cognitive aspects of the discipline.

To enhance the Canadian participation to this event, both the Canadian Psychological Association and the Quebec College of Psychologists had decided not to hold their usual annual meeting in 1996, but to host instead a certain number of their activities and business meetings during the 26th congress. The official languages of the congress were English and French; in keeping with the tradition of previous international congresses to recognize regional linguistic characteristics, Spanish-language poster presentations were also accepted, provided they were accompanied by English- or French-language abstracts.

Besides the very special opening ceremony and the opening reception that immediately followed on August 16, other social and cultural activities were offered to congress participants during the week of the congress. These activities included a private concert by the internationally renowned "I Musici" chamber orchestra, "Le Festin du Gouverneur" (a unique interactive dinner-theatre experience), and a middle of the congress "Soirée Dansante" at Montréal's fashionable Queen Elizabeth Hotel.

The closing ceremony was held on August 21, the last day of the congress, and as in the Olympic tradition (!), most of the attention was oriented toward the next International Congress of Psychology, to be held in Stockholm, Sweden, in July 2000; following the closing addresses, the Swedish Organizing Committee hosted a typical Swedish reception for the congress participants.

Executive Committee and Assembly meetings, Montréal 1996

The outgoing Executive Committee meeting completed its business, reviewing reports and other materials as well as formulating recommendations in preparation for the Assembly. In particular, attention was given to needed Statute amendments, especially the establishment of official biennial Assembly meetings. Heretofore, only the Assembly held in conjunction with International Congresses of Psychology was formally recognized. The Assembly's "mid-term" meeting at the time of the IAAP congress was consultative but it did not have decisional authority. In addition, in submitting his report to the Executive Committee, the Treasurer, Sabourin, accurately forecast the emerging uncertainty about allocation procedures and amounts of grants received from UNESCO through ICSU and ISSC.

The Assembly was attended by 82 delegates from 44 countries; 8 affiliated organizations were represented by 11 persons. Observers from the American Psychological Association, the European Federation of Professional Psychologists Associations, and the International Test Commission were also present, foreshadowing important new collaborations in the coming biennium with each of them.

After reviewing the previous 4 years, President Pawlik offered recommendations for the future. These focused on the increasing demand from other sciences for psychological knowledge in solving problems facing the world, enhanced cooperation with both governmental and non-governmental organizations (e.g., World Health Organization), expanded regional collaboration (e.g., on capacity building for research), the internationalization of publications, and the challenge for psychology of the emerging importance of database archiving for all sciences. Viewed from the perspective of the subsequent 4 years, the outgoing President's vision can be regarded as pertinent as well as prescient.

Statutes and Rules

The Assembly amended the Statutes to establish biennial meetings of the Union's ultimate decisional body. A new procedure for admitting affiliated organizations was also adopted. During the 1996 elections, the Assembly noted certain ambiguities and charged the incoming Executive Committee to review the procedures and propose revisions to facilitate the election process.

Resources and capacity-building

Resources, internal and external, occupied much of the Assembly's attention, a concern that was to be sustained by the Executive Committee in the coming 4 years. To enhance the Union's capacity to better achieve its mission, it overwhelmingly approved (only four abstentions) an increase in dues to US$125 per unit. The intent was to enable greater support of several IUPsyS initiatives. These included collaborative projects in the developing world (e.g., Child rearing practices among low socioeconomic-status women in Turkey; Social integration in southern Africa), as well as extending the projects on Psychological Dimensions of Global Change and on Psychology and Cognitive Science.

In this context, the Assembly endorsed the Executive Committee's work on implementing changes in UNESCO's funding of projects through collaboration with ICSU and ISSC. There was clear recognition that external funding would continue to be essential to the Union's objective of contributing to increasing the capacity of psychological science in all parts of the world.

ARTS

The contribution of the Advanced Research Training Seminars (ARTS) was underscored at the Montréal congress. Two ARTS were offered in 1996 under the coordination of executive member Kagitcibasi. They addressed "Qualitative Research Methods" and "Early Intervention in Families and Other Settings." Both ARTS were very well received and participants benefited from the large financial allocation made by the congress organizers to support attendees from low-income countries. Given their growing importance, a comprehensive review of ARTS was established as a priority for the incoming Executive Committee.

Publications

The *International Journal of Psychology* continued to be the Union's major publication vehicle. The editor, Doré, received 80 manuscripts in the previous year, of which 26 were accepted for publication. A special issue was devoted to "National development of psychology: Factors facili-tating and impeding progress in developing countries." The abstracts of papers presented at the Montréal congress constituted a double special issue.

Scientific meetings

The 26th International Congress of Psychology again demonstrated the Union's capacity to mount a strong and varied program reflecting all the recognized fields and subfields of psychology as a scientific discipline and scientifically based profession. It was attended by over 5000 persons from more than 80 countries. Of these, 4200 were regular delegates with the balance being distinguished guests, accompanying persons, exhibitors, and the media. The growing presence of journalists from the written and electronic popular press signaled a growing perception of the relevance of psychological knowledge and its applications to the general public as well as to society's decision-makers.

The Executive Committee and Assembly both favorably received progress reports on development of the 27th International Congress of Psychology planned for Stockholm (Sweden) in 2000. The continuity of the Union's premier event was assured with the selection of the venue of the 28th congress in 2004. After receiving proposals from three national members, China, Columbia, and Egypt, Beijing (China) was chosen by the

Assembly. This selection underscored the breadth of the Union's international scope; three successive congresses would be held on three different continents with a rich diversity of cultures and history.

Following on the success of the initial regional congress sponsored by IUPsyS in Guangzhou (China), the Union agreed to collaborate with IAAP in supporting a second regional congress to be held in Mexico in 1997. Recognizing that such congresses optimally require several years of planning, it was decided to sponsor a Pan-Arab Regional Congress scheduled for 1999 in Cairo (Egypt).

International collaboration

The historic commitment to promoting and strengthening the global relevance and international character of psychology has long been a strength of IUPsyS. The Union's ability to exercise this responsibility, however, was being tested by emergent changes in the United Nations system as civil society took on a greater share of a wide range of international activities intended to reduce human distress and enhance the wellbeing of all persons. This called for a review of current arrangements leading to renewal of old relationships and the establishment of new partnerships. The coming quadrennium would see considerable progress that was still being envisioned at the time of the Montréal meetings.

An important component focused on the Union's collaboration with the largest individual member-based international organization in psychology, the International Association of Applied Psychology (IAAP). The relationship between IAAP and IUPsyS was addressed at each of the deliberative meetings in Montréal. Both the outgoing and incoming Executive Committees accorded it an important place in their agendas. The Assembly initiated a process to regularize the process of cooperation between the two bodies. The intent was to ensure that certain forms of collaboration would become a matter of common practice and be less dependent on the immediate goodwill of the respective leadership of the respective organizations.

Elections

The Assembly elected Géry d'Ydewalle (Belgium) as President, Cigdem Kagitcibasi (Turkey) and Jan Strelau (Poland) as Vice-Presidents, while Pawlik assumed the position of Past-President. Re-elected members of the Executive Committee were Rubén Ardila (Columbia), Derek Blackman (United Kingdom), Michel Denis (France), Hiroshi Imada (Japan), Lars-Göran Nilsson (Sweden), and Bruce Overmier (USA). Newly elected Members of the Executive Committee for an initial term were John Adair (Canada), Juan José Sanchez-Sosa (Mexico), Houcan Zhang (China), and Ype Poortinga (The Netherlands). Joining the President as officers upon their election by the incoming Executive Committee were a new Secretary-General, Pierre Ritchie (Canada) and, continuing as Treasurer,

Michel Sabourin (Canada). Ritchie had been a delegate to the Assembly since 1988 and served as Secretary-Treasurer of the 26th congress. It was decided to leave the position of Deputy Secretary-General temporarily vacant to allow for broader recruitment.

In a transition year in which the results of much effort were brought to fruition, the Union had put in place leadership that represented a clear blend of continuity and renewal. While broadly diverse, it was keenly aware of gaps that would compel sensitive attention to non-represented regions, especially Africa. There was clearly more to be done to increase the Union's strength on a number of matters beyond geography. The broader climate was also characterized by increased ferment across the whole range of international entities with which the Union had or might collaborate. The newly elected Officers and Executive Committee had no shortage of challenges to maintain and enhance the Union's viability in this quadrennium.

Executive Committee meeting, Stockholm 1997

The 1997 meeting of the Executive Committee was held in Stockholm, Sweden, at the invitation of the 27th congress Organizing Committee, who provided an environment conducive to the business conducted and to an appreciation of the venue of the next congress. A primary activity was a detailed review of plans for the scientific program, including invited keynote speakers, state-of-the art and symposia chairs. As well as the congress President, Lars-Göran Nilsson, International Congress Committee

Executive Committee, Stockholm, July 23–28, 2000—Back row (left to right): Lars Göran Nilsson (President), Örjan Salling (Secretary-General), Arne Öhman (Vice-President, Chair Scientific Committee). Front row (left to right): Birgit Hansson (Vice-President, Chair Organizing Committee), Gunn Johansson (Member, Deputy-Chair Scientific Committee). Not present on picture: Ingvar Lundberg (Member, Deputy-Chair Organizing Committee), Kurt Pawlik (IUPsyS Liaison).

members present for discussion of congress planning were: Arne Öhman (Chair of Scientific Program Committee), Birgit Hansson (Chair of the Organizing Committee), Gunn Johansson (Deputy Chair of the Scientific Program Committee), Britta Sjoblom (Project Coordinator, Stockholm Convention Bureau), and Örjan Salling (Secretary-General of the congress).

International congresses

A site visit to the congress setting as well as the review and accompanying discussion of the various reports led the Executive Committee to the conclusion that the prospects for the 27th congress were excellent. Among prominent features planned for the congress were a health theme as well as a series of seminars focused on diplomacy and psychology. The Organizing and Scientific Program Committees were commended for their excellence.

A report on preliminary planning for the 28th congress in Beijing was also received. The Executive Committee also endorsed the appointment of Professor Qicheng Jing as President of the Congress.

Regional congresses

Concerns about the feasibility of holding the proposed 1999 Pan-Arab Regional Congress grew in 1997. The Executive Committee recognized that its future had become uncertain and charged the President to undertake a further review of the situation.

The International Network of Psychology and the Developing World, with Ardila as Chair, continued to play a role in facilitating the Union's commitment to sponsoring regional congresses, first initiated with China in 1995, followed by Mexico in 1997. Notwithstanding the difficulties encountered in planning a 1999 regional congress, the Union remained committed to the schedule of a major regional congress every 2 years in collaboration with IAAP. Other venues were under consideration for the next several regional congresses.

Organizational matters

Professor Merry Bullock (Estonia/USA) was appointed Deputy Secretary-General. She brought extensive experience as a scientist and expertise in public policy gathered in Canada, Estonia, Germany, and the USA.

One new national member, Georgia and one new affiliate, the International Neuro-psychological Society, were approved in 1997, bringing total membership to 62 countries and 11 affiliates.

The Executive Committee approved a revision to the Rules of Procedure for the creation of an Election Committee, composed of the Past-President as Chair, and two members to be chosen by the Assembly from different countries. The proposal provided for disseminating brief CVs of all candidates for the Executive Committee, including the President and Vice-Presidents. The President asked Pawlik to draft an amendment to the Rules of Procedure for consideration at the Assembly's 1998 meeting.

Pierre L.-J. Ritchie:
Secretary-General of
IUPsyS (1996–); and
Mary Bullock:
Deputy Secretary-
General (1998-).

The Treasurer's report indicated that the financial base of the Union had been enhanced by the new dues and the important surplus generated by the success of the Montréal congress. Under the plan agreed upon earlier, the Canadian National Research Council received US$84,292 as its share of the surplus, and the Union got US$146,848, of which US$73,424 reverted to the Canadian Psychological Association for support of its participation in Union affairs, including the financing of young Canadian psychologists to attend future congresses.

The Executive Committee approved Sabourin's recommendation that the Union's share of the Montréal congress surplus be allocated equally among the 4 years of the current quadrennium. A preliminary budget for fiscal year 1998 was introduced by Sabourin as the first step in developing a multi-year financial planning cycle.

A request for the formation of a Women's Committee (generated by a petition circulated at the Montréal congress) was reviewed. After welcoming the suggestion, there was much discussion but little consensus about the range and scope of the proposed committee's purview. The initial letter requesting a Women's Committee was focused on women in psychology, but the several members of the Executive Committee believed its scope might be broader. They appointed a sub- committee (chaired by Bullock) of the Standing Committee of Psychology as a Science and Profession to seek advice and input from the authors of the letter requesting the Women's Committee and to make a recommendation to the 1998 Executive Committee defining name, scope, range, and topics.

Capacity-building

A comprehensive review of Advanced Research Training Seminars also was completed and its recommendations were discussed and endorsed. The general thrust of the recommendations was to streamline certain procedures and ensure consistent application of basic principles guiding ARTS as a central component of the Union's capacity-building contribution to psychological science in developing countries.

Under the coordination of IUPsyS Executive Committee member John Adair, two ARTS were conducted in 1997, for the first time in conjunction with a Regional Congress of Psychology. One focused on "Multivariate Methods in Psychology: Factor Analysis Structural Models," while the second was on "Research Methods Applied to the Study of Health."

The Standing Committee on the Development of Psychology as a Science and as a Profession, chaired by Vice-President Kagitcibasi, had initiated a review of the role of the Union with respect to its national members, in particular with respect to the Union's objective to promote the science of psychology. The President proposed and the Executive Committee approved a work group, chaired by Kagitcibasi, to develop a draft questionnaire to national members. Information from this questionnaire would be reviewed at the 1998 Assembly and Executive Committee meetings as the basis for further queries and interviews to the national members.

Publications

The editor (Doré) of the *International Journal of Psychology*, in collaboration with the Chair of the Standing Committee on Communication and Publications (Pawlik), initiated a comprehensive review of the *Journal*. This process would continue in two stages for the remainder of the biennium. Ritchie and Bullock now served as associate editors with special responsibility for the International Platform section.

The Proceedings of the 26th International Congress of Psychology were published in two volumes. Volume 1 (Adair, Bélanger, & Dion, 1998) covered cognitive and biological aspects of psychology; Volume 2 (Sabourin, Craik, & Robert, 1998) addressed personality, developmental and social aspects of psychology. Work continued on the preparation of the *International Handbook of Psychological Science* (now called the *International Handbook of Psychology*), due for publication in 2000 under the editorship of Pawlik and Rosenzweig. In anticipation of the imminent 50th anniversary of the IUPsyS, former officers Bélanger, Holtzman, and Rosenzweig were asked to prepare a history of the Union. As this project got underway, Sabourin agreed to join them as a fourth author. The Executive Committee also commissioned a new edition of the IUPsyS *Directory* under the editorship of Overmier.

Special projects

The Standing Committee on the Development of Psychology as a Science and as a Profession completed the project to compile a Bibliography on Psychology Around the World. Authored by Imada (1996), the bibliography was published as an article in the *International Journal of Psychology*. A total of 2497 books, chapters and articles were reported, classified into 3 categories: International: Worldwide, International: Regional, and National, with 157, 203, and 2137 items respectively. An appendix table on "Where and how often can you find country-by-country descriptions of psychology around the world" adds to the bibliography's utility.

Supported by UNESCO through ICSU, the project on Psychology and Cognitive Science completed its initial work. Executive Committee member Denis, as Project Director, authored a comprehensive report providing a detailed analysis of the extensive survey on psychology and cognitive science conducted among the national members of the Union. Responses were received from 31 countries. Given the findings and the potential for interdisciplinary activities, the project was continued with a revised objective. The second stage was to focus on Psychology in a Multi-disciplinary Environment. This dimension was anchored in the unequivocal recognition of the increasing pertinence of a multi-disciplinary environment to psychology and of psychology to other disciplines working in cognitive science. The second stage would prepare the groundwork for a large-scale multi-disciplinary initiative.

Under the auspices of the Union's Ad Hoc Committee for the Psychological Study of Peace, chaired by Michael Wessells, a new venture was launched to address a significant issue of social transformation in sub-Saharan Africa. A far-reaching workshop, "Youth, Political Violence and Conflict Resolution in Southern Africa" was completed in late 1997.

UNESCO grants provided through ISSC in 1997 were allocated to the projects on "Psychological Dimensions of Global Change," "Dealing with Poverty and Social Integration Through Studying Child Rearing Practices of Low Socioeconomic-status Women," and "Youth, Political Violence and Conflict Resolution in Southern Africa." Those provided through ICSU were the projects on "Compiling a Bibliography on Psychology Around the World," "Psychology and Cognitive Science," and "Psychological Dimensions of Global Change".

International collaboration

The evolving relationship with IAAP was again the object of extensive deliberation. A joint IAAP- IUPsyS Officers Committee, formed to explore possible cooperation and collaborative work, met several times to consider areas where the organizations could work together. In his remarks to the Executive Committee, President d'Ydewalle noted that relations with IAAP had improved considerably, with the door open for future initiatives. Nonetheless, there was no expectation of short-term restructuring of the two organizations. The general sense of the Executive Committee's discussion was that any movement toward structural change should be preceded by a long period of developing a successful working relationship. There were questions about what various levels of cooperation might entail. Although there was broad agreement that collaboration and better cooperation are beneficial, there were differences of opinion about how to go about achieving them. Greater proposed integration, particularly suggestions of merger, raised greater conflict.

The Union determined to accord increased attention to the United Nations system in this quadrennium. While wishing to maintain its links to UNESCO, typically in association with ICSU and ISSC, it recognized the pertinence of psychology to a wide range of issues addressed in the UN system. Under the direction of Sabourin, consultative status with the United Nations Department of Public Information was established in 1997. An application for similar standing with the United Nations Economic and Social Council was still pending in 1999. Coordinated by Ritchie, a work plan for co-operation between the World Health Organization and IUPsyS was approved by both organizations in 1997.

Concerns began to be voiced about UNESCO's World Science Conference planned for 1999. This focused on the apparent absence of social science presence in the organization of the conference. This issue would be addressed in collaboration with ISSC.

Assembly and Executive Committee meetings, San Francisco 1998

The wisdom of the decision to hold biennial Assembly meetings was immediately evident in 1998. In addition to enabling the Assembly to affirm the direction being taken by the Executive Committee and securing the contribution of Assembly delegates to current issues, items of official business were also transacted.

A total of 51 delegates representing 38 countries attended the San Francisco Assembly; representatives of 4 affiliates as well as a large number of observers from national members and other organizations were also present.

Organizational matters

Two new national members, Slovakia and Ukraine, were approved in 1998, bringing total membership to 64 countries and 11 affiliates. A growing concern addressed in San Francisco was the increased number of Category 0 countries, that is those who had not paid their dues for at least 3 years; while remaining national members, they no longer had a vote at the Assembly. The matter was referred to the Executive Committee for further consideration.

Among other business, amendments to the Rules of Procedure were approved, creating an Elections Committee as well as revised nominations and elections procedures. The Assembly also approved that the Executive Committee continue exploring research activities and other initiatives to further psychology internationally.

International congresses

The San Francisco meetings expressed their full satisfaction with reports of the planning for the 27th congress. Similarly, the preliminary planning for the 28th congress was proceeding well.

Regional congresses

The doubts previously expressed about the feasibility of holding the proposed 1999 Pan-Arab Regional Congress were unfortunately confirmed. In early 1998, with much regret, the Executive Committee supported the officers' recommendation that IUPsyS withdraw its auspices.

To the good fortune of the international community, the recently constituted Psychological Society of South Africa offered to organize the First African Congress of Psychology. Following an intense period of consultation and negotiation, an agreement was achieved to hold this landmark event under the auspices of the Union with the collaboration of IAAP and the International Association of Cross-Cultural Psychology. The Executive Committee met with the Africa Congress Organizing Committee in San Francisco, yielding a high level of confidence that the event could be mounted notwithstanding the short time-frame.

Capacity-building

Three ARTS were conducted in 1998, again under the coordination of Adair. Two received support from UNESCO via ISSC: "Developing Effective Health Behavior Interventions and Qualitative Approaches in Cross-Cultural Psychology". In addition, "Advances in Cognitive Psychology" was offered. In addition to the funding support of UNESCO/ISSC and the Union itself, ARTS secured financial support from nine national organizations and five other institutions. This underscored the viability and credibility of this activity as a capacity-building vehicle.

Publications

As anticipated, the review of the *International Journal of Psychology* led to revised "Aims and Scope" for the *Journal*. The *Proceedings of the 26th International Congress of Psychology* attracted positive attention and strong dissemination results. Work continued on preparation of the *International Handbook of Psychology* and a book on the History of the Union, both due for publication in 2000. ISSC confirmed that five short articles (boxes) prepared under the auspices of the IUPsyS will be published in the World Social Science Report for release in conjunction with UNESCO's 1999 World Science Conference.

An important new initiative, the Psychology Resource Files, was approved by the 1998 Executive Committee. Under this aegis, materials and texts presenting useful information about psychology and psychologists internationally would be published periodically. It is anticipated that the revised IUPsyS *Directory* will be the initial offering, possibly with other materials to be determined.

The IUPsyS website (http://www.IUPsyS.org), now under the able direction of Deputy Secretary-General Bullock, was considerably enhanced in 1998.

Special projects

The Standing Committee on Research and Special Projects, chaired by Vice-President Strelau, assisted the Assembly and Executive Committee in providing general oversight and policy framework. In 1998, it undertook a preliminary consultation with national members on ideas for future projects, especially those with a goal of promoting capacity-building.

The several international collaborative networks coordinated by IUPsyS continued apace in 1998. Work of the International Network Project on

Psychological Dimensions of Global Change continued with Pawlik as Project Director. The International Network on the Young Child and the Family, coordinated by Vice-President Kagitcibasi, continued its work on several activities including the promotion of psychology as a science and as a profession with national members. In 1998, initial deliberations were held on developing comprehensive data and information on the education and training of psychologists throughout the world. The IUPsyS HealthNet, co-ordinated by Executive Committee member Sanchez-Sosa, embarked on a period of renewal and expansion.

The initiative on Psychology and Cognitive Science completed its current project and concurrently continued planning the new stage of multi-disciplinary work in 1998 with Denis remaining as Project Director. Dissemination of the results of the first stage was facilitated through publication of a Special Issue of the *International Journal of Psychology* edited by Denis (1998). The second stage, which focuses on Psychology in a Multi-disciplinary Environment, was launched to provide a framework for engaging contacts with international bodies representing other disciplines related to psychology. The objective was to explore the possibilities for IUPsyS and other organizations whose objectives partly overlap those of psychology to join their efforts in activities that promote an interdisciplinary view of science. During the 1988 ICSU Extraordinary General Assembly, contacts were made with officers of several Unions, in particular the International Brain Research Organization (IBRO), the International Geographical Union (IGU), and the International Union of the History and Philosophy of Science (IUHPS).

UNESCO grants provided through ISSC in 1997 were allocated to the projects on "Psychological Dimensions of Global Change" and on "Dealing with Poverty and Social Integration Through Studying Child Rearing Practices of Low Socioeconomic-status Women," as well as the ARTS noted earlier. Those provided through ICSU in collaboration with the US National Academy of Sciences were the projects on "Perception and Assessment of Global Environmental Change" and on "Psychology in a Multi-disciplinary Environment."

International collaboration

As a result of a HealthNet initiative, a special IUPsyS liaison, Professor Robert Martin (Canada), had been appointed to the World Health Organization (WHO) in 1997. The initial outcome of this activity was the establishment of a Work Plan approved by both IUPsyS and WHO as a next step toward establishing permanent formal relationship with WHO. The Work Plan emphasized the development of specific outcomes, initially concentrated on producing Behavioral Science Learning Modules as well as communication and information-sharing activities. Collaborative work was expected to focus on a broad range of health psychology activities including the participation of health psychologists in health education, and health promotion as well as traditional areas of mental health. HealthNet and Martin also continued to provide collaboration and assistance to Ritchie as IUPsyS representative to WHO, in implementing the IUPsyS-WHO Work Plan. At the outset, there was evidence of clear support within WHO to develop closer ties with psychology, particularly within a health psychology and behavioral science framework. The renewal of HealthNet was also of considerable interest to WHO.

A major achievement in 1998 was the attainment of Special Consultative status with the United Nations Economic and Social Council (ECOSOC). This was the fruition of considerable effort by Sabourin, the Union's primary representative to UN headquarters, with assistance from current and former Officers. The Union would now be in a position to participate more actively not only in operational tasks, but to contribute to the policy and deliberative process of the UN's senior body on social matters as well.

The President and Secretary-General, together with Denis, represented the Union at ICSU's Extraordinary General Assembly, which adopted changes to ICSU's organization and structure. With the expansion of the Executive Board, the Union hoped to have greater opportunity to participate in the senior level of ICSU's decision-making. The President and Secretary-General also served as delegates to ISSC's biennial General Assembly, at which Pawlik was elected President.

Relations with IAAP remained an important topic. Assembly delegates responded favorably to the President's summary of progress at the San Francisco meeting. The joint IAAP-IUPsyS Committee was now meeting at least once a year and more typically twice. The IAAP Secretary-General, in attendance at the Assembly, endorsed the President's remarks. The Assembly requested a full report at the 2000 Assembly on the steps taken by IAAP and IUPsyS to enhance co-operation between the two organizations.

Executive Committee meeting, Durban 1999

Given the objectives set at the outset of this quadrennium, it was especially fitting that the last Executive Committee meeting prior to the Stockholm congress be held in southern Africa. It was held in conjunction with the First African Congress of Psychology in Durban, South Africa. The congress itself will likely be regarded as one of the more significant events in the history of psychology in sub-Saharan Africa. More than closing the Union's first half-century, it bore testimony to directions for the future.

Regional congresses

Holding the Executive Committee meeting in conjunction with the 1999 regional congress provided concrete affirmation of the Union's capacity and willingness to support psychological science and the application of psychological knowledge to social progress in all areas of the world. Each member of the Executive Committee was invited to contribute to the

Executive Committee (1996–2000) pictured at the 1st African Congress of Psychology, Durban, South Africa, July 1999—Back row (from left to right): Bruce Overmier, John Adair, Rubén Ardila, Houcan Zhang, Lars-Göran Nilsson, Juan José Sanchez-Sosa, Ype Poortinga, and Michel Denis. Front row (left to right): Hiroshi Imada, Michel Sabourin, Jan Strelau, Géry d'Ydewalle, Kurt Pawlik, Cigdem Kagitcibasi, Pierre Ritchie, and Merry Bullock.

congress program. Most participated in two or more events. One of the lasting results of the Union's presence will be the relationships developed between attendees and persons associated with IUPsyS. The work of committees and international networks will be enriched by greater involvement of colleagues from several African countries. The Union secured supplemental grants from both ICSU and ISSC to support its contribution to the African Regional Congress.

Notwithstanding the success of the Durban Regional Congress, it was increasingly clear that the planning and organization of regional congresses is fraught with potential difficulty. Even the African event presented challenges that could not be overcome; for example, it was ultimately not possible to organize an ARTS for the African congress. This issue was the dominant item of discussion at both joint IAAP–IUPsyS officers meetings held in 1999. This led to new common procedures for sponsoring regional congresses.

International congresses

The San Francisco meetings expressed their full satisfaction with reports of the planning for the 27th congress. The organizational framework to support planning for the 28th congress was now in place. A draft contract between the Union and the Chinese organizers was under review, with signing to take place in 2000.

President d'Ydewalle prepared and the Executive Committee ratified guidelines for making an application to hold the Union's international congress. With the increasing number of countries expressing interest in doing so for 2008, this document met an immediate need.

Capacity-building and special projects

Recognizing the importance of preserving the quality of ARTS while being equally cognizant of the large effort required by numerous persons to achieve them, the Executive Committee approved a new policy whereby ARTS will henceforth be offered only every 2 years in conjunction with the two major international congresses. As an alternative, workshops will be encouraged at regional congresses.

The Executive Committee again devoted considerable attention to consideration of various means to support capacity building. While the desire to do so as much as possible in direct collaboration with National Members remained strong, the reality is more often that the Union's limited resources typically preclude such ventures except on an occasional basis. The thrust remains, therefore, on activities that have reasonable prospect of generalization and facilitating collaboration through and within networks. The projects coordinated by Pawlik on psychological dimensions of social change, Kagitcibasi on child rearing practices and literacy, and by Denis in psychology and cognitive science, demonstrate in their diversity and their results the Union's ability to make an important contribution to capacity-building. The issue is expected to remain an important challenge in the next quadrennium and be the object of further deliberation at the 2000 Assembly and Executive Committee meetings.

The Union was informed that it would receive in 2000 the largest grant it has ever been accorded by ICSU for the project "Psychology in a Multi-Disciplinary Environment." In particular, an IUPsyS-IBRO joint symposium and a multi-day training workshop on "Neuroimaging of Cognitive Functions," intended especially for psychologists in developing and Eastern Europe countries, will be held in conjunction with the Stockholm congress. An IUPsyS-IGU joint symposium on "Spatial Cognition and Geographical Knowledge" will also be delivered at the congress.

As a result of networking activities of recent years coordinated by Vice-President Kagitcibasi, a Directory of Centers Involved in Research and Applied Work on the Young Child and the Family in Developing Countries and Eastern Europe was completed and published in the *International Journal of Psychology*. It promised to be a valuable resource for those interested in communicating and collaborating with research centers across the world focusing on the young child and the family.

A highly successful workshop, "Youth and Violence in Southern Africa: Building Cultures of Peace" was offered in conjunction with the First African Congress. It was again organized under the auspices of the Union's Committee on the Psychological Study of Peace with support from UNESCO via ISSC.

Organizational matters

Two new national members, Mongolia and Peru, were approved in 1999, bringing total membership to 66 countries and 11 affiliates.

The growing concern addressed in San Francisco about the larger number of Category 0 countries prompted the Executive Committee to formulate several actions which will be brought to the Stockholm Assembly. In particular, the determination of "good standing" would be based on a more elaborated definition.

An immediate action developed by the Treasurer with the support of the Executive Committee was a request to higher-income countries to consider a voluntary increase in their dues category. Preliminary indications were of a positive response from several national members.

Publications

The most important publications decision of 1999 addressed the language of the *International Journal of Psychology*. Following an extended and vigorous, but unanticipated, debate, the Executive Committee voted to publish the *Journal* as a unilingual English language *Journal* with abstracts in English, French, and Spanish. Implementation will occur in conjunction with the start of the term of a new editor in 2001 since the current editor (Doré) will have completed two terms, the maximum permitted.

Overmier was appointed editor of the new Psychology Resource Files, which will initially be published in 2000 by Psychology Press. Both the *International Handbook* and the book on the history of the Union were also on target for a year 2000 publication.

International collaboration

Along with the relationship with IAAP already described, the relationship with several European entities occupied considerable attention in 1999. At year's end, the Union appeared to have played a constructive role in facilitating greater communication between representatives of the academic and professional psychology communities. It is hoped that EFPPA will be better able to meet the needs of the academic community, and its leadership undertook to consider several mechanisms to enable EFPPA so to do.

The Union was well represented at the World Science Conference with a delegation headed by President d'Ydewalle. It was unclear what the real impact of the Conference will be in the years ahead, with opinions varying between seeing it as the last echo of the outgoing administration and those who saw it as potentially having broader implications for UNESCO and government's science policy agenda.

In the short-term, the Union was unhappy that most of the material it prepared for the World Social Science Report was not retained by UNESCO. This resulted from an apparent misunderstanding between ISSC, which served as the intermediary for all the social sciences, and UNESCO.

Work with United Nations headquarters and with WHO continued to evolve. At an operational level, the Union now has regular representatives to assist it in New York and Geneva. An additional task was added to the

IUPsyS–WHO Work Plan; the Union will develop a policy paper to assist WHO in enunciating the contributions psychologists can make across the health care system. The Behavioral Science Modules on Immunization and Pre-Natal Care were virtually complete and are due to be published and disseminated in 2000.

As the Union receives more requests for involvement, it became increasingly clear that choices will have to be made based on an articulation of the Union's priorities for such involvement. Preparations for the first year of the new millennium underscore the challenge, particularly as the traditional nation-based UN political system begins to consider how to work more collaboratively with agencies of civil society which now undertake much of the work done under UN auspices.

Concluding comment

Although the quadrennium has most of its last year to complete as this is written, it is reasonable to suggest that most of the objectives set at its outset will have been achieved. Notwithstanding the transitions in the Union's own leadership as well as unanticipated challenges which had to be addressed in the short-term, the Union demonstrated sustained focus on its priorities. It continues to grapple with the dilemma of insufficient resources to meet demands and expectations, both those generated internally and those coming increasingly from the wider global community. While those who will assume responsibility for initiating the Union's second half-century after the Stockholm congress will set their own agenda and priorities, it is probable that there will be a good measure of continuity in some of the specifics. They will certainly be faced with having to make ever-harder choices in the allocation of resources while seeking to expand the resource base itself.

References

Adair, J.G., Bélanger, D., & Dion, K.L. (Eds.) (1998). *Advances in psychological science: Vol. 1: Social, personal and cultural aspects.* Hove, UK: Psychology Press.

Denis, M. (Ed.) (1998). Psychology and cognitive science: An international perspective. Special Issue of the *International Journal of Psychology, 33*(6).

Imada, H. (1996). Psychology throughout the world: A selected bibliography of materials published in English 1974–1995. *International Journal of Psychology, 31*(6), 307–368.

Sabourin, M., Craik, F. & Robert, M. (Eds.) (1998). *Advances in psychological science: Vol. 2: Biological and cognitive aspects.* Hove, UK: Psychology Press.

Appendix A

Appendices A.1 to A.12 show the membership of the International Congress of Psychology Committees, 1889–1951; the changing composition of the Committee, and the terms of the members.

Appendix A.1

Members appointed at the 1st congress, Paris, 1889, serving 1889–1892 (N=27)

Beaunis, Henri (France)
Benedikt, —. (Austria)
Bernheim, Hippolyte (France)
Bertrand, —. (France)
Danilewski, —. (Russia)
Delboeuf, Joseph Rémi Léopold (Belgium)
Espinas, Alfred (France)
Ferrari, H. (France)
Forel, August Henri (Switzerland)
Galton, Francis (UK)
Gley, Eugène (France)
Grote, N. (Russia)
Grüber, Edouard (Romania)
Herzen, Pierre (Switzerland)

Hitzig, Eduard (Germany)
James, William (US)
Lomboroso, Cesare (Italy)
Marillier, Léon (France)
Münsterberg, Hugo (Germany)
Myers, Frederick W.H. (UK)
Neiglick, —. (Finland)
Ochorowicz, Julian (Russia)
Ribot, Théodule (France)
Richet, Charles (France)
von Schrenck-Notzing, Albert (Germany)
Sidgwick, Henry (UK)
Sperling, Arthur (Germany)

Appendix A.2

Committee appointed at the 2nd congress, London, 1892, serving 1892–1896 (N=27)

Members newly appointed

Bain, Alexander (UK)
Baldwin, James M. (US)
Donaldson, Henry H. (US)
Ebbinghaus, Hermann (Germany)
Ferrier, David (UK)
Fullerton, George S. (US)
Hall, G. Stanley (US)
Lehmann, Alfred (Denmark)
Liégeois, Jules (France)
Lipps, Theodor (Germany)

Mendelsohn, Maurice (Russia)
Morselli, Enrico (Italy)
Newbold, William R. (US)
Preyer, Wilhelm (Germany)
Schäfer, E.A. (UK)
Stumpf, Carl (Germany)
Sully, James (UK)
Ward, James (UK)
Witmer, Lightner (US)

Members reappointed for a 2nd term

Bernheim, Hippolyte (France)
Delboeuf, Joseph R.L. (Belgium)*
Hitzig, Eduard (Germany)
James, William (US)

Myers, Frederick W.H. (UK)
Richet, Charles (France)
von Schrenck-Notzing, Albert (Germany)
Sidgwick, Henry (UK)

*Member whose death during this term was announced at the next congress.

Appendix A.3

Committee appointed at the 3rd congress, Munich, 1896, serving 1896–1900 (N=38)

Members newly appointed

Binet, Alfred (France)
Brentano, Franz (Italy)
Exner, Sigmund (Austria)
Flechsig, Paul (Germany)
Flournoy, Théodore (Switzerland)
Grote, N. (Russia)
Henschen, S.E. (Sweden)
Hering, Ewald (Germany)
Janet, Pierre (France)
Korsakoff, Serge (Russia)
Lange, Nikolaus (Russia)

Marty, Anton (Austria)
Meinong, Alexius (Austria)
Mingazzini, Giovanni (Italy)
Mosso, Angelo (Italy)
Mourly-Vold, J. (Sweden)
Ramon y Cajal, Santiago (Spain)
Ribot, Théodule (France)**
Sergi, Giuseppe (Italy)
Titchener, Edward B. (US)
Wundt, Wilhelm (Germany)

Members reappointed for a consecutive number of terms

2nd term
Bain, Alexander (UK)
Baldwin, James M. (US)
Ebbinghaus, Hermann (Germany)
Ferrier, David (UK)
Forel, August Henri (Switzerland)**
Hall, G. Stanley (US)
Lehmann, Alfred (Denmark)
Lipps, Theodor (Germany)
Mendelsohn, Maurice (Russia)

Morselli, Enrico (Italy)
Stumpf, Carl (Germany)
Sully, James (UK)

3rd term
James, William (US)
Myers, Frederick W.H. (UK)
Richet, Charles (France)
von Schrenck-Notzing, Albert (Germany)
Sidgwick, Henry (UK)

**Not consecutive terms.

Appendix A.4

Committee appointed at the 4th congress, Paris, 1900, serving 1900–1905 (N=55)

Members newly appointed

Bourdon, Benjamin (France)
Demoor, Jean (Belgium)
Ehrenfels, Christian (Austria)
Ferrari, Giulio Cesare (Italy)
Külpe, Otto (Germany)
Ladd, George, T. (US)
Luciani, Luigi (Italy)
Magaläes, Lemos (Portugal)
Novicow, —. (Russia)

Serebrennikov, Vitali T. (Russia)
Stout, George F. (UK)
Stuart, Anderson (Australia)
Tamburini, Augusto (Italy)
de Tarchanoff, J. (Russia)
Thiery, Armand (Belgium)
Tokarsky, A. (Russia)
Zwaardemaker, Hendrick (Netherlands)

Members reappointed for a consecutive number of terms

2nd term
Binet, Alfred (France)
Brentano, Franz (Italy)
Exner, Sigmund (Austria)
Flechsig, Paul (Germany)
Flournoy, Théodore (Switzerland)

Galton, Francis (UK)**
Henschen, S.E. (Sweden)
Hering, Ewald (Germany)
Janet, Pierre (France)
Lange, Nikolaus (Russia)
Marillier, Léon (France)**

continued →

Members reappointed for a consecutive number of terms (continued)

2nd term (continued)
Marty, Anton (Austria)
Meinong, Alexius (Austria)
Mingazzini, Giovanni (Italy)
Mosso, Angelo (Italy)
Mourly-Vold, J. (Sweden)
Münsterberg, Hugo (US)**
Ramon y Cajal, Santiago (Spain)
Sergi, Giuseppe (Italy)
Titchener, Edward B. (US)
Wundt, Wilhelm (Germany)

3rd term
Bain, Alexander (UK)
Baldwin, James M. (US)
Ebbinghaus, Hermann (Germany)
Ferrier, David (UK)

Forel, August Henri (Switzerland)
Hall, G. Stanley (US)
Lehmann, Alfred (Denmark)
Lipps, Theodor (Germany)
Mendelsohn, Maurice (Russia)
Morselli, Enrico (Italy)
Ribot, Théodule (France)
Stumpf, Carl (Germany)
Sully, James (UK)

4th term
James, William (US)
Myers, Frederick W.H. (UK)
Richet, Charles (France)
von Schrenck-Notzing, Albert (Germany)
Sidgwick, Henry (UK)*

*Member whose death during this term was announced at the next congress.
**Not consecutive terms.

Appendix A.5

Committee appointed at the 5th congress, Rome, 1905, serving 1905–1909 ($N=76$)

Members newly appointed

Aars, Birch Reichenwald (Norway)
Bechterew, V.M. (Russia)
Cattell, V. McKeen (Russia)
Claparède, Edouard (Switzerland)
Dumas, Georges (France)
Heymans, Gerardus (Netherlands)
Höffding, Harald (Denmark)
Höfler, Alois (Austria)
Ladame, Paul (Switzerland)
Looskiy, N.O. (Russia)
McDougall, William (UK)
Motora, Yujiro (Japan)
Patrizi, L. Mariano (Italy)

Retzius, G. (Sweden)
Sakaki, Yasusaburo (Japan)
De Sanctis, Sante (Italy)
Sciamana, Ezio (Italy)*
Séglas, J. (France)
Sollier, Paul (France)
Sommer, Robert (Germany)
Stewart, C.N. (US)
Strong, C. (US)
Toulouse, E. (France)
Vaschide, N. (Romania)*
Winkler, C. (Netherlands)

Members reappointed for a consecutive number of terms

2nd term
Bourdon, Benjamin (France)
Demoor, J. (Belgium)
Ehrenfels, A. (Austria)
Ferrari, Giulio Cesare (Italy)
Külpe, Otto (Germany)
Ladd, George T. (US)

Luciani, Luigi (Italy)
Magaläes, Lemos (Portugal)
Novicow, —. (Russia)
Serebrennikov, Vitali T. (Russia)
Stout, George F. (UK)
Stuart, Anderson (Australia)

continued ➞

Members reappointed for a consecutive number of terms (continued)

2nd term (continued)
Tamburini, Augusto (Italy)
de Tarchanoff, J. (Russia)
Thiery, Armand (Belgium)
Ward, James (UK)**
Zwaardemaker, Hendrick (Netherlands)

3rd term
Binet, Alfred (France)
Brentano, Franz (Italy)
Exner, Sigmund (Austria)
Flechsig, Paul (Germany)
Flournoy, Théodore (Switzerland)
Galton, Francis (UK)**
Henschen, S.E. (Sweden)
Hering, Ewald (Germany)
Janet, Pierre (France)
Lange, Nikolaus (Russia)
Meinong, Alexius (Austria)
Mingazzini, Giovanni (Italy)
Mosso, Angelo (Italy)
Mourly-Vold, J. (Sweden)
Münsterberg, Hugo (US)**

Ramon y Cajal, Santiago (Spain)
Sergi, Giuseppe (Italy)
Titchener, Edward B. (US)
Wundt, Wilhelm (Germany)

4th term
Baldwin, James M. (US)
Ebbinghaus, Hermann (Germany)*
Ferrier, David (UK)
Forel, August Henri (Switzerland)
Hall, G. Stanley (US)
Lehmann, Alfred (Denmark)
Lipps, Theodor (Germany)
Mendelsohn, Maurice (Russia)
Morselli, Enrico (Italy)
Ribot, Théodule (France)
Stumpf, Carl (Germany)
Sully, James (UK)

5th term
James, William (US)
Richet, Charles (France)
von Schrenck-Notzing, Albert (Germany)

*Member whose death during this term was announced at the next congress.
**Not consecutive terms.

Appendix A.6

Committee appointed at the 6th congress, Geneva, 1909, serving 1909–1923 (N=108)

Members newly appointed

Abramowski, Edouard (Russia)
Alrutz, Sydney (Sweden)
d'Arsonval, A. (France)
Asher, Léon (France)
Bernfeld, Pierre (Romania)
Bianchi, Leonardo (Italy)
Bohn, G. (France)
Courtier, Jules (France)
Decroly, O. (Belgium)
Dessoir, Max (Germany)
Fullerton, George S. (US)
Ghéorgov, Ivan (Bulgaria)
Gielecky, Adalbert (Russia)
Heinrich, W. (Russia)
Ioteyko, Iosefa (Belgium)
Larguier des Bancels, Jacques (Switzerland)
Leroy, Bernard (France)
Leuba, James H. (US)

Leuckfeld, Paul (Russia)
Lipmann, Otto (Germany)
Martius, G. (Germany)
Michotte, Albert (Belgium)
Nagel, W. (Germany)
Patini, Ettore (Italy)
Piéron, Henri (France)
Pikler, Julius (Austria)
Prince, Morton (US)
Sanford, Edmund C. (US)
Schuyten, M. (Belgium)
Seris, Homero (Cuba)
Simarro, L. (Spain)
Treves, Zaccaria (Italy)
Tschelpanow, S. (Russia)
Villa, Guido (Italy)
Yourievitch, Serge (France)

continued ➡

Members reappointed for a consecutive number of terms

2nd term

Aars, Birch Reichenwald (Norway)
Bechterew, V.M. (Russia)
Cattell, James McKeen (US)
Claparède, Edouard (Switzerland)
Dumas, Georges (France)
Heymans, Gerardus (Netherlands)
Höffding, Harald (Denmark)
Höfler, Alois (Austria)
Ladame, Paul (Switzerland)
Looskiy, N.O. (Russia)
McDougall, William (UK)
Motora, Yujiro (Japan)
Patrizi, L. Mariano (Italy)
Retzius, G. (Sweden)
Sakaki, Yasusaburo (Japan)
De Sanctis, Sante (Italy)
Séglas, J. (France)
Sollier, Paul (France)
Sommer, Robert (Germany)
Stewart, C.N. (US)
Strong, C.A. (US)
Toulouse, E. (France)
Winkler, C. (Netherlands)

3rd term

Bourdon, Benjamin (France)
Demoor, J. (Belgium)
Ehrenfels, A. (Austria)
Ferrari, Giulio Cesare (Italy)
Külpe, Otto (Germany)
Ladd, George T. (US)
Luciani, Luigi (Italy)
Magaläes, Lemos (Portugal)
Marty, Anton (Austria)**
Novicow, —. (Russia)
Serebrennikov, Vitali T. (Russia)
Stout, George F. (UK)
Stuart, Anderson (Australia)
Tamburini, Augusto (Italy)
de Tarchanoff, J. (Russia)
Thiery, Armand (Belgium)
Ward, James (UK)**
Zwaardemaker, Hendrick (Netherlands)

4th term

Binet, Alfred (France)
Brentano, Franz (Italy)
Exner, Sigmund (Austria)
Flechsig, Paul (Germany)
Flournoy, Théodore (Switzerland)
Galton, Francis (UK)**
Henschen, S.E. (Sweden)
Hering, Ewald (Germany)
Janet, Pierre (France)
Lange, Nikolaus (Russia)*
Meinong, Alexius (Austria)
Mingazzini, Giovanni (Italy)
Mosso, Angelo (Italy)
Münsterberg, Hugo (Germany)**
Ramon y Cajal, Santiago (Spain)
Ribot, Théodule (France)
Sergi, Giuseppe (Italy)
Titchener, Edward B. (US)
Wundt, Wilhelm (Germany)

5th term

Baldwin, James M. (US)
Ferrier, David (UK)
Forel, August Henri (Switzerland)
Hall, G. Stanley (US)
Lehmann, Alfred (Denmark)
Lipps, Theodor (Germany)
Mendelsohn, Maurice (Russia)
Morselli, Enrico (Italy)
Stumpf, Carl (Germany)
Sully, James (UK)

6th term

James, William (US)*
Richet, Charles (France)
von Schrenck-Notzing, Albert (Germany)

*Member whose death during this term was announced at the next congress.
**Not consecutive terms.

Appendix A.7

Committee appointed at the 7th congress, Oxford, 1923, serving 1923–1926 (*N*=105)

Members newly appointed

Aall, A. (Norway)
Adler, Alfred (Austria)
Bartlett, Frederic C. (UK)
Boring, Edwin G. (US)
Bovet, P. (Switzerland)
Brown, William (UK)
Burt, Cyril (UK)
Dodge, Raymond (US)
Drever, James (UK)
Head, Henry (US)
Jaederholm, G.A. (Sweden)
Koffka, Kurt (Germany)

Köhler, Wolfgang (Germany)
Matsumoto, M. (Japan)
Mira, Emilio (Spain)
Moede, Walter (Germany)
Myers, Charles S. (UK)
Pick, A. (Austria)
Pillsbury, Walter B. (US)
Seracky, F. (Austria)
Spearman, Charles (UK)
Thurstone, Louis L. (US)
Warren, Howard C. (US)
van Wayenberg, G. (Netherlands)

Members reappointed for a consecutive number of terms

2nd term
Alrutz, Sydney (Sweden)
d'Arsonval, A. (France)
Asher, Léon (Switzerland)
Bernfeld, Pierre (Romania)
Bianchi, Leonardo (Italy)
Bohn, G. (France)
Courtier, Jules (France)
Decroly, O. (Belgium)
Dessoir, Max (Germany)
Dumas, Georges (France)**
Fullerton, George S. (US)
Ghéorgov, Ivan (Bulgaria)
Gielecky, Adalbert (Russia)
Heinrich, W. (Russia)
Ioteyko, Iosefa (Belgium)
Larguier des Bancels, Jacques (Switzerland)
Leroy, Bernard (France)
Leuba, James H. (US)
Leuckfeld, Paul (Russia)
Lipmann, Otto (Germany)
Martius, G. (Germany)
Michotte, Albert (Belgium)
Patini, Ettore (Italy)
Piéron, Henri (France)
Pikler, Julius (Austria)
Prince, Morton (US)
Sanford, Edmund C. (US)
Schuyten, M. (Belgium)
Seris, Homero (Cuba)
Treves, Zaccaria (Italy)
Tschelpanow, S. (Russia)

Villa, Guido (Italy)
Yourievitch, Serge (France)

3rd term
Bechterew, V.M. (Russia)
Cattell, James McKeen (US)
Claparède, Edouard (Switzerland)
Heymans, Gerardus (Netherlands)
Höffding, Harald (Denmark)
Looskiy, N.O. (Russia)
McDougall, William (US)
Patrizi, L. Mariano (Italy)
Sakaki, Yasusaburo (Japan)
De Sanctis, Sante (Italy)
Séglas, J. (France)
Sollier, Paul (France)
Sommer, Robert (Germany)
Stewart, C.N. (US)
Strong, C.A. (US)
Toulouse, E. (France)
Winkler, C. (Netherlands)

4th term
Bourdon, Benjamin (France)
Demoor, J. (Belgium)
Ehrenfels, A. (Austria)
Ferrari, Giulio Cesare (Italy)
Luciani, Luigi (Italy)
Magaläes, Lemos (Portugal)
Marty, Anton (Austria)
Novicow, —. (Russia)

continued →

Members reappointed for a consecutive number of terms (continued)

4th term (continued)
Serebrennikov, Vitali T. (Russia)
Stout, George, F. (UK)
Stuart, Anderson (Australia)
de Tarchanoff, J. (Russia)
Thiery, Armand (Belgium)
Ward, James (UK)**
Zwaardemaker, Hendrick (Netherlands)

5th term
Flechsig, Paul (Germany)
Henschen, S.E. (Sweden)
Janet, Pierre (France)
Lange, Nikolaus (Germany)
Mingazzini, Giovanni (Italy)

Ramon y Cajal, Santiago (Spain)
Sergi, Giuseppe (Italy)

6th term
Baldwin, James M. (US)
Forel, August Henri (Switzerland)**
Hall, G. Stanley (US)
Mendelsohn, Maurice (Russia)
Morselli, Enrico (Italy)
Stumpf, Carl (Germany)

7th term
Richet, Charles (France)
von Schrenck-Notzing, Albert (Germany)

**Not consecutive terms.

Appendix A.8

Committee appointed at the 8th congress, Groningen, 1926, serving 1926–1929 (N=110)

As stated in the Proceedings of the 8th congress, members of the committee are listed by city of residence.

Permanent Secretary
Edouard Claparède

Members newly appointed

Bühler, Karl (Vienna)
Keisow, Federico (Turin)
Langfeld, Herbert S. (Princeton)
Lévy-Bruhl, M. (Paris)
Ley, August (Brussels)
Pear, T.H. (Manchester)
Ponzo, Mario (Turin)

Revault d'Allones (Paris)
Roels, E. (Utrecht)
Rubin, Edgar (Copenhagen)
Stern, William (Hamburg)
Thouless, Robert H. (Manchester)
Wertheimer, Max (Berlin)

Members reappointed for a consecutive number of terms

2nd term
Aall, A. (Christiana)
Adler, Alfred (Vienna)
Bartlett, Frederic C. (Cambridge, UK)
Boring, Edwin G. (Cambridge, MA)
Bovet, P. (Geneva)
Brown, William (Oxford)
Burt, Cyril (London)
Dodge, Raymond (Washington)
Drever, James (Edinburgh)
Head, Henry (London)
Jaederholm, G.A. (Gothenberg)

Koffka, Kurt (Giessen)
Köhler, Wolfgang (Berlin)
Matsumoto, M. (Tokyo)
Mira, Emilio (Barcelona)
Moede, Walter (Berlin)
Myers, Charles S. (London)
Pillsbury, Walter B. (Ann Arbor)
Seracky, F. (Prague)
Spearman, Charles (London)
Thurstone, Louis L. (Washington)
Warren, Howard C. (Princeton)

continued →

Appendix A.9

Committee appointed at the 9th congress, Yale, 1929, serving 1929–1932 (*N*=106)

Permanent Secretary
Édouard Claparède

Members newly appointed

Angell, James R. (New Haven, CT)
Aveling, F. (London)
Blachowski, S. (Poznan)
Borovski, V.M. (Moscow)
Bott, Edward A. (Toronto)
Bouman, L. (Utrecht)
Edgell, Beatrice (London)
Gopalswami, M.V. (Mysore)
Grünbaum, A.A. (Amsterdam)
Hunter, T.A. (Wellington, New Zealand)
Hunter, Walter S. (Worcester, MA)
Jastrow, Joseph (New York)
Kafka, Gustav (Dresden)
Katz, David (Rostock)

Klemm, Otto (Leipzig)
Lashley, Karl S. (Chicago, IL)
Lewin, Kurt (Berlin)
Pavlov, Ivan P. (Leningrad)
Piaget, Jean (Geneva)
Ranschburg, Paul (Budapest)
Roxo, Henrique (Rio de Janeiro)
Salkind, A.B. (Moscow)
Spielrein, I. (Moscow)
Thorndike, Edward L. (New York)
Washburn, Margaret F. (Poughkeepsie, NY)
Wirth, Wilhelm (Leipzig)
Woodworth, Robert S. (New York)
Wynn-Jones, L. (Leeds)

Members reappointed for a consecutive number of terms

2nd term

Adler, A. (Vienna)
Bühler, Karl (Vienna)
Keisow, Federico (Turin)
Langfeld, Herbert S. (Princeton)
Lévy-Bruhl, M. (Paris)
Ley, August (Brussels)
Pear, T.H. (Manchester)
Ponzo, Mario (Turin)
Revault d'Allones (Paris)
Roels, E. (Utrecht)
Rubin, Edgar (Copenhagen)
Stern, William (Hamburg)
Thouless, Robert H. (Manchester)
Wertheimer, Max (Berlin)

3rd term

Aall, A. (Oslo)
Asher, Léon (Bern)
Bartlett, Frederic C. (Cambridge, UK)
Boring, Edwin G. (Cambridge, MA)
Bovet, P. (Geneva)
Brown, William (Oxford)
Burt, Cyril (London)
Dodge, Raymond (New Haven, CT)
Drever, James (Edinburgh)
Head, Henry (London)

Jaederholm, G.A. (Gothenburg)
Koffka, Kurt (Northampton, MA)
Köhler, Wolfgang (Berlin)
Matsumoto, M. (Tokyo)
Mira, Emilio (Barcelona)
Moede, Walter (Berlin)
Myers, Charles S. (London)
Pillsbury, Walter B. (Ann Arbor, MI)
Seracky, F. (Prague)
Spearman, Charles (London)
Thurstone, Louis L. (Chicago, IL)
Warren, Howard C. (Princeton, NJ)

4th term

d'Arsonval, A. (Paris)
Bernfeld, P. (Bucharest)
Bohn, G. (Paris)
Courtier, Jules (Paris)
Decroly, O. (Brussels)
Dessoir, Max (Berlin)
Dumas, Georges (Paris)**
Ghéorgov, Ivan (Sofia)
Gielecky, Adalbert (Cracow)
Heinrich, W. (Cracow)
Larguier des Bancels, Jacques (Lausanne)
Leroy, Bernard (Paris)

continued →

Appendix A.9

Committee appointed at the 9th congress, Yale, 1929, serving 1929–1932 (*N*=106)

Permanent Secretary
Edouard Claparède

Members newly appointed

Angell, James R. (New Haven, CT)
Aveling, F. (London)
Blachowski, S. (Poznan)
Borovski, V.M. (Moscow)
Bott, Edward A. (Toronto)
Bouman, L. (Utrecht)
Edgell, Beatrice (London)
Gopalswami, M.V. (Mysore)
Grünbaum, A.A. (Amsterdam)
Hunter, T.A. (Wellington, New Zealand)
Hunter, Walter S. (Worcester, MA)
Jastrow, Joseph (New York)
Kafka, Gustav (Dresden)
Katz, David (Rostock)

Klemm, Otto (Leipzig)
Lashley, Karl S. (Chicago, IL)
Lewin, Kurt (Berlin)
Pavlov, Ivan P. (Leningrad)
Piaget, Jean (Geneva)
Ranschburg, Paul (Budapest)
Roxo, Henrique (Rio de Janeiro)
Salkind, A.B. (Moscow)
Spielrein, I. (Moscow)
Thorndike, Edward L. (New York)
Washburn, Margaret F. (Poughkeepsie, NY)
Wirth, Wilhelm (Leipzig)
Woodworth, Robert S. (New York)
Wynn-Jones, L. (Leeds)

Members reappointed for a consecutive number of terms

2nd term
Adler, A. (Vienna)
Bühler, Karl (Vienna)
Keisow, Federico (Turin)
Langfeld, Herbert S. (Princeton)
Lévy-Bruhl, M. (Paris)
Ley, August (Brussels)
Pear, T.H. (Manchester)
Ponzo, Mario (Turin)
Revault d'Allones (Paris)
Roels, E. (Utrecht)
Rubin, Edgar (Copenhagen)
Stern, William (Hamburg)
Thouless, Robert H. (Manchester)
Wertheimer, Max (Berlin)

3rd term
Aall, A. (Oslo)
Asher, Léon (Bern)
Bartlett, Frederic C. (Cambridge, UK)
Boring, Edwin G. (Cambridge, MA)
Bovet, P. (Geneva)
Brown, William (Oxford)
Burt, Cyril (London)
Dodge, Raymond (New Haven, CT)
Drever, James (Edinburgh)
Head, Henry (London)

Jaederholm, G.A. (Gothenburg)
Koffka, Kurt (Northampton, MA)
Köhler, Wolfgang (Berlin)
Matsumoto, M. (Tokyo)
Mira, Emilio (Barcelona)
Moede, Walter (Berlin)
Myers, Charles S. (London)
Pillsbury, Walter B. (Ann Arbor, MI)
Seracky, F. (Prague)
Spearman, Charles (London)
Thurstone, Louis L. (Chicago, IL)
Warren, Howard C. (Princeton, NJ)

4th term
d'Arsonval, A. (Paris)
Bernfeld, P. (Bucharest)
Bohn, G. (Paris)
Courtier, Jules (Paris)
Decroly, O. (Brussels)
Dessoir, Max (Berlin)
Dumas, Georges (Paris)**
Ghéorgov, Ivan (Sofia)
Gielecky, Adalbert (Cracow)
Heinrich, W. (Cracow)
Larguier des Bancels, Jacques (Lausanne)
Leroy, Bernard (Paris)

continued →

Members reappointed for a consecutive number of terms (continued)

4th term (continued)
Leuba, James H. (Bryn Mawr, PA)
Leuckfeld, Paul (Kharkov)
Lipmann, Otto (Berlin)
Michotte, Albert (Louvain)
Patini, Ettore (Naples)
Piéron, Henri (France)
Pikler, Julius (Budapest)
Schuyten, M. (Antwerp)
Seris, Homero (Havana)
Tschelpanow, S. (Moscow)
Villa, Guido (Pavia)
Yourievitch, Serge (Paris)

5th term
Cattell, James McKeen (New York)
Claparède, Edouard (Geneva)
Heymans, Gerardus (Groningen)
Höffding, Harald (Copenhagen)
Looskiy, N.O. (Prague)
McDougall, William (Durham, NC)
Patrizi, L. Mariano (Modena)
Sakaki, Yasusaburo (Fukuoka)
De Sanctis, Sante (Rome)
Séglas, J. (Paris)
Sollier, Paul (Paris)
Sommer, Robert (Giessen)
Strong, C.A. (Florence)

Toulouse, E. (Paris)
Winkler, C. (Utrecht)

6th term
Bourdon, Benjamin (Rennes)
Demoor, J. (Brussels)
Ehrenfels, A. (Prague)
Ferrari, Giulio Cesare (Bologna)
Magaläes, Lemos (Lisbon)
Stout, George, F. (St Andrews, UK)
Stuart, Anderson (Sydney)
Thiery, Armand (Louvain)
Zwaardemaker, Hendrick (Utrecht)

7th term
Forel, August Henri (Yvorne, Switzerland)
Henschen, S.E. (Stockholm)
Janet, Pierre (Paris)
Mingazzini, Giovanni (Rome)
Ramon y Cajal, Santiago (Madrid)
Sergi, Giuseppe (Rome)

8th term
Baldwin, James M. (Paris)
Mendelsohn, Maurice (Paris)
Stumpf, Carl (Berlin)

9th term
Richet, Charles (Paris)

**Not consecutive terms.

Appendix A.10

Committee appointed at the 10th congress, Copenhagen, 1932, serving 1932–1937 (*N*=84)

Permanent Secretary
Edouard Claparède

Assistant Secretary
Herbert S. Langfeld

Members newly appointed

Dale, Paulis (Riga)
Foucault, Marcel (Montpellier)
Gemelli, Agostino (Milan)
Lafora, G.R. (Madrid)

Miles, Walter (New Haven, CT)
Seashore, Carl E. (Iowa City)
Wallon, Henri (Paris)

Members reappointed for a consecutive number of terms

2nd term
Angell, James R. (New Haven, CT)
Aveling, F. (London)
Blachowski, S. (Poznan)

Borovski, V.M. (Moscow)
Bott, Edward A. (Toronto)
Bouman, L. (Utrecht)*
Edgell, Beatrice (London)

continued ➔

Members reappointed for a consecutive number of terms (continued)

2nd term (continued)
Gopalswami, M.V. (Mysore)
Hunter, T.A. (Wellington, New Zealand)
Hunter, Walter S. (Worcester, MA)
Jastrow, Joseph (New York)
Kafka, Gustav (Dresden)
Katz, David (Rostock)
Klemm, Otto (Leipzig)
Lashley, Karl S. (Chicago, IL)
Lewin, Kurt (Berlin)
Pavlov, Ivan P. (Leningrad)*
Pear, T.H. (Manchester)
Piaget, Jean (Geneva)
Ranschburg, Paul (Budapest)
Roxo, Henrique (Rio de Janeiro)
Spielrein, I. (Moscow)
Thorndike, Edward L. (New York)
Washburn, Margaret F. (Poughkeepsie, NY)
Wirth, Wilhelm (Leipzig)
Woodworth, Robert S. (New York)
Wynn-Jones, L. (Leeds)

3rd term
Bühler, Karl (Vienna)
Keisow, Federico (Turin)
Langfeld, Herbert S. (Princeton)
Ley, August (Brussels)
Ponzo, Mario (Turin)
Roels, E. (Utrecht)
Rubin, Edgar (Copenhagen)
Stern, William (Hamburg)
Thouless, Robert H. (Manchester)
Wertheimer, Max (Frankfurt)

4th term
Aall, A. (Oslo)
Bartlett, Frederic C. (Cambridge, UK)
Boring, Edwin G. (Cambridge, MA)
Brown, William (Oxford)
Burt, Cyril (London)
Dodge, Raymond (New Haven, CT)
Drever, James (Edinburgh)
Jaederholm, G.A. (Gothenburg)*
Koffka, Kurt (Northampton, MA)

Köhler, Wolfgang (Berlin)
Mira, Emilio (Barcelona)
Moede, Walter (Berlin)
Myers, Charles S. (London)
Pillsbury, Walter B. (Ann Arbor, MI)
Seracky, François (Prague)
Spearman, Charles (London)
Thurstone, Louis L. (Chicago, IL)
Warren, Howard C. (Princeton, NJ)*

5th term
Decroly, O. (Brussels)*
Dumas, Georges (Paris)**
Gielecky, Adalbert (Cracow)
Heinrich, W. (Cracow)
Larguier des Bancels, Jacques (Lausanne)
Leuba, James H. (Bryn Mawr, PA)
Lipmann, Otto (Berlin)*
Michotte, Albert (Louvain)
Piéron, Henri (Paris)
Tschelpanow, S. (Moscow)*
Yourievitch, Serge (Paris)

6th term
Cattell, James McKeen (New York)
Claparède, Edouard (Geneva)
McDougall, William (Durham, NC)
De Sanctis, Sante (Rome)*
Sollier, Paul (Paris)*

7th term
Bourdon, Benjamin (Rennes)
Ferrari, Giulio Cesare (Bologna)*
Stout, George, F. (St Andrews, UK)

8th term
Janet, Pierre (Paris)
Sergi, Giuseppe (Rome)*

9th term
Stumpf, Carl (Berlin)*

10th term
Richet, Charles (Paris)*

*Members of the committee whose deaths during this term were announced at the 11th congress
**Not consecutive terms.

Committee appointed at the 11th congress, Paris, 1937, serving 1937–1948 (N=84)

Executive Committee

Edouard Claparède, *Permanent Secretary*
Herbert S. Langfield, *Assistant Secretary*
Karl Bühler
Otto Klemm

Charles S. Myers
Henri Piéron
Mario Ponzo

Members newly appointed

Antipoff, Hélène (Bello Horizonte, Brazil)
Baley, Stefan (Warsaw)
Beebe-Center, John (Cambridge, MA)
Berger, Hans (Jena)
Blondel, Charles (Paris)*
Bonaventura, Enzo (Florence)*
Bühler, Charlotte (Vienna)
Carmichael, Leonard (Rochester, NY)
Guillaume, Paul (Paris)

Hull, Clark L. (New Haven, CT)
Kretschmer, Ernst (Marburg)
Luquet, G.H. (Paris)
Meyerson, Ignace (Paris)
Orbeli, Leon (Leningrad)
Rikimaru, Y. (Tohoku)
Thurnwald, Richard (Berlin)
Wolters, Albert W.P. (Reading, UK)

Members reappointed for a consecutive number of terms

2nd term

Dale, Paulis (Riga)
Foucault, Marcel (Montpellier)*
Gemelli, Agostino (Milan)
Lafora, G.R. (Madrid)
Miles, Walter (New Haven, CT)
Seashore, Carl E. (Iowa City)
Wallon, Henri (Paris)

Roxo, Henrique (Rio de Janeiro)
Spielrein, I. (Moscow)*
Thorndike, Edward L. (New York)
Washburn, Margaret F. (Poughkeepsie, NY)*
Wirth, Wilhelm (Leipzig)
Woodworth, Robert S. (New York)
Wynn-Jones, L. (Leeds)

3rd term

Angell, James R. (New Haven, CT)
Aveling, F. (London)*
Blachowski, S. (Poznan)
Borovski, V.M. (Moscow)
Bott, Edward A. (Toronto)
Edgell, Beatrice (London)
Gopalswami, M.V. (Mysore)
Hunter, T.A. (Wellington, New Zealand)
Hunter, Walter S. (Providence, RI)
Jastrow, Joseph (New York)*
Kafka, Gustav (Dresden)
Katz, David (Stockholm)
Klemm, Otto (Leipzig)*
Lashley, Karl S. (Chicago, IL)
Lewin, Kurt (Cambridge, MA)*
Pear, T.H. (Manchester)
Piaget, Jean (Geneva)
Ranschburg, Paul (Budapest)*

4th term

Bühler, Karl (Vienna)
Keisow, Federico (Turin)*
Langfeld, Herbert S. (Princeton, NJ)
Ley, August (Brussels)
Ponzo, Mario (Turin)
Roels, E. (Utrecht)
Rubin, Edgar (Copenhagen)
Stern, William (Durham, NC)*
Thouless, Robert H. (Glasgow)
Wertheimer, Max (Berlin)

5th term

Bartlett, Frederic C. (Cambridge, UK)
Boring, Edwin G. (Cambridge, MA)
Brown, William (Oxford)
Dodge, Raymond (New Haven, CT)*
Drever, James (Edinburgh)
Koffka, Kurt (Northampton, MA)*
Köhler, Wolfgang (Swarthmore)

continued →

Appendix A.11 *continued*

Members reappointed for a consecutive number of terms (continued)

5th term (continued)
Moede, Walter (Berlin)
Myers, Charles S. (London)*
Pillsbury, Walter B. (Ann Arbor, MI)
Seracky, François (Prague)*
Spearman, Charles (London)*
Thurstone, Louis, L. (Chicago, IL)

6th term
Gielecky, Adalbert (Cracow)
Heinrich, W. (Cracow)
Leuba, James H. (Bryn Mawr, PA)*
Michotte, Albert (Louvain)

Piéron, Henri (Paris)
Yourievitch, Serge (Paris)

7th term
Cattell, James McKeen (New York)*
Claparède, Edouard (Geneva)*
McDougall, William (Durham, NC)*

8th term
Bourdon, Benjamin (Rennes)*

9th term
Janet, Pierre (Paris)*

*Members of the committee whose deaths during this term were announced at the 12th congress.

Appendix A.12

Committee appointed at the 12th congress, Edinburgh, 1948, serving 1948–1951 (*N*=80)

Executive Committee

Herbert S. Langfeld, *Permanent Secretary*
Jean Piaget, *Assistant Secretary*
Stefan Baley
Frederic C. Bartlett
Leonard Carmichael
Gustav Kafka
David Katz

Albert Michotte
T.H. Pear
Henri Piéron
Mario Ponzo
Géza Révész
Edgar Rubin
Henri Wallon

Members newly appointed

von Allesch, Johannes (Göttingen)
Anderberg, Rudolf (Upsala)
Banissoni, Ferruccio (Rome)
Bujas, Zoran (Zagreb)
Buytendijk, F. (Utrecht)
Cantril, Hadley (Princeton)
Coucheron-Jarl, Vidkunn (Oslo)
Debesse, Maurice (Strasbourg)
Drever, James Jr (Edinburgh)
Elmgren, John (Göteborg)
Erismann, Thomas (Innsbruck)
Fraisse, Paul (Paris)
Germain, José (Madrid)
Graham, Clarence (New York)
Harding, D.W. (London)

Humphrey, George (Oxford)
Klineberg, Otto (New York)
Knight, Rex (Aberdeen)
Lagache, Daniel (Paris)
Lasaga, José I. (Havana)
Luria, Alexander R. (Moscow)
MacNeill, Florence (Manchester)
Mäki, Niilo (Helsinki)
Marquis, Donald G. (Ann Arbor, MI)
Marzi, Alberto (Florence)
Meili, Richard (Zurich)
Mira y Lopez, E. (Rio de Janeiro)
Nuttin, Joseph (Louvain)
Ou, Tsuing-Chen (Peking)
Poyer, Georges (Paris)

continued →

Members newly appointed (continued)

Révész, Géza (Amsterdam)

Skinner, Burrhus Frederick
   (Cambridge, MA)

Tolman, Edward C. (Berkeley, CA)

Vana, T. (Prague)

Viteles, Morris S. (Philadelphia)

Wolfle, Dale W. (Washington)

Members reappointed for a consecutive number of terms

2nd term

Antipoff, Hélène (Rio de Janeiro)

Baley, Stefan (Warsaw)

Beebe-Center, John (Cambridge, MA)

Berger, Hans (Jena)

Bühler, Charlotte (Hollywood)

Carmichael, Leonard (Medford, MA)

Guillaume, Paul (Paris)

Hull, Clark L. (New Haven, CT)

Kretschmer, Ernst (Marburg)

Luquet, G.H. (Paris)

Meyerson, Ignace (Paris)

Orbeli, Leon (Leningrad)

Rikimaru, Y. (Tohoku)

Wolters, Albert W.P. (Reading, UK)

3rd term

Dale, Paulis (Riga)

Gemelli, Agostino (Milan)

Miles, Walter (New Haven, CT)

Seashore, Carl E. (Iowa City)*

Wallon, Henri (Paris)

4th term

Blachowski, S. (Poznan)

Edgell, Beatrice (London)

Hunter, Walter S. (Providence, RI)

Kafka, Gustav (Würzburg)

Katz, David (Stockholm)

Lashley, Karl S. (Orange Park, FL)

Pear, T.H. (Manchester)

Piaget, Jean (Geneva)

Woodworth, Robert S. (New York)

Wynn-Jones, L. (Leeds)

5th term

Bühler, Karl (Hollywood)

Langfeld, Herbert S. (Princeton, NJ)

Ley, August (Brussels)

Ponzo, Mario (Rome)

Rubin, Edgar (Copenhagen)*

Thouless, Robert H. (Cambridge, UK)

6th term

Bartlett, Frederic C. (Cambridge, UK)

Boring, Edwin G. (Cambridge, MA)

Drever, James Sr (Edinburgh)*

Köhler, Wolfgang (Swarthmore)

Pillsbury, Walter B. (Ann Arbor, MI)

Thurstone, Louis, L. (Chicago, IL)

7th term

Heinrich, W. (Cracow)

Michotte, Albert (Louvain)

Piéron, Henri (Paris)

---

*Members of the committee whose deaths during this term were announced at the 13th congress.

   The members of the 12th International Committee were designated as the Assembly of the 13th International Congress of Psychology with the exception of the following: James Drever Sr, Gustav Kafka, Tsuing-Chen Ou, Edgar Rubin, Carl Seashore, and L. Wynn-Jones. The following additional members were appointed to the Assembly: Cyril Burt (London), Jesper Florander (Copenhagen), Philip Lersch (Munich), and Fillmore Sanford (Washington, DC)

Appendix B

1951–1954

Elected President
Piéron, H. (France)

Vice-President
Bartlett, F.C. (UK)

Treasurer
Katz, D. (Sweden)

Secretary-General
Langfeld, H.S. (USA)

Deputy Secretary-General
Piaget, J. (Switzerland)

Elected Executive Committee
Baley, S. (Poland)
Germain, J. (Spain)
Klineberg, O. (USA)
Lersch, P. (FRG)
Michotte, A. (Belgium)
Pear, T.H. (UK)
Ponzo, M. (Italy)
Rasmussen, T. (Denmark)
Révész, G. (Netherlands)
Wallon, H. (France)

1954–1957

Elected President
Piaget, J. (Switzerland)

Vice-President
Rasmussen, T. (Denmark)

Treasurer
Mailloux, N. (Canada)

Secretary-General
Klineberg, O. (USA)

Deputy Secretary-General
Germain, J. (Spain)

Elected Executive Committee
Bartlett, F.C. (UK)
Drever, J. Jr (UK)
Duijker, H.C.J. (Netherlands)
Elmgren, J. (Sweden)
Langfeld, H.S. (USA)
Michotte, A. (Belgium)
Piéron, H. (France)

1957–1960

Elected President
Michotte, A. (Belgium)

Vice-President
Drever, J. Jr (UK)

Treasurer
Mailloux, N. (Canada)

Secretary-General
Klineberg, O. (USA)

Deputy Secretary-General
Duijker, H.C.J. (Netherlands)

Elected Executive Committee
Bartlett, F.C. (UK)
Mäki, N. (Finland)
Nuttin, J. (Belgium)
Piaget, J. (Switzerland)
Piéron, H. (France)
Russell, R.W. (USA)
Skard, A. (Norway)

1960–1963

Elected President
Klineberg, O. (USA)

Vice-President
Duijker, H.C.J. (Netherlands)

Treasurer
Mailloux, N. (Canada)

Secretary-General
Russell, R.W. (USA)

Deputy Secretary-General
Westerlund, G. (Sweden)

Elected Executive Committee
Drever, J. Jr (UK)
Fraisse, P. (France)
Leontiev, A.N. (USSR)
Nuttin, J. (Belgium)
Piaget, J. (Switzerland)
Sato, K. (Japan)
Skard, A. (Norway)

1963–1966

Elected President
Drever, J. (UK)

Vice-President
Fraisse, P. (France)

Treasurer
Mailloux, N. (Canada)

Secretary-General
Russell, R.W. (USA)

Deputy Secretary-General
Westerlund, G. (Sweden)

Elected Executive Committee
Duijker, H.C.J. (Netherlands)
Klineberg, O. (USA)
Leontiev, A.N. (USSR)
Nuttin, J. (Belgium)
O'Neil, W.M. (Australia)
Piaget, J. (Switzerland)
Sato, K. (Japan)
Summerfield, A. (UK)
Tomaszewski, T. (Poland)

continued ➡

1966–1969

Elected President
Fraisse, P. (France)

Vice-Presidents
Leontiev, A.N. (USSR)
Russell, R.W. (USA)

Treasurer
Mailloux, N. (Canada)

Secretary-General
Jacobson, E.H. (USA)

Deputy Secretary-General
Nielsen, G. (Denmark)

Elected Executive Committee
Klineberg, O. (USA)
Luria, A.R. (USSR)
Nuttin, J. (Belgium)
Pfaffmann, C. (USA)
Piaget, J. (Switzerland)
Sato, K. (Japan)
Summerfield, A. (UK)
Tomaszewski, T. (Poland)
Yela, M. (Spain)

1969–1972

Elected President
Russell, R.W. (USA)

Vice-Presidents
Luria, A.R. (USSR)
Nuttin, J. (Belgium)

Treasurer
Mailloux, N. (Canada)

Secretary-General
Jacobson, E.H. (USA)

Deputy Secretary-General
Nielsen, G. (Denmark)

Elected Executive Committee
Bruner, J. (USA)
Duijker, H.C.J. (Netherlands)
Fraisse, P. (France)
Leontiev, A.N. (USSR)
O'Neil, W.M. (Australia)
Pfaffmann, C. (USA)
Summerfield, A. (UK)
Tanaka, Y. (Japan)
Tomaszewski, T. (Poland)
Westerlund, G. (Sweden)

1972–1976

Elected President
Nuttin, J. (Belgium)

Vice-Presidents
Summerfield, A. (UK)
Tanaka, Y. (Japan)

Treasurer
Mailloux, N. (Canada)

Secretary-General
Holtzman, W.H. (USA)

Deputy Secretary-General
Montmollin, G. de (France)

Elected Executive Committee
Bruner, J. (USA)
Fraisse, P. (France)
Jacobson, E.H. (USA)
Klix, F. (GDR)
Leontiev, A.N. (USSR)
Lomov, B.F. (USSR)
Rosenzweig, M.R. (USA)
Russell, R.W. (USA)
Tomaszewski, T. (Poland)
Westerlund, G. (Sweden)

continued ➡

1976–1980

Elected President
Summerfield, A. (UK)

Vice-Presidents
Diaz-Guerrero, R. (Mexico)
Lomov, B.F. (USSR)

Treasurer
Mailloux, N. (Canada) 1976–77
Bélanger, D. (Canada) 1977–80

Secretary-General
Holtzman, W.H. (USA)

Deputy Secretary-General
Montmollin, G. de (France) 1976–78
Pawlik, K. (FRG) 1978–80

Elected Executive Committee
Durojaiye, M.O.A. (Nigeria)
Fraisse, P. (France)
Frankenhaeuser, M. (Sweden)
Guevera, J. (Cuba)
Klix, F. (GDR)
Nuttin, J. (Belgium)
Rosenzweig, M.R. (USA)
Russell, R.W. (USA)
Tanaka, Y. (Japan)
Tomaszewski, T. (Poland)

1980–1984

Elected President
Klix, F. (GDR)

Vice-Presidents
Rosenzweig, M.R. (USA)
Tomaszewski, T. (Poland)

Treasurer
Bélanger, D. (Canada)

Secretary-General
Holtzman, W.H. (USA)

Deputy Secretary-General
Pawlik, K. (FRG)

Elected Executive Committee
Azuma, H. (Japan)
d'Ydewalle, G. (Belgium)
Diaz-Guerrero, R. (Mexico)
Durojaiye, M.O.A. (Nigeria)
Lomov, B.F. (USSR)
Montmollin, G. de (France)
Sinha, D. (India)
Summerfield, A. (UK)
Taft, R. (Australia)
Takala, M. (Finland)

1984–1988

Elected President
Holtzman, W.H. (USA)

Vice-Presidents
Diaz-Guerrero, R. (Mexico)
Lomov, B.F. (USSR)

Treasurer
Bélanger, D. (Canada)

Secretary-General
Pawlik, K. (FRG)

Deputy Secretary-General
Farr, R. (UK) 1984–87
d'Ydewalle, G. (Belgium) 1987–88

Elected Executive Committee
Azuma, H. (Japan)
Durojaiye, M.O.A. (Nigeria)
d'Ydewalle, G. (Belgium)
Jing, Q. (China)
Klix, F. (GDR)
Montmollin, G. de (France)
Rosenzweig, M.R. (USA)
Sinha, D. (India)
Taft, R. (Australia)
Takala, M. (Finland)

continued →

1988–1992

Elected President
Rosenzweig, M.R. (USA)

Past-President
Holtzman, W.H. (USA)

Vice-Presidents
Azuma, H. (Japan)
Takala, M. (Finland)

Treasurer
Bélanger, D. (Canada)

Secretary-General
Pawlik, K. (FRG)

Deputy Secretary-General
d'Ydewalle, G. (Belgium)

Elected Executive Committee
Diaz-Guerrero, R. (Mexico)
Gelman, R. (USA)
Hogan, T.P. (Canada)
Jing, Q. (China)
Kagitcibasi, C. (Turkey)
Klix, F. (GDR)
Lomov, B.F. (USSR) 1988–89
Nilsson, L.G. (Sweden)
Sheehan, P.W. (Australia)
Sinha, D. (India)

1992–1996

Elected President
Pawlik, K. (Germany)

Past-President
Rosenzweig, M.R. (USA)

Vice-Presidents
Jing, Q. (China)
Nilsson, L.G. (Sweden)

Treasurer
Bélanger, D. (Canada) 1992
Sabourin, M. (Canada) 1993–96

Secretary-General
d'Ydewalle, G. (Belgium)

Deputy Secretary-General
Overmier, J.B. (USA)

Elected Executive Committee
Abou-Hatab, F. (Egypt)
Ardila, R. (Colombia)
Blackman, D. (UK)
Denis, M. (France)
Gelman, R. (USA)
Hogan, T.P. (Canada)
Imada, H. (Japan)
Kagitcibasi, C. (Turkey)
Sinha, D. (India)
Strelau, J. (Poland)

continued →

1996–2000

Elected President
d'Ydewalle, G. (Belgium)

Past-President
Pawlik, K. (Germany)

Vice-Presidents
Kagitcibasi, T. (Turkey)
Strelau, J. (Poland)

Treasurer
Sabourin, M. (Canada)

Secretary-General
Ritchie, P. (Canada)

Deputy Secretary-General
Bullock, M. (Estonia/USA)

Elected Executive Committee
Adair, J.G. (Canada)
Ardila, R. (Colombia)
Blackman, D. (UK) 1996–98
Denis, M. (France)
Imada, H. (Japan)
Nilsson, L.G. (Sweden)
Overmier, J.B. (USA)
Poortinga, Y.H. (Netherlands)
Sanchez-Sosa, J.J. (Mexico)
Zhang, H. (China)

Appendix C

Statutes of the International Union of Scientific Psychology, 1951

Section 1. Nature, aims, headquarters and duration of the Union

Article 1. The International Union of Scientific Psychology is a group uniting the National Societies and Associations of the adhering countries, having for their aim the development of studies and scientific researches in psychology, whether biological or social, normal or pathological, pure or applied.

Article 2. The aims and objects of the Union are as follows:

(a) To contribute to the development of intellectual exchange and scientific relations between psychologists of different countries and in particular for the organization of Congresses whether general or specialized on definite subjects to be determined.

(b) To contribute to psychological documentation by fostering international exchange of publications, of books, and of reviews, of film and of bibliographies.

(c) To aid scholars of different countries to go abroad to universities, laboratories and libraries, etc.

(d) To foster the exchange of students and of young research workers.

Article 3. The Union may receive subsidies or donations from governments, from intergovernmental organizations, from private or special sources for its general functioning or for the accomplishment of any special tasks which are in accordance with the general aims set out in these statutes.

Article 4. The Central Headquarters of the Union will be fixed by a decision of the General Assembly.

Article 5. No limit will be set to the duration of the Union. Its dissolution can only be decided at a meeting of the General Assembly by a majority of two-thirds.

Section II. Composition of the Union

Article 6. The members of the Union shall be national societies or associations of psychology, regularly established, of those countries adhering to the Union.

Article 7. A country may support the Union either through its principal academy or through its National Research Council, or through some other national institution or association, or in the absence of these, through its government.

The term "country" is to be understood as including dominions, diplomatic protectorates and any dependency in which independent scientific activity has been developed.

Article 8. The existing Executive Committee of the International Congress of Psychology shall take initiative in establishing the Union by securing and accepting members, by fixing the time and

continued ➔

place of the first meeting of the Assembly, by appointing the President for this meeting, and by submitting the present draft of the Statutes for adoption or amendment by the Assembly.

Article 9. Additional members of the Union may be accepted by a majority vote of any meeting of the Assembly, or by a mail vote of the members of the Assembly.

Article 10. The unit dues shall be ten dollars. The number of units assigned to a country shall depend upon the number of psychologists in the societies or associations of that country, but shall not exceed 40 units for any one country. In each country the organizations adhering to the Union shall be responsible for the payment of the dues.

Article 11. The membership of any society or association in the Union shall be terminated:

  (a) by resignation subject to a year's notice;
  (b) by a vote of exclusion adopted by not less than two thirds of the entire membership of the
       Assembly, after charges have been presented and an opportunity given for a hearing.
  (c) A resigning or excluded group forfeits all claim to any funds in the treasury of the Union.

Section III. Government of the Union

Article 12. Ultimate authority for the operation of the Union is vested in the Assembly, which consists of representatives of the member societies, duly attested, each representative having equal power in discussion and voting. Each society is entitled to one representative if its membership is less than 500, and to two representatives if its membership is 500 or more. Vacancies among the representatives occurring between assemblies are to be filled by the society concerned.

Article 13. The duties and powers of the Assembly include the following:

  (a) to elect a President and Vice-President for a term beginning at the close of the current meeting
       and to extend to the close of the next meeting. Each member organization is entitled to
       nominate one candidate for President and Vice-President. The President and Vice-President
       shall not be eligible for re-election immediately.
  (b) to elect the members of the Executive Committee.
  (c) to elect and exclude member societies as provided in Articles 9 and 11 (b).
  (d) to adopt a budget to be submitted by the Executive Committee.
  (e) to determine the time and place of the following meeting of the Assembly, subject to change
       by the Executive Committee in case of necessity.
  (f) to amend its Statutes by a two-thirds vote of its members, present and voting.
  (g) to establish its own rules of procedure.

Article 14. Except as otherwise ordered in Articles 5, 13 (f), and 11 (b), questions coming before the Assembly shall be decided by a majority of representatives present and voting, or by a mail vote of the members of the Assembly when considered necessary by the President.

Article 15. For administering the affairs of the Union the Assembly shall elect by secret ballot from its membership an Executive Committee of ten to fourteen members; no more than two shall be from any one country. The election ballot shall consist of names proposed by the constituent societies to the extent of their representation on the General Assembly. The members of the Executive Committee shall be elected at each meeting of the Assembly and shall serve until their successors are elected.

Article 16. The duties and powers of the Executive Committee are the following:

  (a) to choose from its membership its own Chairman, a General Secretary and Assistant Secretary
       of the Union, and a Treasurer.
  (b) to authorize expenditures in conformity with the budget adopted by the Assembly.
  (c) to determine the agenda of business to be transacted at the regular meeting of the Assembly.

continued →

   (d) to arrange for congresses and colloquia.

   (e) to call a special meeting of the Assembly in an emergency and to alter the time and place of a regular meeting as provided in Article 13 (e).

   (f) to present a report to the next meeting of the Assembly.

   (g) to appoint special committees for the discussion and recommendations concerning any questions falling within the purview of the Union.

   (h) in general, subject to the superior authority of the Assembly, to make all decisions necessary for the operation of the Union and the realization of its aims, in the intervals between meetings of the Assembly.

Article 17. The President of the Union shall preside at all meetings of the General Assembly. He and the Vice President shall be ex-officio members of the Executive Committee.

Article 18. The duties and powers of the General Secretary are the following:

   (a) to authorize particular expenditures in accordance with general instructions from the Executive Committee.

   (b) with the approval of the Chairman of the Executive Committee to call meetings of that Committee or to arrange for mail ballots of its members, whenever a decision of the Committee is necessary or desirable.

   (c) to record the meetings of the Executive Committee and of the Assembly and to arrange for records of the scientific congresses and colloquia of the Union.

   (d) in general, to perform the customary duties of his office and to represent the Union as required by action of the Executive Committee.

Article 19. The duties and powers of the Treasurer are the following:

   (a) to present a budget for adoption by the Executive Committee and the General Assembly.

   (b) to bank the fees, subsidies or donations.

   (c) to authorize payments on the decision of the General Secretary conformable to the items of the budget.

   (d) to present his accounts annually to the Executive Committee for approval and to the General Assemblies at their regular meetings.

   (e) to send out due bills annually to the adhering countries or organizations.

Appendix C2

The International Union of Psychological Science (IUPsyS): Statutes and Rules of Procedure (as revised and adopted by the Assembly of the Union in 1998)

Statutes

Section I. Nature and aims of the Union

Article 1. The International Union of Psychological Science is an organization comprised of National Members (see Article 6) whose aim is the development of psychological science, whether biological or social, normal or abnormal, pure or applied.

Article 2. The aims and objects of the Union are as follows:

(a) To develop the exchange of ideas and scientific information between psychologists of different countries, and in particular to organize International Congresses and other meetings on subjects of general or special interest in psychology.

(b) To contribute to psychological documentation in different countries by fostering exchange of publications of all kinds, including reviews, films and biographies.

(c) To aid scholars of different countries to go abroad to universities, laboratories, libraries, and other institutions.

(d) To foster the exchange of students and of young research workers.

(e) To collaborate with other international and national organizations in matters of mutual interest.

(f) To engage in such other activities as will further the development of the science of psychology.

Article 3. The Union may receive subsidies or donations from governments and from private or special sources for its general functioning or for the accomplishment of any special tasks which are in accordance with the general aims set out in these statutes.

Article 4. The Union has a legal venue in Montréal, Canada.

Article 5. No limit shall be set to the duration of the Union. Its dissolution shall only be decided at a meeting of the Assembly (see Article 12) by a majority of two-thirds of the entire membership of the Assembly, voting by correspondence being permitted.

Section II. Membership of the Union

Article 6. The Union shall consist of National Members elected in accordance with Article 7, not more than one member organization coming from any one country. Such a National Member shall be a national society of scientific psychology, regularly established, or a federation or association of such societies, or, alternatively, a national academy of sciences, national research council, or similar organization. In case the National Member is a national society of scientific psychology of a federation or association of such societies, no change to another form of representation for that country shall be made unless that society, federation, or association agrees to such change. The term 'country' shall be understood to include dominions, protectorates, and non-autonomous territories in which independent scientific activity in psychology has been developed. Federated states shall be considered single countries.

Article 7. Members of the Union shall be elected by the Assembly according to procedures specified in Article 13. The National Member for a country may change from one form of organization, as described in Article 6, to another of the forms described as in the same article, with the consent of the Assembly.

Article 8. Each National Member of the Union shall pay an annual subscription in accordance with the category to which the Members belongs. There shall be thirteen (13) categories, as follows:

continued →

Category 0. These Members pay no annual dues, do not vote on issues, and have an observer status at the meetings of the Assembly. They are otherwise Members of the Union and are provided with the regular services to Members. This is an exceptional form of membership accorded in the expectation that such Members will eventually become regular dues-paying Members.

Category A. The annual dues are based on one (1) unit and the Member is entitled to one (1) delegate to the Assembly.

Category B. The annual dues are based on three (3) units and the Member is entitled to one (1) delegate to the Assembly.

Category C. The annual dues are based on five (5) units and the Member is entitled to one (1) delegate to the Assembly.

Category D. The annual dues are based on ten (10) units and the Member is entitled to two (2) delegates to the Assembly.

Category E. The annual dues are based on fifteen (15) units and the Member is entitled to two (2) delegates to the Assembly.

Category F. The annual dues are based on twenty (20) units and the Member is entitled to two (2) delegates to the Assembly.

Category G. The annual dues are based on thirty (30) units and the Member is entitled to two (2) delegates to the Assembly.

Category H. The annual dues are based on forty (40) units and the Member is entitled to two (2) delegates to the Assembly.

Category I. The annual dues are based on fifty (50) units and the Member is entitled to two (2) delegates to the Assembly.

Category K. The annual dues are based on sixty (60) units and the Member is entitled to two (2) delegates to the Assembly.

Category L. The annual dues are based on eighty (80) units and the Member is entitled to two (2) delegates to the Assembly.

Category M. The annual dues are based on one hundred (100) units and the Member is entitled to two (2) delegates to the Assembly.

Each National Member chooses the category to which it wishes to belong, subject to approval by the Executive Committee. A revision of the classification will be made periodically.

The Assembly can change by a two-thirds majority of those entitled to vote the value of a unit.

Article 9. The membership of any National Member in the Union may be terminated either:

(a) (by resignation subject to a year's notice, or

(b) by non-payment of three annual subscriptions, whether in successive years or not, providing that the Member concerned has been given annual notices of subscriptions due, and a final notice that termination of its membership is to be considered by the Assembly, or

(c) by a vote of exclusion adopted by not less than two-thirds of those entitled to vote in the Assembly, whether present or not, after charges have been presented and an opportunity given for a hearing. A National Member whose membership has terminated shall forfeit all claim to any funds in the treasury of the Union.

Section III. Affiliation

Article 10. The following kinds of international organizations of scientific psychology may be given the title of 'Affiliated Organization' by a vote of the Assembly:

(a) worldwide or regional international organizations whose members are individuals, and

(b) regional international organizations whose members are national associations.

continued ➡

Each organization accepted as an Affiliated Organization shall be invited to send a observer with no voting rights to meetings of the Assembly.

Article 11. The Union may become affiliated with international scientific organizations whose aims are in accordance with Articles 1 and 2 of the Statutes.

Section IV. Administration of the Union

Article 12. Ultimate authority of the operation of the Union is vested in the Assembly, which consists of delegates of the National Members and of Executive Committee Members, each representative having equal power in discussion and voting. The Assembly shall meet biennially, normally at the occasion of an international congress.

In the event that a delegate from a National Member to the Assembly becomes a member of the Executive Committee, that National Member shall be entitled to an additional delegate to the Assembly.

At least three months' notice shall be given of the business to be transacted at a meeting of the Assembly; new issues, raised during the three months prior to a meeting of the Assembly, may be placed on the agenda for consideration provided that their discussion is approved by a two-thirds majority of those who are entitled to vote and are present at the Assembly meeting.

Article 13. The duties and powers of the Assembly include the following:

(a) To elect in accordance with the rules of procedure a President and two Vice-Presidents for a term beginning at the close of an International Congress and continuing to the close of the next International Congress. The President and the two Vice-Presidents shall not be eligible for immediate re-election to the same office. They must be elected by an absolute majority of the members of the Assembly present and voting.
(b) To elect and exclude National Members as provided in Articles 7 and 9.
(c) To consider budgets submitted by the Executive Committee.
(d) To determine the time and place of the next meeting of the Assembly, subject to change by the Executive Committee in case of necessity.
(e) To decide all matters relating to these statutes. Alterations or amendments to these statutes shall require a two-thirds majority of those entitled to vote in the Assembly, whether present or not.
(f) To establish rules of procedure.

Article 14. Except as otherwise ordered, questions coming before the Assembly shall normally be decided by a simple majority if at least half of those entitled to vote are present and voting. When the Assembly is not in session, or if less than half of those entitled to vote are present, the President may arrange for voting by correspondence. Approval of an issue voted upon by correspondence shall require a two-thirds majority of the votes, and shall not be valid unless at least half of the possible votes is received.

Article 15. For administering the affairs of the Union the Assembly shall elect an Executive Committee of ten members, of which at least eight shall be chosen from the Assembly, but not more than one from any one country. These shall be elected in accordance with the rules of procedure at a meeting of the Assembly held at the time of an International Congress, and shall serve until the close of the next International Congress. The President of the Union shall be Chairman of the Executive Committee. The President, the Vice-Presidents, and the immediate Past-President shall be members of the Executive Committee. All members of the Executive Committee shall be members of the Assembly.

The Executive Committee shall meet, if finances permit, on at least one occasion between two successive International Congresses.

continued ➡

Article 16. The duties and powers of the Executive Committee are the following:

    (a) To appoint, not necessarily from among the delegates to the Assembly, a Secretary-General, a Deputy Secretary-General, and a Treasurer of the Union. These shall be voting members of the Executive Committee and of the Assembly.

    (b) To authorize expenditure in conformity with the budget adopted by the Assembly.

    (c) To propose the agenda of business to be transacted at meetings of the Assembly.

    (d) To arrange for congresses and colloquia.

    (e) To call a special meeting of the Assembly in an emergency, and to alter the time and place of a regular meeting as provided for in Article 13(d).

    (f) To present a report to each meeting of the Assembly.

    (g) To appoint members of the three Standing Committees—the Committee on Research, the Committee on Communication and Publications, and the Committee on the Development of Psychology as a Science and as a Profession. Chairmen of Standing Committees, if not already serving as Executive Committee members, shall be *ex officio* members of the Executive Committee.

    (h) To appoint special committees to discuss and to make recommendations concerning any questions falling within the purview of the Union.

    (i) In general, subject to the superior authority of the Assembly, to make all decisions necessary for the operation of the Union and the realization of its aims, in the intervals between meetings of the Assembly.

Article 17. The President of the Union shall preside at all meetings of the Assembly. If the President is unable to do so, the senior Vice-President shall preside. If both are absent, the Assembly shall choose its own presiding officer.

Article 18. The duties and powers of the Secretary-General shall be:

    (a) To authorize particular expenditure in accordance with general instructions from the Executive Committee.

    (b) With the approval of the President of the Union to call meetings of the Executive Committee or to arrange for a vote of its members by correspondence.

    (c) To prepare and circulate agenda for meetings of the Assembly and of the Executive Committee.

    (d) To prepare and circulate minutes of meetings of the Assembly and of the Executive Committee, and to arrange for records of the scientific congresses and colloquia of the Union.

    (e) In general, to perform the customary duties of his or her office, and to represent the Union as required by the Executive Committee.

Article 19. The duties of the Deputy Secretary-General shall be to aid the Secretary-General and to deputize for him or her when necessary.

Article 20. The duties and powers of the Treasurer shall be:

    (a) To keep the accounts of the Union.

    (b) To bank all fees, subsidies and donations.

    (c) To present a budget and statement of accounts annually to the Executive Committee, and to each meeting of the Assembly.

    (d) To make payments on the authority of the Secretary-General in accordance with the budget.

    (e) To collect dues annually from the National Members.

Rules of Procedure

Section I. Organization of International Congresses

(1) Beginning with the Congress in 1972, the interval between two International Congresses shall normally be four years unless the Assembly decides otherwise. *continued* →

(2) International Congresses will be held under the auspices of the Union, which will delegate the detailed organization of each Congress to the National Member in whose country it is held, in accordance with the following procedure:

    (a) The President of an International Congress shall be a psychologist who, except under special circumstances, is a resident of the country in which the Congress is held. The choice of President shall be made after consultations between representatives of the National Member and the President, Vice-Presidents and Secretary-General of the Union.

    (b) In advance of each International Congress, all National Members should be consulted regarding the psychological problems which they would like to have discussed. The choice among the topics suggested will be made by the Program Committee, which normally shall be established by the host. The President of the Union, in consultation with the Executive Committee, shall appoint a delegate to have advisory and liaison functions on the Program Committee of an International Congress; the delegate appointed by the Union should participate in the planning of the Congress.

    (c) The Union should aid in the preliminary financing of each International Congress by advancing a loan of funds where necessary. Such funds are to be repaid when the financial accounts of the Congress have been finally audited to the extent there is a surplus (of Congress revenues over Congress expenditures). Any surplus which is left over after this audit must be reported to the Treasurer of the Union; the Executive Committee of the Union should be consulted on the nature of the expenditure involved.

    (d) The reports of the International Congress should be published in a uniform manner.

(3) The Assembly shall meet for at least two sessions on two separate days during the International Congress.

Section II. Subscriptions

(1) The annual subscription payable in respect of each unit (Article 8) shall be US$125, effective 1 January 1997.

(2) One year preceding each International Congress, the Treasurer prepares a budget based, in part, on the value of the units of contributions expected from the National Members. After consideration of this budget, the Executive Committee makes a recommendation regarding the value of a unit. This recommendation is sent by the Secretary-General to the delegates of the National Members who will be called upon to vote on this recommendation at the Assembly.

(3) The annual subscription is due on the first of January of the year to which it applies.

(4) The Executive Committee can, in special cases, make different arrangements regarding the dues of a National Member, such arrangements to be valid for one year only; any prolongation would call for a revision of the category status of that Member.

Section III. Nominations and elections

(1) At a meeting between two International Congresses of Psychology the Assembly sets up an Election Committee. It consists of the Past President (*ex-officio*) as Chair and two persons elected by the Assembly at that meeting. No member of the Election Committee can be a candidate in the election under the purview of this Committee.

(2) At least 9 months in advance of an International Congress of Psychology, the Secretary-General shall request nominations for President, Vice-Presidents, and Executive Committee members from National Members holding voting rights in the Assembly. Each nomination must be accompanied by a one-page curriculum vitae of the person nominated and by a signed statement expressing that person's agreement to be nominated and to serve if elected. Nominations shall be

continued →

submitted to the Chair of the Election Committee by a deadline to be set by the Secretary-General and no less than seven months in advance of an International Congress of Psychology.

(3) The Election Committee shall collate all nominations received. Upon unanimous decision, it may request additional information on a nomination.

(4) At least 5 months in advance of an International Congress of Psychology, the Election Committee shall send a first report to National Members. This report includes full documentation on all nominations received in good order. A National Member may request the Election Committee to provide further information on a nomination.

(5) The Assembly may decide to receive additional nominations at the time of its first session during an International Congress of Psychology. In that case, the Election Committee shall present an up-dated second report to the Assembly in the beginning of its second session during that International Congress of Psychology.

(6) Election of the Executive Committee shall be in accordance with the following procedures:

  (a) All elections shall be conducted by secret ballot; each delegate entitled to vote in the Assembly has as many votes as positions to be filled in a ballot.

  (b) Each nomination for a member to be elected only from among Assembly Members needs to be seconded by at least one further Assembly Member at the first session of the Assembly during an International Congress of Psychology. Additional nominations may be made by the same procedure at the second session of the Assembly. In order to be valid, each nomination must include a cv and the written agreement by the person nominated in accordance with Rule III.2 above.

  (c) Following completion of these nominations, the Election Committee shall present a final report at the second Assembly session.

  (d) Election of the President and Vice-Presidents shall take place immediately after this report.

  (e) Election of eight members of the Executive Committee from the Assembly shall take place immediately after election of the President and Vice-Presidents. If in the election of these eight members of the Executive Committee two or more candidates from the same country receive an absolute majority of votes, only the candidate with the highest number of votes shall be elected.

  (f) Two additional members of the Executive Committee, for a total of ten members, shall be elected in a separate ballot after election of eight members described in paragraph (e). Following a brief recess, nominations for these two positions shall be made by the joint proposal of at least four other members of the Assembly present and voting at its second session. Candidates for these two additional members of the Executive Committee may be drawn from outside the Assembly.

  (g) The President and Vice-Presidents shall be elected by the highest number of votes. The eight members elected under (d) shall be elected in no more than two ballots. In the first ballot a member is elected by absolute majority of votes. If a second ballot is necessary in order to obtain sufficient members, the second ballot will consist of no more than twice as many candidates as the number of positions to be filled in the second ballot. For this second ballot the remaining list of candidates is reduced to this number by striking out any candidate coming from a country already represented among those elected in the first ballot; if necessary, the number of candidates for the second ballot is reduced further by striking out those who received the lowest number of votes in the first ballot. In this second ballot those with the highest number of votes shall be elected. The two members elected under (e) shall be elected by the highest number of votes.

continued →

(h) No speeches favoring any candidate shall be made although factual information of a biographical nature may be presented when deemed desirable by the President and when Assembly members ask for it.

Section IV. Order of Assembly business

A motion for termination of the membership of any society or association in the Union (Article 9) shall be made the first order of business. The vote on such a motion shall take effect immediately.

Section V. Standing Committees

The chairperson of the three Standing Committees, the Committee on Research, the Committee on Communication and Publications, and the Committee on the Development of Psychology as a Science and as a Profession, will usually be chosen by the Executive Committee from among its members. In order to assure continuity, they may be co-opted from outside the Committee.

Appendix D

Appendix D

Locations, dates, and presidents of the International Congresses of Psychology

Location	Time	President
1. Paris	August 6–10, 1889	Jean Martin Charcot (Acting, Théodule A. Ribot)
2. London	August 2–6, 1892	Henry Sidgwick
3. Munich	August 4–7, 1896	Carl Stumpf
4. Paris	August 20–25, 1900	Théodule A. Ribot
5. Rome	April 26–30, 1905	Giuseppé Sergi (Honorary, Leonardo Bianchi)
6. Geneva	August 2–7, 1909	Théodore Flournoy
7. Oxford	July 26–August 2, 1923	Charles S. Myers
8. Groningen	September 6–11, 1926	Gerardus Heymans
9. Yale	September 1–7, 1929	James McKeen Cattell
10. Copenhagen	August 22–27, 1932	Edgar Rubin*
11. Paris	July 25–31, 1937	Henri Piéron (Honorary, Pierre Janet)
12. Edinburgh	July 23–29, 1948	James Drever Sr
13. Stockholm	July 16–21, 1951	David Katz
14. Montréal	June 7–12, 1954	Edward A. Bott and Edward C. Tolman
15. Brussels	July 28–August 3, 1957	Albert Michotte
16. Bonn	July 31–August 6, 1960	Wolfgang Metzger (Honorary, Karl Bühler)
17. Washington	August 20–26, 1963	Otto Klineberg (Honorary, Edwin G. Boring)
18. Moscow	August 4–11, 1966	Alexei N. Leontiev
19. London	July 27–August 2, 1969	George C. Drew
20. Tokyo	August 13–19, 1972	Moriji Sagara
21. Paris	July 18–25, 1976	Paul Fraisse
22. Leipzig	July 6–12, 1980	Friedhart Klix
23. Acapulco	September 2–7, 1984	Rogelio Diaz-Guerrero
24. Sydney	August 28–September 2, 1988	Peter Sheehan
25. Brussels	July 19–24, 1992	Paul Bertelson and Géry d'Ydewalle
26. Montréal	August 18–23, 1996	David Bélanger
27. Stockholm	July 23–28, 2000	Lars-Göran Nilsson

*Harald Höffding designated but died before the meetings.

Appendix E

Years in which national organizations were elected to IUPsyS

1951

Charter Members
Belgium
Federal Republic of Germany
France
Italy
Japan
Netherlands
Norway
Sweden
Switzerland
United Kingdom
United States of America

Admitted later in 1951
Brazil
    Membership terminated in 1996 after
    adhering organization became defunct.
Canada
Cuba
    Membership lapsed 1963; re-admitted 1966.
Denmark
Egypt
    Soon became inactive; reinstated in 1986.
Finland
Israel
Spain
Uruguay

1954
Yugoslavia
    Membership terminated in 1992 after
    Yugoslavia disbanded.

1957
Australia
    Formerly represented by British
    Psychological Society.

1957 (continued)
New Zealand
    Formerly represented by British
    Psychological Society
Poland
Turkey
USSR
    Membership terminated in 1991 after
    Union of Soviet Socialist Republics
    disbanded.

1962
South Africa
    Readmitted with new adhering
    body, 1996.
Venezuela
    Membership lapsed 1956; re-admitted 1962.

1963
Czechoslovakia
    Membership terminated in 1994 after
    Czechoslovakia separated into Czech
    Republic and Slovakia. Czech Republic
    admitted 1996; Slovakia admitted 1998.

1965
Philippines

1966
German Democratic Republic
    Merged with German Psychological
    Federation, 1992.
Hungary
India
Mexico
Romania

continued →

1969
Colombia
Iran

1972
Bulgaria
Hong Kong

1973
Korea

1974
Ireland
    Withdrew in 1988; readmitted 1996.

1975
Argentina

1976
Panama

1979
Dominican Republic

1980
China

1984
Nicaragua

1985
Zimbabwe

1987
Pakistan

1988
Indonesia
Nigeria

1992
Estonia
Greece
Portugal
Singapore

1994
Chile
Malta

1995
Croatia
Slovenia
Vietnam

1996
Albania
Austria
Bangladesh
Czech Republic
Morocco
Russia
Uganda

1997
Georgia

1998
Slovakia
Ukraine

1999
Mongolia
Peru

Index

Beijing
  Executive Committee
  meeting (1987), 186–189
  28th International Congress
  of Psychology (2004),
  230–231, 233, 241
Bekman, Sevda, 5, 214
Bélanger, David, 160, 162, 168,
  192, 193, 197, 198, 205, 214,
  223
Belgian Society of Psychology,
  84, 88, 202
Bellagio, Executive Committee
  meeting (1964), 110–112
Bellingham, Advanced
  Research Training Seminar
  (1998), 5
Belyaeva, Alexandra, 201
Berkeley, Executive
  Committee meeting (1991),
  198–202
Berlin, Advanced Research
  Training Seminar (1992), 5,
  196
Bernheim, Hippolyte, 20, 21,
  23
Bertelson, Paul, 202, 203
Bianchi, Leonardo, 37
Bibliography of Psychology in
  the World, 114, 221, 235
Biesheuvel, Simon, 115, 116,
  128
Binet, Alfred, 24
Blackman, Derek, 205, 213, 231
Bloch, Vincent, 157
Boehnke, Klaus, 196
Boivin, Michael, 5
Bonn
  Assembly (1960), 95–98
  Executive Committee
  meeting (1960), 98–99
  16th International Congress
  of Psychology (1960), 91–95
Boring, Edwin G., 24, 48, 102,
  103
Bott, Edward A., 72, 74, 75
Bower, T.G.R., 158
Brayfield, Arthur, 103
Brazilian Psychological

Society, 76, 79, 83, 99, 108,
  111, 153, 223
Brissaud, Edouard, 18
British Journal of Psychology, 44
British National Committee
  for Psychological Science,
  191
British Psychological Society,
  56, 88, 111, 114, 122, 126, 134,
  191
Broadbent, Donald E., 135
Brown, William, 45
Bruner, Jerome, 139, 143, 149
Brussels
  Advanced Research
  Training Seminar (1992), 5
  Assembly (1957), 88–89
  Assembly (1992), 203–206
  Executive Committee
  meeting (1957), 89–90
  Executive Committee
  meeting (1989), 196–197
  15th International Congress
  of Psychology (1957), 84–88
  25th International Congress
  of Psychology (1992),
  202–203
Bühler, Charlotte, 24, 55
Bühler, Karl, 24, 55, 91, 92
Bulgarian Psychological
  Society, 140
Bullock, Merry, 233, 235, 240

Cairo, see Pan-Arab Regional
  Congress
Cajal, Ramon y, see Ramon y
  Cajal, Santiago
Canadian National Committee
  for Psychology, 180
Canadian Psychological
  Association, 67–68, 72, 73,
  74, 215, 223, 234281
Canberra, behavioral
  toxicology conference
  (1988), 184

Caracas, Executive Committee
  meeting (1981), 170–172
Career development, 218
Carmichael, Leonard, 98, 101,
  107
Cattell, James McKeen, 24, 41,
  48–49, 54
CD-ROM, 6, 7–8
Charcot, Jean-Martin, 18, 20
Charns, Albert, 173
Child and human
  development project, 170,
  188
Child rearing, 154, 235, 239
Child research centers, 171,
  181–182
China
  Executive Committee
  meeting (1987), 186–189
  Executive Committee
  meeting (1995), 219–221
  28th International Congress
  of Psychology (2004),
  230–231, 232, 241
  Regional Congress (1995),
  218, 221–222
Chinese–English Dictionary,
  188, 201
Chinese Psychological Society,
  168, 187, 218
Claparède, Edouard, 9, 38, 39,
  45, 46, 47, 48, 51, 52, 59,
CODATA, 213
Cognitive Bases of Education,
  219, 220–221
Cognitive science, 206, 235,
  238–239
Cognitive Science, Artificial
  Intelligence and
  Neuroscience, 182, 188
Cole, Michael, 201
Collins, Mary, 63
Colombian Federation of
  Psychologists, 139, 140
Colombian National
  Committee of Psychology,
  204
Committees, see also Executive
  Committee

Wilson, John T., 103
Windsor
  Executive Committee
    meeting (1967), 127–130
  Executive Committee
    meeting (1977), 161–162
Witte, W., 99
Women's Committee, 233–234
Women's Role and Status
  project, 164–165
Woodworth, Robert S., 24
World Health Organization
  (WHO), 1, 181, 184, 186, 236,
  240, 243
World Science Conference,
  236, 243

World Social Science Report,
  238, 243
World Social Science Year, 110
World War I, 43
World War II, 43, 55–56, 62
Wundt, Wilhelm, 11, 19, 24, 30
  Special Fund, 168
Wundtke, Hans, 200

Yale, 9th International
  Congress of Psychology
  (1929), 47–50
Yela, Mariano, 121
Young, Martha, 5
Young Child and Family
  network, 238

Directory, 242
Young Child and the
  Family Environment
  project, 199–200, 206,
  211
Young Psychologists'
  Program, 101, 102–103, 107,
  190
Yugoslavian Psychological
  Society, 76

Zazzo, René, 158
Zhang, Houcan, 219, 231,
  240
Zurich, Executive Committee
  meeting (1986), 183–186

*For Product Safety Concerns and Information please contact
our EU representative GPSR@taylorandfrancis.com Taylor & Francis
Verlag GmbH, Kaufingerstraße 24, 80331 München, Germany*

T - #0174 - 270225 - C0 - 216/172/18 - PB - 9781138877399 - Gloss Lamination